Earl Leslie Griggs (1899–1975) in 1961

Reading Coleridge

APPROACHES AND APPLICATIONS

EDITED BY

Walter B. Crawford

CORNELL UNIVERSITY PRESS

ITHACA AND LONDON

First published 1979 by Cornell University Press.
Published in the United Kingdom by
Cornell University Press Ltd.,
2-4 Brook Street, London W1Y 1AA.

International Standard Book Number 0-8014-1219-6
Library of Congress Catalog Card Number 79-7616
Printed in the United States of America
*Librarians: Library of Congress cataloging information
appears on the last page of the book.*

To the memory of
EARL LESLIE GRIGGS,
admired teacher and beloved friend;
editor of the
Collected Letters of Samuel Taylor Coleridge,
indispensable reference point
of all modern Coleridge scholarship

Contents

Preface

It is an act of personal homage for me to present this volume of Coleridge studies in memory of Earl Leslie Griggs (1899–1975), who died in an automobile accident on 26 November 1975 in his seventy-seventh year. Across twenty-five years our connection grew from a mutually appreciative student-teacher relationship to a close personal friendship. In my feelings of affection and professional respect for Earl Griggs, I know I am representative of many others who have been warmed by his friendship and inspired by his scholarship—of many others, indeed, who would have contributed to this volume had circumstances made it possible. Let the volume stand, then, as a permanent memorial to Earl in a form which one of his own books (see Bibliography, below) proves he understood and valued.

My thanks are due to many persons who have helped make this volume possible. Marilyn Gaull and Richard Haven gave valuable advice and support at the outset. Each of the contributors responded understandingly, cooperatively, and helpfully to my many queries. Special thanks are due to John Beer and Carl Woodring, who with me have made up the editorial board responsible for the volume. To Evelyn Griggs I am indebted for the photograph of her late husband used for the frontispiece. To her and to Alwyne H. B. Coleridge, present head of the family of the poet's direct descendants and lifelong friend of

Earl and Evelyn, I owe thanks for continual encouragement and support.

Grateful acknowledgment is made for the use of copyrighted material quoted extensively in this volume. Mr. A. H. B. Coleridge of Devonshire has granted permission to quote from unpublished Coleridge and Sara Coleridge manuscripts at the British Library; Humanities Research Center, The University of Texas at Austin; the Henry W. and Albert A. Berg Collection, The New York Public Library, Astor, Lenox and Tilden Foundations; and Victoria University Library, Toronto. Dr. Walter Knowlton Hall of Georgia has granted permission to quote from unpublished papers in the James Marsh Collection, Guy W. Bailey Library, University of Vermont. Permission to quote from these materials has also been granted by the libraries named. The John Payne Collier MS Notes on Coleridge's lectures are quoted by permission of the Folger Shakespeare Library, Washington. Mr. Jonathan Wordsworth of Oxford has granted permission to quote from an unpublished transcript of the text of his forthcoming Norton Critical Edition of *The Prelude* by William Wordsworth. The Trustees of Dove Cottage have granted permission to quote from MS 18A of their collection.

Permission to reprint quotations from the following publications has been granted by Princeton University Press and by Routledge & Kegan Paul Ltd.: *The Notebooks of Samuel Taylor Coleridge,* ed. Kathleen Coburn (Bollingen Series 50, Volume 1 © 1957 by the Bollingen Foundation, Volume 2 © 1961 by the Bollingen Foundation, Volume 3 © 1973 by Princeton University Press); *The Collected Works of Samuel Taylor Coleridge,* Kathleen Coburn, General Editor; Bart Winer, Associate Editor (Bollingen Series 75): Volume 1, *Lectures 1795: On Politics and Religion,* ed. Lewis Patton and Peter Mann (© 1971 by Routledge & Kegan Paul Ltd.), Volume 4, *The Friend,* ed. Barbara E. Rooke (© 1969 by Routledge & Kegan Paul Ltd.), Volume 6, *Lay Sermons,* ed. R. J. White (© 1972 by Routledge & Kegan Paul Ltd.),

Volume 10, *On the Constitution of the Church and State,* ed. John Colmer (© 1976 by Princeton University Press).

Permission to reprint quotations from the following publications has been granted by Oxford University Press: Samuel Taylor Coleridge, *Biographia Literaria,* ed. J. Shawcross (2 volumes, © 1907); *Collected Letters of Samuel Taylor Coleridge,* ed. Earl Leslie Griggs (6 volumes, © 1956, 1959, and 1971); *The Complete Poetical Works of Samuel Taylor Coleridge,* ed. Ernest Hartley Coleridge (2 volumes, © 1912); *The Poetical Works of William Wordsworth,* ed. Ernest de Selincourt and Helen Darbishire (5 volumes, © 1940–49, corrected editions to 1969); and William Wordsworth, *The Prelude,* ed. Ernest de Selincourt and Helen Darbishire (© 1959). Permission has also been granted by Routledge & Kegan Paul Ltd. to reprint quotations from *Coleridge on Shakespeare: The Text of the Lectures of 1811-12,* ed. R. A. Foakes (© 1971), and by Miss Kathleen Coburn of Toronto to reprint quotations from *Inquiring Spirit: A New Presentation of Coleridge from His Published and Unpublished Prose Writings,* ed. Kathleen Coburn (New York: Pantheon Books; London: Routledge & Kegan Paul, © 1951).

W. B. C.

Long Beach, California

Abbreviations

Coleridge's Works Frequently Cited in This Volume

BL *Biographia Literaria.* Ed. with his aesthetical essays by J[ohn] Shawcross. 2 vols. Oxford: Clarendon Press, 1907. Often reprinted. First published 1817.

CL *Collected Letters of Samuel Taylor Coleridge.* Ed. Earl Leslie Griggs. 6 vols. Oxford: Clarendon Press, 1956–71.

CPW *The Complete Poetical Works of Samuel Taylor Coleridge.* Including poems and versions of poems now published for the first time. Ed. with textual and bibliographical notes by Ernest Hartley Coleridge. 2 vols. Oxford: Clarendon Press, 1912. Often reprinted, with some minor omissions.

CS *On the Constitution of the Church and State.* Ed. John Colmer. *The Collected Works of Samuel Taylor Coleridge,* 10. (Bollingen Series, 75.) London: Routledge & Kegan Paul; Princeton: Princeton University Press, 1976. After the second of two editions, 1830.

F *The Friend.* Ed. Barbara E. Rooke. *The Collected Works of Samuel Taylor Coleridge,* 4. (Bollingen Series, 75.) 2 vols. London: Routledge & Kegan Paul; Princeton: Princeton University Press, 1969.

IS *Inquiring Spirit: A New Presentation of Coleridge from His Published and Unpublished Prose Writings.* Ed. Kathleen Coburn. New York: Pantheon Books; London: Routledge & Kegan Paul, 1951.

L *Lectures 1795: On Politics and Religion.* Ed. Lewis Patton and Peter Mann. *The Collected Works of Samuel Taylor Coleridge,* 1. (Bollingen Series, 75.) London: Routledge & Kegan Paul; Princeton: Princeton University Press, 1971.

Abbreviations

LS   *A Lay Sermon.* In *Lay Sermons.* Ed. R. J. White. *The Collected Works of Samuel Taylor Coleridge,* 6. (Bollingen Series, 75.) London: Routledge & Kegan Paul; Princeton: Princeton University Press, 1972. First published 1817.

N   *The Notebooks of Samuel Taylor Coleridge.* Ed. Kathleen Coburn. (Bollingen Series, 50.) Vols. I and II, New York: Pantheon Books; London: Routledge & Kegan Paul, 1957, 1961. Vol. III, Princeton: Princeton University Press, 1973. Angle brackets indicate passages added later by Coleridge.

OM   Opus Maximum MS, Victoria University Library, Toronto.

SM   *The Statesman's Manual.* In *Lay Sermons.* Ed. R. J. White. *The Collected Works of Samuel Taylor Coleridge,* 6. (Bollingen Series, 75.) London: Routledge & Kegan Paul; Princeton: Princeton University Press, 1972. First published 1816.

TT   *Specimens of the Table Talk of the Late Samuel Taylor Coleridge.* Ed. Henry Nelson Coleridge. First published 1835. Cited by date.

Introduction

"Reading Coleridge" was chosen as the title of this volume because the various approaches to Coleridge and the various readings of various aspects of Coleridge's thought presented herein are of special interest in light of the explicit treatment in the first two essays of the problem of how Coleridge ought to be read.

In "Explaining Coleridge's Explanation," an essay "Toward a Practical Methodology for Coleridge Studies," Laurence S. Lockridge finds genetic interpretation at least an indispensable adjunct to historical and structural interpretation. Even if one's method involves primarily one of the latter, Lockridge says, Coleridge's "thought is better expounded not as some isolable and either coherent or incoherent body of ideas but rather as a play of ideas emanating from a living personality—Coleridge thinking, feeling, sensing." "If one focuses on passages that have arisen directly from personal struggle, immediate observation, and obvious intellectual perplexity at the moment of composition, one will find a vitality of inquiry and of language that may elsewhere fail Coleridge." More derivative or abstract passages, though they "may seem to lend themselves to exposition of what Coleridge thinks," at the same time "misrepresent his quality of mind." For Coleridge's own "treatment of subjects from mathematics and science to religion and cosmology is insistently psychogenetic," which gives him "an arresting modernity. The scholar need not import Freudian or Jungian categories to begin to explain him, or for that matter Hegelian, Heideggerian, or Derridean. The greater service is to let Coleridge explain himself."

Thomas McFarland's "Complex Dialogue," however, examines Coleridge's doctrine of polarity against the broad background of its European contexts. He explicates this doctrine in Heraclitus and Bruno, to whom Coleridge said it was fundamental, compares the Coleridgean formulation with those of Hegel, Schelling, and Goethe, extends his survey to the treatment of the idea by other Europeans, and concludes that "the Romantic commitment to reconciled oppositions is, in largest description, an attempt to cope with the increasing incompatibility of the data that impinged on cultural consciousness."

A significant part of McFarland's essay is his extended justification of his approach to his subject, in contradistinction to the approach of John Appleyard and Owen Barfield, which, as Appleyard puts it, considers Coleridge "on his own terms and not as a representative of something else"—an oversimplified approach, says McFarland, which can "never be more than an heuristic device." "Strictly speaking," McFarland argues, "neither Coleridge nor any other philosopher can be said 'on his own terms' to have thought anything at all": both formulation and terminology he derives from his intellectual culture, without which "there would be no thought." A philosopher's thought "is 'the outgrowth of a social act.' Only if it is heard as a voice in a complex dialogue with his forebears and contemporaries can its meaning be ascertained."

The vexing question of Coleridge's plagiarism arises, of course, in both McFarland's and Lockridge's essays, and also in that by Max F. Schulz. It enters briefly into McFarland's discussion of method, and it is treated at length by Lockridge, especially in his discussion of historical interpretation, in which he illustrates his points by examining specific passages showing different degrees of Coleridge's dependence upon and acknowledgement of the ideas and language of others. Schulz argues (in his note 6) that since he makes no special claims for the intellectual status of Coleridge's ideas of paradise, he need not raise the question of Coleridge's use of others' writings.

Though it is Lockridge and McFarland who in this volume provide the most fuel for the continuing debate on fundamental questions of critical methodology and of Coleridge's originality as a thinker, the other essays may also be considered in relation to those questions.

Max F. Schulz's "Coleridge and the Enchantments of Earthly Paradise" is concerned with the idea of polarity or reconciliation of opposites as it is manifested in Coleridge's writings in one of the most insistent forms it took in the Romantic period—"a harking back to paradise, to a time when man lived in a golden age of harmony with himself, his fellow man, and God." Schulz uses all three of the approaches discussed by Lockridge, but especially the historical, treating Coleridge's ideas of paradise as part of the centuries-long development of a tradition, and the genetic, drawing extensively on passages from notebooks and letters that have arisen—as Lockridge suggests—directly from personal engagement with the ideas at the moment of composition. At one point (note 12) Schulz rejects certain structural interpretations of "The Eolian Harp" focusing narrowly on grammatical points "when the poem is otherwise calling for a reading that embraces its whole statement." Concentrating mainly on Coleridge's poetry, Schulz treats his subject first in terms of the time-space continuum and then in terms of the garden enclosure, and concludes: "Given his pre-nineteenth-century sense of social activism and piety, and his personal guilt over his sloth, failed promise, and sensual addition to drink and drugs, there is little wonder that Coleridge uneasily feared that every flowery bower was in reality an enchanted garden, and the paradisal breadth and depth of earth and sky a barren void."

In "Coleridge and Wordsworth: The Vital and the Organic,"

by John Beer, the focus is, even more than in Schulz's essay, on the poet (in this case, two poets) as person "thinking, feeling, sensing"—to quote Lockridge again. Beer eschews the tendency to treat the two sides of Coleridge's activity—the poetic and the philosophic—in separate compartments. He examines the intricate relationship between Coleridge's early poetry and his theories of organicism and vital energy, believing "that *all* his writings, particularly in the years when he was intimate with Wordsworth, grew from a common matrix of intellectual and poetic exploration which found its center in the need to rediscover for his age a significant relationship with nature, and that the poetry originally embodied a view of nature about which he later came to have reservations," as he realized that "energies can be destructive as well as constructive." A similar examination of Wordsworth's early poetry—particularly the two-part *Prelude* of 1799—leads to the belief "that reflection on Coleridge's ideas gave new substance to Wordsworth's memories of his early physical nature and its development." He concludes also that "by insisting that language, like all natural process, consisted of an interplay between forms and energies, Coleridge gave himself and his friend a way of looking at experience which in turn liberated their own poetry-making powers."

Some of the technical problems posed for modern editors of Coleridge texts—and therefore for readers of them—by the work of his earliest editors are discussed in the study by R. A. Foakes, "What Did Coleridge Say? John Payne Collier and the Reports of the 1811–12 Lectures," which refines and extends the findings presented in his 1971 edition, *Coleridge on Shakespeare: The Text of the Lectures of 1811–12.* Somewhat similar problems are being dealt with currently by the editors (for the *Collected Coleridge*) of the *Table Talk* and the contents of the *Literary Remains,* originally edited by Henry Nelson Coleridge.

Rather than a reading of thought, Carl Woodring offers a reading of a person—Coleridge's daughter and editor, and author in her own right, Sara—and some of her distinctive accomplishments. His focus is on the remarkable woman who emerged from what can only be recognized as an unusual childhood, a Cinderella figure growing up with the beauties and sublimities of Lakeland scenery outside her windows and endless learning and literary labor in the Southey household inside; on her *Phantasmion: A Fairy Tale* (1837), which exemplifies the law—important for Sara as for her father—that imagination, not moral precept, is growth; and on her contributions as editor and interpreter of her father's prose and to the question of the correct copy-text of the poems.

Since it was primarily as a thinker rather than as a poet that Coleridge was regarded during the nineteenth century, and the growth of Victorian studies is not unconnected with some current directions in Coleridge studies, it is appropriate that this book contains two essays concerned with Coleridge's nineteenth-century influence in England and America. Many mid-nineteenth-century Americans read Coleridge under the guidance of his first American editor, and Anthony John Harding's study, "James Marsh as Editor of Coleridge," helps us understand their combined influence. As Coleridge's Kantianism is often said to be more Coleridgean than purely Kantian, so, Harding indicates, Marsh's Coleridgeanism was more Marshian than purely Coleridgean. The widespread influence of Coleridge's *Aids to Reflection* in the United States owed as much to Marsh's presentation of the master's ideas, in his long "Preliminary Essay" to his edition of *Aids* (1829), as to the ideas as they were presented by Coleridge.

Instances of even more extended or divergent readings of Coleridge was discussed in Stephen Prickett's essay on Coleridge's idea of the clerisy, which traces the Victorian reaction and the development of the idea up to Eliot. By the time the Victorians had developed, altered, and spread this idea, it had become a good deal less than the pure original Coleridgean idea, but "part of a tradition of which we have still not seen the end."

The essays in *Reading Coleridge*, then, examine the content

Reading Coleridge

] 1 [

Explaining Coleridge's Explanation: Toward a Practical Methodology for Coleridge Studies

Laurence S. Lockridge

Scholarly and critical work on Coleridge as a thinker has only begun to take advantage of the rich materials his editors have been making available in recent years. One senses a lag not wholly explained by the usual period required for the assimilation of new texts. The publication in 1973 of the monumental Volume 3 of the *Notebooks,* for example, has not created the stir in the profession that one might expect from an event of significance not only to Coleridge studies but to the study of nineteenth-century thought generally. Apparently the feeling persists among students and experienced scholars alike that to venture into Coleridge's prose is dangerous business.

The reasons for this hesitation are familiar ones, but they seem to have become even more stubborn lately. First among them is, of course, the issue of plagiarism. Whatever judgment one makes of it, Norman Fruman's *Coleridge, The Damaged Archangel* (1971) has made the larger intellectual community doubtful of claims made for Coleridge as a creative figure in the history of ideas. Answers to Fruman have had neither the simplicity nor the publicity of his thesis and have therefore had less impact; many still fear that Coleridge is a desultory follower of Kant and Schelling who would take one down his mazy path to a dead end. The related problem of German scholarship is perhaps even more inhibiting: isn't it necessary to undergo a twenty-year apprenticeship in Kant, Schiller, Fichte, Schelling, Schleiermacher, Tetens, Herder, the brothers Schlegel, and lord knows who else before one can presume to speak about Coleridge? Students of literature fear their lack of philosophical expertise, while philosophers prefer to take their Kant straight. How can one ever be sure a brilliant passage crucial to one's argument is written by Coleridge, and not by Steffens or Ritter or Maass?

Beyond this is the suspicion that Coleridge is not only difficult but fundamentally muddle-headed and that any effort to find clarity in opacity will be scholarly and critical superimposition: the author's Coleridge, not Coleridge himself. Especially in his early years, he contradicts himself or changes his mind from one day to the next; linear development is often problematic. One tendency in Coleridge studies, in response to this disjointedness, has been to focus on isolated passages, to probe them as if they were conundrums or bits of prose trying to be poetry, and to forego the elucidation Coleridge himself might provide elsewhere in the vast, untidy corpus. The result in scholarship is a certain repetitiveness, wherein the same passages reappear in discussion time and again, the most familiar, of course, the definitions of imagination and fancy in *Biographia Literaria,* Chapter XIII. (In Volume 3 of the *Notebooks* alone, there are several other passages defining or describing these concepts, especially 4066, but also 3247, 3744, 3820, 3827, 4111–15, 4176, 4397, and 4498.) The entire issue of his philosophy of literature and practical literary criticism might more profitably be pursued if those key "definitions" in *Biographia Literaria* were retired for awhile. *Biographia Literaria,* incidentally, gives most students their first taste of his prose, and it frequently gives them a strong impression that he cannot be read, that his prose is elephantine, that he cannot for the life of him stay on the subject, and that, as Carlyle says, he spends all his time assembling "precautionary and vehiculatory gear" but never finally sets out. A significant scholarly question raised by the prose works Coleridge published in his lifetime, many of them dull or irritating in the reading, is how and where one finds life and drama in these ruminations. How does one make Coleridge move?

What is needed now, I think, is a statement of the practical methodology best suited to his *kind* of mind. In outlining such a methodology, I will take a cue from Richard Haven's designations, as they relate to Coleridge, of three kinds of interpretation—the genetic, the historical, and the structural—and will, for convenience' sake alone, illustrate my points with reference to my own work with his moral thought.[1] That his moral thought might in some respects constitute a special case not permitting methodological extensions to other areas of his thought I will keep in mind and will speak to in conclusion. My aim is to make the prospect of working with Coleridge the thinker less formidable, and perhaps even enticing.

Genetic Interpretation

By genetic interpretation I refer to criticism of two closely related kinds: one, linking Coleridge's thought with its sources in his own life and personality, views an idea as a biographical or psychological consequent of sorts; the other focuses on his own treatment of the genetic, his psychogenetic accounts of, for example, art, philosophical ideas, and his own behavior. An example of the first, in the main, is Walter Jackson Bate's critical biography, *Coleridge* (1968), and of the second, Richard Haven's *Patterns of Consciousness* (1969).

[1]Richard Haven, *Patterns of Consciousness: An Essay on Coleridge* (Amherst: University of Massachusetts Press, 1969), pp. 7–8; Lockridge, *Coleridge the Moralist* (Ithaca: Cornell University Press, 1977). This methodological essay may be supplemented by a largely bibliographical one, George Whalley's "On Reading Coleridge," in *S. T. Coleridge*, ed. R. L. Brett, Writers and Their Background (London: G. Bell, 1971), pp. 1–44.

Coleridge is his own best biographer and analyst, not as one who tells his story from A to B but as one who describes closely—despite a few notable silences—the important moments of his life, whether events as such or intellectual and emotional mutations. He is at his best when personally and actively engaged in the matter of his observation and when his exploratory powers are exercised in the informal context of notebook entries, letters, conversation, and marginalia. This point can be extended emphatically to become the first tenet of a Coleridge methodology: it can work as a principle of selection, as a means of deciding which of his many reflections on a particular subject one will emphasize in an exposition of his thought. If one focuses on passages that have arisen directly from personal struggle, immediate observation, and obvious intellectual perplexity at the moment of composition, one will find a vitality of inquiry and of language that may elsewhere fail Coleridge. Such failure tends to come about not when he jumps off the deep end (there he swims not so badly with those "logical swim-bladders" Carlyle derides), but when he forsakes active mental exploration for pompous holding forth or attitudinizing, when he simply manipulates an acquired vocabulary of "sum-m-mjects" and "om-m-mjects," when he plagiarizes, when he begins to speak with his mind already made up, or when he has lost that sense of self that tells him and us that it is *Coleridge* speaking. The airless writing that results may seem the more useful to a scholar, because it often is concerned with summaries or comprehensive definitions or larger pronouncements. Such passages may seem to lend themselves to expositions of what Coleridge thinks, but at the same time they misrepresent his quality of mind. When he keeps in view the experiential data of his own life, his observation of a scene before him, or his direct encounter with another author, the result may be a decrease in summary statement but a gratifying increase in animation and sense of exploration.

Let two contrasting passages—though scores could be

marshaled—illustrate this point, both for what they say in substance and for how they are written. A notebook entry of 1805 records what he feels when he argues with a utilitarian or materialist:

> Now if I say to a Paleyan or Priestleyan my *mist,* my delving & difficulty, & he answers me in a set of parrot words, ⟨quite satisfied, clear as a pike-staff,—nothing *before* & *nothing behind*—a stupid piece of mock-knowlege, having no *root* for then it would have feelings of dimness from *growth,* having no buds or twigs, for then it would have yearnings & strivings of obscurity from *growing,* but a dry stick of Licorish, sweet tho' mawkish to the palate of self-adulation,⟩ acknowleging no sympathy with this delving, this feeling of a wonder/then I must needs set him down for a Priestleyan, Paleyan, Barbouldian, &c &c &c &c &c—from Lock to Mackintosh. [*N*, II, 2509]

The passage expresses deep personal irritation at a lack of sympathy with intellectual perplexity; the banality of the "Paleyan or Priestleyan" is itself a matter of great perplexity to him. The multiple metaphoric extensions, characteristically to plants (brilliantly juxtaposed to that "dry stick of Licorish"), reveal the essential Coleridge, who turns to metaphor not as decoration but as a powerful tool of exploration. Though not dressed in the language of philosophy, the inquiry is provocative in its philosophical implications. It links intellectual and moral growth with sublime feeling and with acts of willful appropriation, not simple mental acquiescence; and it questions the sufficiency of clarity as an intellectual ideal. The attack, by implication, is not only on materialists or utilitarians but on Cartesian rationalists for their reliance on "clear and distinct conceptions." It has obviously been provoked by actual encounters with such lunkheads, though the exact occasion is unclear. Invested as the passage is with his voice and personality, it makes us sensitive to its genetic properties, the author behind it, and his strong sense of the occasions that have given birth to it.

Contrast this notebook passage now with one in *The Friend:*

To examine any thing wisely, two conditions are requisite: first, a
distinct notion of the desirable ENDS, in the complete accomplish-
ment of which would consist the perfection of such a thing, or its
ideal excellence; and, secondly, a calm and kindly mode of feeling,
without which we shall hardly fail either to overlook, or not to
make due allowances for, the circumstances which prevent these
ends from being all perfectly realized in the particular thing which
we are to examine. For instance, we must have a general notion
what a MAN can be and ought to be, before we can fitly proceed to
determine on the merits or demerits of any one individual. [*F,* I,
249-50]

One might be tempted to employ such a passage in an exposition
of his thought, because it categorizes conveniently and has an
authoritative conclusiveness about it. And that is one problem
with it, for though it might serve as a summary statement, it is
also dull. More than this: its appearance of a wise summing up is
illusory. As we have just seen, Coleridge is not always so
enamoured of "a calm and kindly mode of feeling" as a prerequisite for intellectual inquiry; what he values more is perplexity,
delving, and strong feeling, the "feeling of a wonder." And his
characteristic method is not to proceed from "general notions"
to particulars, but quite the reverse. I suggest we get a better
idea of Coleridge as a vital mind if we lay aside, or at least
deemphasize, passages such as this one; when he speaks as a wise
man he frequently cheats on his better insights.

The personal observation that contradicts the weighty speculation often leads Coleridge to revision and adjustment, a pattern in which one may find not muddle-headedness but mental
drama. The drama is found, for example, in his reflections on
the nature of duty, a theme central to much of his life and
thought. In *Lectures 1795, The Friend, Lay Sermons,* and *Aids,* one
finds much heady and ominous talk of the necessity of "*bottoming
on fixed Principles,*" of following Luther's example, who "did his
duty, come good come evil!," of observing Kant's categorical

imperative (which he quotes in *The Friend* without attribution), of renouncing "WORLDLY PRUDENCE" (*L*, p. 5; *F*, I, 49, 194; *CL*, I, 171). With no trace of irony he tells Southey he will marry Sarah Fricker, whom he does not love, because it "still remains for me to be externally Just though my Heart is withered within me." "Mark you, Southey!—*I will do my Duty*" (*CL*, I, 132, 145). Walter Pater observes that Coleridge's "pathetic history pleads for a more elastic moral philosophy than his, and cries out against every formula less living and flexible than life itself."[2] But Coleridge learns some hard lessons here—the marriage, for one thing, proves a curse on both parties—and in extensive writings on the subject he develops his own elasticity. Late in life he advises his young friend Thomas Allsop against running into an imprudent marriage, because "Self may be moodily gratified by *Self*-sacrifice," and a sense of duty that does not embrace personal inclination and prudence is likely to be self-defeating. "A morality of consequences I, you well know, reprobate—but to exclude the necessary *effect* of an action is to take away all meaning from the word, action—to strike Duty with blindness" (*CL*, V, 177–78; see also 182). In the truly moral person duty and inclination are harmonized, and Coleridge sees this as a real moral and psychological possibility, for others if not for him—it is not merely the hypothetical "holy will" that, according to Kant, transcends moral categories altogether. His experience with "supermoralists" such as his authoritarian older brother George or the punctilious Southey or the occasionally severe Wordsworth makes his own talk of fixed principles seem hollow to him when it is not dangerous. One can see the same mind faulting Southey for his moral austerity (the "smiles, the emanations, the perpetual Sea-like Sound & Motion of Virtuousness, which is Love, is wanting"), Wordsworth for his "Ode to Duty," to which he is tempted to respond with an "Ode to Pleasure,"

---

[2]Walter Pater, *Appreciations* (1889; rpt. London: Macmillan, 1901), pp. 103–04.

and Marat and Robespierre for their ruthlessness as "conscientious Persecutors."[3]

A scholar who admits genetic analysis into his discussion can argue that Coleridge's biographical circumstances and psychological make-up—his dependency on authority figures and readiness to feel guilt—give rise to his preoccupation with and reflections on duty, conscience, and principle; he can argue this without necessarily denying that these reflections have intrinsic intellectual interest apart from what gives rise to them. He can also argue that Coleridge's rejection of supermoralism comes about from his response to too great a dose of it in others. Thus, with reference to their sources in Coleridge's life and personality, the scholar can give a coherent account of both aspects of Coleridge's thinking on duty and principle—his "supermoralism" on the one hand and his moral liberalism on the other—and present what might otherwise be thought simple intellectual contradiction or muddle-headedness as dramatic vacillation or even a change of mind dearly won. Genetic interpretation proves here and elsewhere one way of finding continuity, movement, and drama in what may otherwise appear to be miscellaneous or contradictory reflections by anchoring them in a life and personality which, though tormented and crippled, still offer their own kind of elucidation.

Coleridge's own interest in genetic interpretation is everywhere apparent—in such a familiar instance as the distinction he makes between "poem" as an objective construct and "poetry," the act of the "whole soul" that may or may not give rise to a poem; or in the famous Preface to "Kubla Khan," purporting to account for the poem; or, more generally, in his fascination with the psychological origins of ideas and behavior. He is a better psychologist than epistemologist, and he thinks that "in Psychology Kant is but suspicious Authority" (*N*, I, 1710). Be-

[3]*N*, I, 1815; *N*, II, 2091, 2531; *IS*, pp. 128-30, 276-77; Notebook 29, Berg Collection, New York Public Library, ff. 112-19ᵛ.

sides his various epistemological formulations, such as the reason/understanding distinction he urged so polemically on his contemporaries, one might pursue his direct observation of the human mind, its "envy," "indolence," "dread," "sympathy," "guilt," or need of "confirmation." In this kind of psychological observation he gives us something we rarely find in the German or even the British philosophers. If in his promotion of "reason" he celebrates the powers of the human mind, in his observations of habit, indolence, and motivation he sounds like a modern skeptic: "Thought or the Act of Thinking has no *transitive* power," the mind cannot create a "drawbridge from Thought to Thing" (*N,* I, 1500n). He laments the "*thinking* disease" that results in mere self-involution "instead of Actions, Realizations, *things* done & as such externalized & *remembered.* On such meagre Diet as ⟨feelings evaporated⟩ embryos interrupted in their progress to *Birth,* no moral Being ever became Healthy" (*N,* III, 4012).

This kind of psychogenetic inquiry gives Coleridge an arresting modernity. The scholar need not import Freudian or Jungian categories to begin to explain him, or for that matter Hegelian, Heideggerian, or Derridean. The greater service is to let Coleridge explain himself, to employ a method that would— taking up on Byron's quip—help him explain his explanation. A Coleridgean psychogenetic account, whether of his own life, of art, or of human experience generally, may not ultimately satisfy us. When he looks inward, for example, he has some blind spots (though despite a reluctance to examine closely his own sexuality, aggressions, or plagiarism, he does frequently provide a grammar of interpretation for such phenomena by witnessing and describing them in other people). When he attempts to describe the function of human mind generically, he sometimes resorts to the very faculty psychology he deplores or he hypostatizes mental powers or he corrupts phenomenological description with prescriptive categories often reflecting that "bump of reverence" of which Owen Barfield speaks. A Freudian critic might wish to substitute for Coleridge's talk of dejection, envy, dread, or love his own vocabulary of repression, projection, castration anxiety, or cathexis; an existentialist might wish to read *The Ancient Mariner* as an exercise in ontological anguish, not Coleridgean remorse or guilt or bad conscience; a Marxian critic might see in Coleridge's chronic "self-inquisition" a display of liberal-bourgeois individualism. But before bringing in other modalities, we might profitably follow him on his own terms as far as he can take us.

For Coleridge's more provocative psychogenetic explorations, one will turn less often to *The Friend* or *Aids* or even *Biographia Literaria* than to the *Notebooks* and *Letters*, which texts, I suggest, should supersede, for a time at least, the works Coleridge published in his lifetime or that have otherwise already become familiar to us. The *Notebooks* and *Letters* have color and immediacy and a focus on the personal that are frequently lost when he clumsily tries to find his voice in public.

A naive use of the genetic approach, whether it focuses on the origins of Coleridge's thought in his own life and personality or on his own psychogenetic writings, may result in the genetic fallacy: the invalid attempt wholly to explain a phenomenon by means of its antecedents. Before expounding the internal structure of Coleridge's thought, Barfield argues against genetic analysis on this basis.[4] A recent book, Molly Lefebure's *Samuel Taylor Coleridge: A Bondage of Opium* (1974), demonstrates the perils of genetic analysis: the author attempts to explain virtually everything about Coleridge in terms of his opium addiction. A biographer could perhaps say that opium brutally forces him to his speculations on the nature of conscience, guilt, and dread, but these speculations have interest apart from what may have led him to make them; and, in any event, opium may act more as catalyst than as cause. Genetic accounts sometimes trivialize the

---

[4]Owen Barfield, *What Coleridge Thought* (Middletown, Conn.: Wesleyan University Press, 1971), pp. 3-10.

subject by not so much explaining as explaining away real intellectual perplexity—by, for example, reducing it to mere psychological conflict, just as Coleridge himself attempts to reduce "Kubla Khan" to a mere "psychological curiosity."

To this objection, one can reply, first, that there is intrinsic interest in accounting for something; one should simply have the tact not to offer an account of origins as a sufficient explanation. How many of us still dismiss literary biography as irrelevant to the interpretation of literature? Second, one can argue that Coleridge is particularly susceptible of genetic interpretation, because he himself insists that the structure of a phenomenon is a function of the mind that half-perceives and half-creates it. As Haven says, especially with regard to Coleridge, "Genetic interpretation involves structural analysis insofar as structure is genetically determined" (p. 8). To see a continuity between the genetic and the structural is to be true to one of the most salient tendencies of his mind.

My position, then, is that Coleridge is an exception to any rule limiting or forbidding genetic interpretation. His thought is better expounded not as some isolable and either coherent or incoherent body of ideas but rather as a play of ideas emanating from a living personality—Coleridge thinking, feeling, sensing. Any treatment of his thought may profitably be anchored in the drama of his life and personality—for the sake not only of rhetorical color but also, as we have seen in his reflections on duty, of clarity. One may indeed follow a line of thought as it unfolds according to an internal continuity, but if one has selected those passages rhetorically freshest and most improvisatory, one's exposition will already be tinged with the personal. His entire argument on most subjects could not be presented with such passages alone—one wishes there were even more of them, especially in the very late notebooks and in the Opus Maximum—but they can well be the basis of any presentation. Furthermore, Coleridge's own psychogenetic bent—whether in his writings on epistemology, psychology, science, religion, or art—is a major characteristic of his method; to practice it oneself is to be sympathetic, in a strict sense, to the Coleridgean situation.

Historical Interpretation

By historical interpretation I refer to criticism that places Coleridge in the history of ideas with regard either to the ways in which he has been influenced by other figures, past and present, or to the kinds of overt commentary he makes on these figures. Technically, historical interpretation is not separate from genetic interpretation on the one hand, since it deals with the question of origins and antecedents, or from structural interpretation on the other, since it must structure its data, whether diachronically or synchronically. It will be useful to violate an old Coleridgean dictum here, however, and both distinguish and separate historical interpretation from these. The first mode of historical inquiry has often dwelt on unacknowledged sources Coleridge has used in a way that many would call plagiarism; the second, on Coleridge as a critical mind who comments on a wealth of other cultural and intellectual figures. Fruman's *Coleridge, The Damaged Archangel* is an example of the first, Thomas McFarland's *Coleridge and the Pantheist Tradition* (1969) of the second. Fruman does not expressly draw the conclusion his study seems to suggest—that Coleridge's heavy and neurotically dishonest reliance on other thinkers makes futile the kind of enterprise in which McFarland and others are engaged. By and large, though, he is in the line of scholarship going back to René Wellek's *Immanuel Kant in England* (1931), which argues, in effect, that Coleridge's mind is precisely what he himself most inveighed against: "a leaden cistern," "a mere repository or banqueting-room," and not "the germinal power that craves no knowledge but what it can take up into itself, what it can appropriate and re-produce in fruits of its own" (*F*, I, 473).

I suggest that one will find a great amount of material better described as Coleridge's than as Kant's or Schelling's or Jean Paul's if one develops an ear for the Coleridgean rhetoric of intellectual exploration. One can begin to develop this if the genetic perspectives of which I have already been speaking are kept in mind: one can to a large extent isolate and deemphasize purely derivative material if one selects for analysis or constructive exposition those passages in which Coleridge has left concrete traces of himself in the act of thinking, those ruminations that have obviously been triggered by some moment itself recorded and incorporated. When he *is* thus engaged, he is not simply translating or furtively stealing from the Germans. One could isolate the unacknowledged translations or close paraphrases (or plagiarisms, according to one's view of the controversy), or, as McFarland has suggested, simply put quotation marks around them, and still have an enormous residue of *Coleridge*.

However one may choose to deemphasize passages closely tied to unacknowledged sources, they cannot and should not be eliminated from consideration. I suggest a three-part schema of such passages as a basis for deciding how they may be employed in constructions of Coleridge's thought. His moral character or sanity is not the issue here, and the extent to which the word "plagiarism" applies to these categories would be disputed.

First, there is the verbatim translation or very close paraphrase of an unacknowledged source, which translation or paraphrase is not fully and visibly absorbed into an argument Coleridge is developing, or which is not put into perspective by his direct and substantial commentary on it. Since we are not here attempting to decide what should be called "plagiarism" and what should not, we can include in this category both those passages he published in his lifetime, or intended to publish, and those in notebooks and letters, where, in a strict sense, the issue of plagiarism would not arise, or at least not in the same way. The most famous instance of this first category is, of course, the direct translation and close paraphrase in *Biographia Literaria,*

[35]

Chapter XII, of many passages from Schelling's *Abhandlungen zur Erläuterung des Idealismus der Wissenschaftslehre* (1796–97) and *System des transzendentalen Idealismus* (1800). Many scholars would want to include in this category such texts as *Theory of Life,* which contains many close paraphrases of Schelling and Henrik Steffens, or "On Poesy or Art," again of Schelling, or those portions of *The Philosophical Lectures* heavily indebted to the German historian of philosophy, Tennemann. In the *Notebooks* one finds many translations and close paraphrases from the Germans without documentation of source and without substantial commentary.

Many scholars would argue that such passages may properly be used alongside passages not directly attributable to a source in constructions of Coleridge's thought. They would point out that the fact he may have derived an idea from another thinker does not mean he does not assent to it. Once he adopts the idea as his own, he *thinks* it, after all, quite apart from the question of where the idea originated or whether he was honest or dishonest in the way he appropriated and presented it. Then too, the idea may have intrinsic interest to us without reference to its origin. The issue is a difficult one, but I would argue that these passages, to the extent one can spot them in advance, should serve mostly a corroborative role in such constructions. Though they usually indicate what Coleridge agrees with, they may not so indicate, or they may do so only in a general, not a precise way. And may they not sometimes merely suggest what he finds interesting? In the *Notebooks* he has translated or closely paraphrased without acknowledgment many sources with scant indication of agreement or disagreement (e.g., *N,* III, 3673, 4088, 4186, 4287–97), and there are instances throughout the corpus where one might assume some disagreement (e.g., portions of the manuscript *Logic,* of *Biographia Literaria,* Chapter XII, or even of *N,* III, 4397, beyond the departures from source that Kathleen Coburn has documented). In works he published or in lectures he delivered, one would with more confidence assume agreement than in works not expressly intended for the public, but the very issue I am touching on here concerning the nature and degree of intellectual assent—an especially cumbersome issue in Coleridge's case with which to have to deal peripherally—would still arise. Does "agreement" mean "commitment"? Does a conduit necessarily absorb? The scholar might have to make assumptions about Coleridge's degree of commitment that a skeptical mind would regard as gratuitous.

More important, such passages do not in themselves reveal Coleridge as a *creative* thinker. I use "creative" quite apart from the narrower word "original," for how often can we identify with certainty a given figure as the originator of an idea? Without attempting a comprehensive definition of "creative" as it relates to expository prose, I think it could be said that one criterion is that the author has presented a line of thought in his or her own language, albeit based perhaps on the thought of others, and has ordered it sentence by sentence, paragraph by paragraph, according to his or her way of seeing the subject matter. A translated or closely paraphrased passage does not in itself satisfy this criterion. A creative reader, a creative translator, or, for that matter, a creative plagiarist is not necessarily a creative thinker, and to present Coleridge's translations or paraphrases as expressive of his creative thought—and is it not one's first interest, in most cases, to seek *this* out?—is to dilute the distinctive qualities of his mind.

Metaphorically, in distinguishing translated or paraphrased passages from those in which Coleridge is more creatively engaged, one is not grossly dividing him but rather seeking out his core. In practice this methodological recommendation amounts to a question of emphasis, since passages translated or closely paraphrased may still serve important functions in scholarly or critical exposition—they help to fill out the intellectual context from which Coleridge drew nourishment and in light of which he did his own creative thinking. In the *Notebooks* I came across a passage which began: "The moral Law referred to the empirical human being, or Man the φαινομενον)+ [as contradistinguished from] Homo Νουμενον, has a determinate *commencement* (punctum incipiens) of its career, viz. the definite sphere or circumscription in which the Individual finds himself at the time he first finds himself, i.e. at the first exertion of reflective Self-consciousness" (*N*, III, 3673). The passage seemed to sum up one aspect of Coleridge's thinking on this subject, but it had an odor about it that suggested the headier formal writings of the German idealists; it was a passage with verbal and logical discrimination but little color or movement. It did promise a good summary linkage in the argument I was constructing, however, and I set it aside for that purpose. It was merely a hunch and some luck that took me to the passage in Fichte's *System der Sittenlehre* (1798) of which it is a nearly verbatim translation.[5] The source discovered, I did not feel the passage wholly disqualified from use, but it seemed appropriate to use it only to corroborate those arguments developed elsewhere with a much more Coleridgean accent. Since Coleridge says nothing about the passage in context, it would have been idle, even presumptuous, to argue from it or on the basis of it.

As a disseminator of ideas through translation and paraphrase whether the source is acknowledged or not, Coleridge is a pivotal figure in the history of ideas. In the Opus Maximum manuscript he gives us, *with* acknowledgment, the first translation in English of Kant's opening passage in *Grundlegung zur Metaphysik der Sitten* (1785): "There is, observes the great restorer of the Stoic Moral Philosophy, nothing in the world, yea! nothing out of the world within the power of human conception that can without qualification or limit be regarded as good, save the Good Will alone" (OM, B₂, ff. 63–66). A scholar might rightly praise him here for being the first writer in English to single out, and intend to make available to his compatriots, a passage that

---

[5] Johann Gottlieb Fichte, *Werke*, ed. Fritz Medicus, 6 vols. (Leipzig: Fritz Eckardt, 1908–12), II (1908), 560.

has subsequently proved to be one of the most famous in the literature of ethics. If Coleridge had not documented the passage, the same scholar might unhesitatingly accuse him of plagiarism, and let it go at that. But one could then reply to this scholar that Coleridge at least has good taste in sources, and probably an impulse to teach as well as to steal.

Unacknowledged translations or close paraphrases can be used, then, if sparingly, as linkages in argument, as suggestions of affinities and contexts, or as illustrations of what Coleridge read. They may vary in length from a sentence or two to whole paragraphs to the better part of whole treatises. The best way of spotting them, besides direct recall of the sources themselves, is to be alert to a shift of style, often an attenuation of rhetorical verve. No matter how keen an ear one develops for this sort of thing, some passages will probably get by; most Coleridge scholars from time to time claim for him a passage that he has only translated or paraphrased.

I would propose a second category consisting of passages based on unacknowledged sources that have been absorbed into and redirected by Coleridge's argument, but not to the extent that one could speak of them simply as unacknowledged influences. I discovered one such passage in an unpublished and never delivered "college commemoration sermon" of 1799, in which he silently adapts the argument of a compatriot, not a German. In the preface to his *Fifteen Sermons* (1726), Joseph Butler notes that the subject of morals may be treated by beginning either with "the abstract relations of things" or with one's observation of "what the particular nature of man is." Coleridge echoes Butler directly here without using his exact words and agrees with him that one should begin with observation of the particular nature of man but, as Butler argues, only insofar as that "nature" embraces the very reasoning power the rationalist enlists as *his* first premise. Butler continues by noting that the Stoics were correct to view human nature as "an one or a whole, made up of several parts; but yet, that the several parts even considered as a whole, do not complete the idea, unless in the notion of a whole, you include the relations and respects, which those parts have to each other. Every work both of nature and of art is a system. . . ." Coleridge follows Butler closely and writes that the "opinion of the wisest ancients that virtue consists in following nature is safe and well-founded, if by the word nature be understood not any single appetite, affection, passion, or quality, but the *system* of our nature: that is those relations and correspondencies which these several parts bear, each to all, and all to each."[6] Several other parallels and echoes of phraseology put the source identification beyond dispute. This use of Butler is significant, whether or not one calls it plagiarism. It gives us one of the few direct indications in Coleridge's work that he actually studied Butler and used him, and it corroborates internally Hazlitt's statement that in 1798 Coleridge had been reading the *Fifteen Sermons* and that he had pronounced Butler to be one of England's greatest metaphysicians.[7] Furthermore, the use of Butler is significant because it links Coleridge with an important element of the liberal moral tradition in Great Britain; he has appropriated an author who contributes to a conception of the human being as an organism possessed of many powers that should be freely developed, not repressed. And more important here, the passage demonstrates how Coleridge can direct a source to his own end: updating the context, he employs Butler in beginning a lengthy argument against the Godwinians (of whom Butler knew nothing, of course), who reduce the essential human personality to its reasoning function and downgrade the emotional life. In passages such as this one, Coleridge may not pass out credit to his predecessors, and he may even directly echo another's language and precise argument, but he may in so

[6]LT 29, Victoria University Library, Toronto; *Fifteen Sermons*, in *British Moralists*, ed. D. D. Raphael, 2 vols. (Oxford: Clarendon Press, 1969), I, 325–30.
[7]William Hazlitt, "My First Acquaintance with Poets," in *Works*, ed. P. P. Howe, 21 vols. (London: J. M. Dent, 1933), XVII, 113.

doing redirect the argument interestingly and reveal a creative intelligence at work. When using such passages, the scholar might focus on this strategy of redirection, or on the way the passage means something different in the context Coleridge provides for it from what it meant in its original context. The argument that he employs an unusual method of composition—one which results in a "mosaic" of sources and his reflections on them—would most suitably pertain to passages of this category, in my judgment.[8]

A third category includes those passages indebted to unacknowledged sources that have been fully absorbed and used and redirected. Here we are speaking of unacknowledged influences, not direct translations or paraphrases. In his moral thought the most important, usually unacknowledged sources or influences are Kant's *Grundlegung zur Metaphysik der Sitten* (1785), *Kritik der praktischen Vernunft* (1788), and *Metaphysik der Sitten* (1797) for their treatment of the means by which one arrives at a moral judgment; Schiller's *Über Anmut und Würde* (1793) for its argument against Kant's account of duty and inclination as contraries, and his *Briefe über die ästhetische Erziehung des Menschen* (1794–1795) for the relation of personality to time; Fichte's *System der Sittenlehre* for its account of ego, alienation, and self-consciousness, and *Die Bestimmung des Menschen* (1800) for its account of conscience; and Schelling's *Das Wesen der menschlichen Freiheit* (1809) for its discussion of will and evil. Two examples of this kind of influence may suffice. In a notebook Coleridge rewrites the Decalogue in Kantian terms: "Thou shalt have no other gods before me" becomes "Let the Will obey the pure Reason *exclusively* & *unconditionally*"; not making graven images becomes "Preserve the pure Reason pure—& debase it not by any mixture of *sens*uality"; not taking the name of the Lord in vain becomes "Preserve the faculty of Discourse ... in

---

[8]See Thomas McFarland, *Coleridge and the Pantheist Tradition* (Oxford: Clarendon Press, 1969), pp. xxii–xl, 1–52.

strict awe & allegiance to the pure Reason," etc. (*N*, III, 3293). This use of Kant is a good example of Coleridge's perennial effort to reconcile German idealism with Judeo-Christian doctrine, and it occasionally reveals distortion or augmentation of source, as when he insists on "worship of," not simply rational respect for, the "distinction between the Noumenon & the Phænomenon." A rhetorically more vivid adaptation of German sources is a notebook entry in which he weighs the relative weight of the self's power to create and of circumstance and nature to control and inhibit. His argument is an informal adaptation of the Kantian doctrine of the centrality of human mind, its principle of freedom despite the rigidly predetermined phenomenal world in which mind finds itself. In describing this phenomenal world, he admits each human being is

> influenced & determined (caused to be what he is, qualis sit = qualified, *bethinged*) by Universal Nature, its elements & relations.—Beyond this ring-fence he cannot stray, of these circummurations he can seldom overleap the lowest & innermost, and the outermost is his apparent horizon, & insurmountable— from this Skein of necessities he cannot disentangle himself, which surrounds with subtlest intertwine the slenderest fibres of his Being, while it binds the whole frame with chains of adamant. [*N*, III, 4109]

The passage has special relevance to one who feels himself so often trapped by circumstance, who broods on the degree of his own culpability. It also reveals the rhetorical strain and distention, the tendency toward neologism and hypotaxis, the use of the dash (he calls punctuation marks "dramatic *directions* representing the process of Thinking & Speaking conjointly" [*N*, III, 3504])—all symptoms of Coleridge's being engaged in, even trapped by, real intellectual perplexity. The passage has too much of his own accent to be labeled "derivative," even though one might describe it as loosely Kantian in its fundamental orientation. Such passages may be used without reservation in constructions of Coleridge's creative thought.

To argue that passages based on unacknowledged sources—whether influences or plagiarisms—can be profitably used is not to dismiss them as a problem; they remain the thorniest problem confronting the Coleridge scholar and critic. But they can be turned to some advantage.

How knowledgeable must one be of German philosophy and literature before setting out? The question is in a real sense inappropriate because one becomes knowledgeable *by virtue of studying* Coleridge, if this is an aspect of his thought that arrests one. He will continue to perform his historic teaching function by leading one into what may be strange seas of thought. Before avoiding any interdisciplinary topic involving him, one might keep this point in mind. In addition, historical scholarship that focuses on analogues, influences, sources, and plagiarisms has the somewhat ironic result of freeing those who would prefer to concentrate on genetic or structural interpretation. The import of McFarland's *Coleridge and the Pantheist Tradition,* with its extensive investigation of Continental sources and analogues, is not that all studies of Coleridge's thought must similarly scout through this massive literature; indeed it is almost the opposite. This study demonstrates Coleridge's independence of Spinoza and Schelling, the figures with whom he wrestles in arriving at his own theological position on pantheism. They are sources, to be sure, but sources he uses and departs from over a period of years. One could, in theory, construct his theological position on pantheism internally with scant reference to them, or, as Barfield might say, with only Coleridge's references to them, thereby abrogating the historical/comparative method, the success of which has made itself no longer methodologically imperative. Barfield, who is knowledgeable in German philosophy, sets out to construct, with only occasional references to the Germans, what Coleridge thought. Ideally one would have a thorough acquaintance with German philosophy and literature, but it is not, in any event, a prerequisite for all scholarly projects, especially if one takes advantage of the possibilities inherent in a genetic and/or structural approach. Some familiarity *is* necessary, and here Coleridge himself will be helpful.

Historical scholarship that focuses on Coleridge's treatment of a broad expanse of the Western intellectual tradition is an enormous undertaking, as Kathleen Coburn's notes on the *Notebooks* make clear. It appears that Coleridge somehow managed to comment on most of what he read and learned. A large volume has been compiled on what he said about the seventeenth century, and book-length studies could be made of that material alone.[9] The *Collected Marginalia,* when its publication has been completed, will be a great contribution to this aspect of historical interpretation. And, incidentally, when Coleridge comments directly on other texts plagiarism as such ceases to be an issue.

As a critic of other minds he is acute, but his powers of analysis have been underestimated because of his poor powers of sustained exposition. For example, his critique of the dominant British moral schools of his day—hedonism, egoism, and utilitarianism—is remarkably subtle, once the scattered writings, published and unpublished, have been consolidated. A few passages combine to produce a striking anticipation of G. E. Moore's famous open-question argument, which was the center of debate among ethicists during the first half of this century. Coleridge writes that the "sum total of Moral philosphy is found in this one question—Is 'good' a superfluous word?—or lazy synonime for the pleasurable, and its causes? at least, a mere modification to express degree & comparative duration ⟨of pleasure?⟩—/—Therefore we may more unanswerably state the question—Is 'good' superfluous as a word exponent of a *kind?*"

---

[9]*Coleridge on the Seventeenth Century,* ed. Roberta Florence Brinkley (Durham, N.C.: Duke University Press, 1955).

(*N*, III, 3938). We find the question in the *Notebooks* but must turn to the Opus Maximum and *The Philosophical Lectures* for a full answer. In these texts he argues, against the hedonists, that "good" is a more inclusive term than "pleasure": "If I say pleasure is a good and pain an evil, will it be pretended that I convey the same impression and am talking as childishly as if I had said black is black & white is white? Shall I not be as intelligible to all men, as when I say, that green is a colour and an octave a sound?" (OM, B$_2$, ff. 61–62). The hedonist himself would not utter the truism that there is "no pleasure but pleasure and no pain but pain," and he knows the substitution of "pleasure" for "good" changes the meaning of most sentences, for pleasure is only *a* good. Moore uses this same "argument from trivialization" in attempting to undermine "naturalistic ethics."[10] The historical approach therefore lends itself just as provocatively to "anticipations" as to "derivations." Coleridge's argument, thus constructed, reveals the kind of critical acumen of which he is capable and which he continues to bring to bear in arguments against egoists and utilitarians.

The more closely one follows his argument, the more Coleridge is likely to elude easy placement in the history of ideas. His criticism of utilitarianism, for example, is that it is

> no less *ideal* than that of any former system: that is, it is no less incapable of receiving any external experimental proof, compulsory on the understandings of all men, such as criteria exhibited in chemistry. Yet, unlike the elder Systems of Morality, it remains in the world of the senses, without deriving any evidence therefrom. The agent's mind is compelled to go out of itself in order to bring back *conjectures*, the probability of which will vary with the shrewdness of the individual. [*F*, I, 317]

His argument for this is presented at length in *The Friend*, and it may strike one as both ironic and puzzling that this "idealist"

[10]G. E. Moore, *Principia Ethica* (Cambridge: Cambridge University Press, 1903; rpt. 1959), pp. 1–21.

Coleridge, whom Carlyle thought lost in a Kantian "haze-world" of "vacant air-castles and dim-melting ghosts and shadows," should criticize a philosophical position because it is too "ideal." What exactly is the fundamental orientation from which he could make this criticism? To pursue such a question is to discover in him a freedom of speculation that resists fixed ideas and that tends to view opposing intellectual currents synthetically. The important consequence of this recognition is often to thwart the reduction of Coleridge to any particular historical "school of thought."

In a notebook entry we find a clue to how he regards his own "idealism": he seeks the most concrete and tangible approach to reality, he says, and it is indeed the opposing empirical and utilitarian traditions that forsake concreteness. The law of conscience to which he subscribes "knits us to earth, to the flesh and blood of our human nature with all its food and fuel of Affections, local attachments, predilections of Language & Country," whereas Bentham's and Paley's law of expediency "inevitably unloosens the Soul from its centripetal Instincts, makes a man a thing of generalities and ideal abstractions, Shadows in which no life is, no power . . . . Like a spherical Balloon we float between earth & heaven without belonging to either" (N, III, 3875). As for egoism, he writes in another note, Hobbes's doctrine that self-interest is the motive-spring of all human actions is today one of the "accredited facts, almost universally considered as universal Experience, which yet neither or ever were actually experienced." This error comes about, he says surprisingly, when we rely too much on tradition and "the habit of referring to notions formed from books . . . , instead of trying them by our experience & actual Observation" (N, III, 3856). Such comments make us realize that Coleridge himself hopes to unite the so-called Coleridgean and Benthamite schools of thought that John Stuart Mill thinks listen too little one to the other.

Perhaps some tidy historical generalizations are unsettled when one gets up close to Coleridge—who turns out in this case to be neither "idealist" nor "empiricist"—but the compensation for this is the intellectual renewal that such revisions often imply and to which Coleridge, a nexus of so many warring traditions, can continue to contribute.

Structural Interpretation

Since Coleridge left his work in such disorder, the structural critic will be engaged in an act of construction, not reconstruction, not even completion of a monument he left unfinished. As a construction, Coleridge's thought never gets off the ground. Yet he admires Godwin for demonstrating the "most important of all important Truths, that Morality might be built up on it's own foundation, like a Castle built *from* the rock & *on* the rock" (*CL*, III, 313-14). An overt attempt to expound coherent internal principles in Coleridge is Barfield's *What Coleridge Thought*, which, as I have said, deliberately minimizes psychological or biographical or historical interpretation in its search for internal continuities.

A structural approach has much to commend it in that, for its purposes, the difficult question of the chronological evolution of Coleridge's thought becomes secondary. Trying to decide when he thought what, and in what way he changed his mind from one year to the next, is sometimes as futile as it is exhausting. Successful chronological accounts of this development, such as J. A. Appleyard's *Coleridge's Philosophy of Literature* (1965), are rare. Though there are, of course, many fundamental changes over the years in what Coleridge *believed,* the essential pattern of his thought is not confined in a linear temporal axis; rather it is a multidimensional consideration and reconsideration of images, issues, and ideas, often progressive, sometimes retrogressive. His habit of mind is a curious mixture of radical discontinuity in exposition, yet a powerful sense of interrelationship—a mixture that results in ideas picked up and dropped for periods of time, then picked up and dropped again, though usually not without

[47]

some augmentation or undercut or qualification. Thus the best approach to Coleridge may be one in which passages written even decades apart are spliced together. I suggest that the structural critic is performing his or her most important task by presenting Coleridge spliced together, by performing, at least on one level, as a vigorous editor. Accordingly, the ideal way to *read* Coleridge would not be to begin with the first installment of *The Friend* or the first volume of the Opus Maximum or Chapter I of *Biographia Literaria,* let alone entry 1 of the *Notebooks,* and then plow on through. Rather one would read him after his scattered speculations have been assembled and interpreted by the scholar, who has provided something of the unified construction which Coleridge so admired and did not himself achieve. To this end, the scholar who builds with Coleridge should also literally *present* him, quoting extensively and avoiding paraphrase as much as possible. When thus spliced together Coleridge's writings on any topic will reveal continuities—the continuities of an internal dialogue, as it were—more than total consistency in doctrine or steady development toward some settled point of view. Whether he may or may not be called a Hartleian or Kantian or Unitarian or Trinitarian at any particular moment becomes less important than the articulation of this dynamic continuity.

How may we view as Coleridge's structure what he himself never constructed? An illustration may be found in his writings on self-realization. He is highly critical, as I have mentioned, of both Kantian formalism and British utilitarianism, two major schools of moral thought that represent radically opposed bases for judgment of human conduct. These theories do agree, however, that the primary concern is moral action, not the character of the agent, let alone such questions as whether his personality is fully realized, his sensibility refined, his creative powers fully employed, his capacity for love evidenced. These questions are addressed in moral theories we would classify as "self-realization" theories, which are concerned with "virtues" or human powers, the total character of the agent over and beyond the acts he may perform. At no point in his life does Coleridge state that he criticizes Kantian formalism and British utilitarianism from the viewpoint of a self-realization ethic (though he does occasionally use the term "self-realization" more than half a century before F. H. Bradley); rather this is an implicit tendency in his thought from the beginning, even before he reads the Germans and comes under the sway of Kant's "giant's hand." From his earliest years to his latest he is possessed by the ideas of wholeness of self and harmony of function, concerns he thinks Kantian formalism and British utilitarianism either neglect or violate. To argue that he is working toward a self-realization ethic on a temporal axis would be to impose a false teleology; rather he is thinking *as* a self-realizationist throughout his life.

Again, in what sense is a study of Coleridge which presents the major contours of his moral thought as a dramatic conflict among these three major schools his structure, and in what sense is it the critic's? He never defines the conflict in precisely this way. Structure must not be confused with scaffolding, however, and what the structural critic attempts is to provide scaffolding that permits the implicit structure to be seen. My assumption, and it is a Coleridgean one, is that intellectual structure is not necessarily an orderly assemblage of ideas, but is necessarily an explicit *or implicit* system of interrelationships of which the author is aware and in terms of which he continually conducts his inquiry. Coleridge has awareness of system in this sense—implicit where it is not explicit awareness. His critiques of Kant and of Bentham (or more frequently Paley) are there on view. His extensive writings on self-realization have only to be connected one with another. It is, many scholars would agree, characteristic of Coleridge that these writings suggest their own interrelationships and fall together gracefully. Once connected, they implicitly but clearly argue the moral view from which Kantian formalism and British utilitarianism are both found inadequate: the Kantian idea of the self is insufficiently respectful of human powers other than the rational; the utilitarian idea of the self is limited by its usually quantitative notion of happiness and by its psychologically naive confidence that happiness is something that can be sought. Wellek complained in *Immanuel Kant in England* that Coleridge does not distinguish among incompatible modes of thought. One can agree with Wellek that because he never expounds his thought in an orderly way, he does not deserve the name philosopher, moral or otherwise; but he does discriminate among incompatible modes of thought, and to provide scaffolding for implicit structure can be not distortion or scholarly willfulness but elucidation.

A structural approach can combine, I have suggested, with a genetic, and it remains to be demonstrated more precisely how this may be. In brief, a genetic focus provides an effective way of selecting many of the mental episodes the structural critic uses as his "content" and about which he then asks the question of "form." Genetic interpretation—perhaps surprisingly, since it often deals with questions of biography and development—can go hand in hand with nonchronological construction in Coleridge studies. Consider further his theory of self-realization. This theory powerfully and continuously informs his mental life with regard to the judgments he makes of character and action; it is a theory lived and tested, one that finds confirmation, sadly, in his sense of his deficiencies and those of others. Of his son Hartley he writes, "It is the absence of a Self, it is the want or torpor of Will, that is the mortal Sickness of Hartley's Being, and has been for good & evil, his character—his moral *Idiocy*—from his earliest Childhood." Hartley is the "relationless, unconjugated, and intransitive Verb Impersonal with neither Subject nor Object, neither governed or governing" (*CL*, V, 232). That he is "absent to the present" means he can imbibe glass after glass of wine with no awareness of what he is doing. Coleridge wishes Hartley "could but promise himself to be a *Self* and to construct a circle by the circumvolving line" (*CL*, VI, 551). Out of his own emptiness Coleridge formulates his views of the "educed" or educated self, in whom a sense of power and free-dom combines with habit and discipline, and for whom love—the strong sense of self ironically experienced in giving the self to another—is still possible. The contrast he himself provides to this ideal self is described in similar terms throughout his life. As a young man of 23 he complains to Josiah Wade that his past life seems "a feverish dream! all one gloomy huddle of strange ac-tions, & dim-discovered motives"; at 31 he observes, "I have no rooted thorough thro' feeling—& never exist wholly present to any Sight, to any Sound, to any Emotion"; at 38 he notes that he is "whirled about without a center—as in a nightmair—no gravity—a vortex without a center"; and at 50 he tells Thomas Allsop that his love affair with Sara Hutchinson left him with "a Self emptied—a gourd of Jonas."[11]

The lived—or painfully unlived—theory of self-realization is expressed in this kind of commentary, in which the experiential continually leads to the theoretical, to the ever-present view of the self as the "band or copula" of human powers sensed within as unity and harmony, but a harmony achieved, if it is, through growth and alienation and a suffering that can be so intense that the evolution of the self, his own or that of his Mariner, is ar-rested. The commentary that expresses the theory accumulates over a lifetime; this view of the self is implicit in writings from "This Lime-tree Bower My Prison" and *The Ancient Mariner* to his deathbed letters. The structural critic would rightly perceive chronology to be of secondary importance here. A coherent structure of thought centered in self-realization informs almost everything Coleridge says about morality, and also everything he *does* about it. That the theory is lived suggests in itself the blend-ing of the structural with the genetic, and a structural account of the theory that did not pay attention to its genesis in his own life and personality would be needlessly eviscerated. Whatever the subject matter, the structural critic might keep in mind that ideas

[11]*CL*, I, 184; *N*, II, 2000; *N*, III, 3999; *CL*, V, 250.

for Coleridge are not an academic matter; rather they are entwined with "the living Substance," and, as he so often reminds us, entwined with his own (*IS,* p. 80).

Concluding Remarks

Which method is most appropriate depends partly on personal critical preference, partly on what one wishes to discover. Most topics could benefit, in varying degrees, from the different kinds of contribution each method makes. I would suggest that some use of a genetic approach in the sense I have outlined would always be beneficial, even though one's primary method might be historical or structural. That morality is intimately connected with human action and psychology and insists on correlations between theory and practice (unless, of course, one maintains a strict metaethical detachment) argues that genetic interpretation would lend itself to this subject more readily than it would to most others. This is true, I think, but the question is merely one of degree. Coleridge's treatment of subjects from mathematics and science to religion and cosmology is insistently psychogenetic, as his "Essay on Method" makes clear. The other methodological procedure of genetic criticism—its emphasis on the relation of Coleridge's life and personality to his thought— may be more difficult to apply to many subjects than it is to his moral thought. The general recommendation that one seek as much as possible those passages rhetorically invested in some way with his personality would still obtain. Beyond this, one suspects that correlations between life and thought will be both possible and illuminating in most subject matters. For example, such correlations might help to account for puzzling aspects of his political philosophy. His shift from the radical liberalism of Pantisocracy days to despair at the passage of the first Reform Bill in 1832 might be in part accounted for by his psychological ambivalence toward authority, seen, for instance in his dealings with his older brother George, and might corroborate what some scholars have argued: that Coleridge's basic political orientation from early years to late does not alter so much as has been assumed. His literary criticism would frequently admit of genetic commentary. The correlation between his reading of Hamlet and his self-concept is well known, but that kind of correlation can be found elsewhere—in his reading of Donne, of whose willfulness he, as the indolent man, is in awe, or in his mostly negative response to Dr. Johnson, who may in many ways mirror him disconcertingly.

These days, with the literary profession paying so much attention to the relation of literature and philosophy, Coleridge studies should be especially germane. No figure in English literature is so engrossed in philosophical issues as he. Publication of essential texts will make all the more tempting new studies of such topics as his theories of language, psychology, history, and religion. Volume 3 of the *Notebooks* constitutes one of the profoundest contributions to nineteenth-century thought in the English language, and volumes 4 and 5 (with subject index), the five volumes of the *Collected Marginalia,* and the Opus Maximum will only add to this scholarly opportunity. The poetry will continually find new contexts in the prose as it becomes available. His theory of will and evil, for example, though developed many years after composition of "The Ancient Mariner," confirms certain interpretations of the poem, if it cannot be used actively to interpret it. Unlike his prose, the familiar corpus of poetry will not increase significantly, but the Coleridgean commentary that can be brought to bear on it will. Once again Coleridge may be instrumental in explaining Coleridge.

Probably he should have the last word on method, about which he published his own treatise, after all, in the 1818 revision of *The Friend* (I, 448–524). The method he propounds there is notably a combination of the genetic and the structural, with an emphasis on synchronic over diachronic ordering. The methodical person finds order in experience by means of "a primary act positively *originating* in the mind itself, and prior to

[53]

the object in order of nature, though co-instantaneous in its manifestation," a primary act he calls variously a "*leading Thought*" or "INITIATIVE" or "intuition." It is "the sense of a principle of connection given by the mind, and sanctioned by the correspondency of nature," a correspondence that prevents method from becoming mere subjective imposition (*F,* I, 471). This genetic approach combines with a structural: method "becomes natural to the mind which has been accustomed to contemplate not *things* only, or for their own sake alone, but likewise and chiefly the *relations* of things, either their relations to each other, or to the observer, or to the state and apprehension of the hearers." The methodical person denies time as succession or temporality, and instead "realizes its ideal divisions," "organizes the hours, and gives them a soul: and that, the very essence of which is to fleet away, and evermore *to have been,* he takes up into his own permanence . . . " (*F,* I, 450–60).

The "Essay on Method" corroborates much of what we have been saying here; in fact, Coleridge appears tacitly to be telling us what we will have to bring to bear on him if he is to make sense. Unlike Mistress Quickly, who is bound by a mere succession of "events and images as such, and independent of any power in the mind to classify or appropriate them," Hamlet, with whom Coleridge elsewhere proclaims his kinship, has an "exuberance of mind" that "interferes with the *forms* of Method." But unlike Polonius, who has all the form but none of the substance of method, Hamlet's apparent discontinuities disguise a powerful, methodical intellect. Coleridge, similarly, may seem "fantastical" and discontinuous—he lacks the form or scaffolding of method—yet he would argue that "however irregular and desultory his talk, there is *method* in the fragments" (*F,* I, 449–54).

It is up to the scholar and critic, with his or her own apt method, to seek out this methodical core or structure and to provide a format of presentation. At the intellectual center of the Romantic movement in England and responsive to the great figures on the Continent, Coleridge can well provide a power of initiative and *"path of Transit"* for Romantic studies, if only we hear him out and, with patience and imagination, provide for him the means by which his spirit of inquiry may become our own.

]2[

A Complex Dialogue: Coleridge's Doctrine of Polarity and Its European Contexts

Thomas McFarland

"In all subjects of deep and lasting Interest," wrote Coleridge in 1820, "you will detect a struggle between two opposites, two polar Forces, both of which are alike necessary to our human Well-being, & necessary each to the continued existence of the other" (*CL*, V, 35). What he here enunciated was an ineradicable characteristic and compelling urgency of his thought. As a commentator has emphasized:

> Coleridge's conception of genre is based upon the method of the reconciliation of opposites, which embodies the characteristic method of his thought. . . . The reconciliation of opposites, indeed, is the Archimedes lever of Coleridge's criticism. His procedure and his terminology are dialectical or "polar." Reality is always organic unity or wholeness, but this reality can only be discursively revealed as two, in the form of polar opposites reconciled, or of centripetal and centrifugal forces in equilibrium.[1]

More recently, Owen Barfield, in his study entitled *What Coleridge Thought*, has seen the doctrine of polarity as the Ar-

---

[1]Richard Harter Fogle, *The Idea of Coleridge's Criticism* (Berkeley: University of California Press, 1962), p. 4.

chimedes lever not merely of Coleridge's criticism, but of the entirety of his mental activity: "polarity," summarizes Barfield, "is at the root of what Coleridge thought"; "the apprehension of polarity is itself *the basic act of imagination.*"[2]

Explicit testimony from Coleridge himself amply supports such assessments of the importance of polarity in his intellectual commitment. We may isolate a single comprehensive statement: "EVERY POWER IN NATURE AND IN SPIRIT *must evolve an opposite, as the sole means and condition of its manifestation:* AND ALL OPPOSITION IS A TENDENCY TO RE-UNION. This is the universal Law of Polarity or essential Dualism, first promulgated by Heraclitus, 2000 years afterwards re-published, and made the foundation both of Logic, of Physics, and of Metaphysics by Giordano Bruno" (*F,* I, 94 n). Coleridge's description of the provenance of the doctrine of polarity is historically admissible (if we except possibly even earlier formulations by thinkers of the Orient), and his awareness of Heraclitus's priority and Bruno's reassertion both indicates the lodgment of the doctrine in transmissions and indebtedness-es going back to the origins of Western philosophy, and some-what paradoxically suggests a continual rebirth in differing epochs as dictated by evolving needs and disparate intellectual situations.

Heraclitus promulgated the doctrine fully, albeit cryptically. In their reduction of his thought to fourteen rubrics, Kirk and Raven devote no fewer than four to his involvement in the doc-trine of polarity;[3] and among the Heraclitean fragments brought forward to illustrate the first of them ("Different types of example of the essential unity of opposites"), they cite such statements as

---

[2]Owen Barfield, *What Coleridge Thought* (Middletown, Conn.: Wesleyan University Press, 1971), pp. 145, 36.

[3]G. S. Kirk and J. E. Raven, *The Presocratic Philosophers: A Critical History with a Selection of Texts* (Cambridge: Cambridge University Press, 1971), pp. 189–95.

Sea is the most pure and the most polluted water; for fishes it is drinkable and salutary, but for men it is undrinkable and deleterious.

Again:

The path up and down is one and the same.

And yet again:

Disease makes health pleasant and good, hunger satiety, weariness rest. [p. 189]

Diels's great collection can supply us with additional examples of Heraclitus's conception of polarity. For instance:

That which is in opposition is in concert, and from things that differ comes the most beautiful harmony.[4]

Again:

They do not understand how that which differs with itself is in agreement: harmony consists of opposing tensions, like that of the bow and the lyre. [p. 162, B51]

And once more:

And what is in us is the same thing: living and dead, awake and sleeping, as well as old and young; for the latter having changed becomes the former, and this again having changed becomes the latter. [pp. 170-71, B88]

How central was the principle of reconciled opposition to Heraclitus's dark understanding may be further emphasized by

[4]Hermann Diels, *Die Fragmente der Vorsokratiker,* 6th ed., ed. Walther Kranz (Dublin, Zurich: Weidmann, 1971), I, 152 (B8).

a collage of quotations from Burnet's classic study of early Greek philosophy:

> A glance at the fragments will show that the thought of Herakleitos was dominated by the opposition of sleeping and waking, life and death, and that this seemed to him the key to the traditional Milesian problem of the opposites, hot and cold, wet and dry.... We see further that there is a regular alternation of the two processes; sleep alternates with waking, and life with death.... Such, so far as we can make it out, is the general view of Herakleitos, and now we may ask for his secret, the one thing to know which is wisdom. It is that, as the apparent strife of opposites in this world is really due to the opposite tension which holds the world together, so in pure fire, which is the eternal wisdom, all these oppositions disappear in their common ground.[5]

Guthrie—to add a more modern authority—interprets the harmony of opposites as one part of a threefold rationale for the Heraclitean "Logos": "Harmony is always the product of opposites, therefore the basic fact in the natural world is strife."[6] Heraclitus's doctrine, Guthrie further observes, was in fact a special realization of a more general intellectual preoccupation of his time:

> The Heraclitean doctrine of the simultaneity of opposites and its paradoxical consequences is the result of intense concentration on a mental phenomenon common in the early Greek world, to which the name "polarity" has been given. Thus for example H. Fränkel writes of "a thought-form which after Homer, in the archaic period of Greece, was the dominant one, namely the polar mode of thought: qualities cannot be conceived otherwise than together with their contraries." [p. 446]

[5] John Burnet, *Greek Philosophy: Thales to Plato* (1914; rpt. London: Macmillan; New York: St. Martin's Press, 1968), pp. 47, 49.
[6] W. K. C. Guthrie, *A History of Greek Philosophy* (Cambridge: Cambridge University Press, 1962–), I, 435.

As Coleridge was correct about Heraclitus's priority in focusing the polar doctrine of the harmony of opposites, so was he also correct about Bruno's reestablishment of that doctrine. "Harmony," writes Bruno, "is not effectuated except where there is contrariety. The spherical does not repose on the spherical, because they touch each other at a point; but the concave rests on the convex." The "*coincidenza de contrarii*," as Bruno calls it, is an arcane knowledge that may fairly be thought to provide, as Coleridge says it does, "the foundation both of Logic, of Physics, and of Metaphysics": "if the matter is considered physically, mathematically, and morally, one sees that that philosopher who has arrived at the theory of the 'coincidence of contraries' has not found out a small thing, and that that magician who knows how to look for it where it exists is not an imbecile practitioner." To this statement Bruno's narrator, Sophia, responds with nothing less than a paean to the importance of contraries: "the beginning, the middle, and the end, the birth, the growth, and the perfection of all that we see, come from contraries, through contraries, into contraries, to contraries. And where there is contrariety, there is number, there is order, there are degrees, there is succession, there is vicissitude".[7]

In his great treatise *De la causa, principio e uno*, again, Bruno concludes that "contraries coincide in unity (p. 335)" and that "he who wants to know the greatest secrets of nature should regard and contemplate the minima and maxima of contraries and opposites. It is a profound magic to know how to draw out the contrary after having found the point of union" (p. 340).

The contemplation of the minima and maxima of contraries and opposites, and the finding of their point of union, were for Coleridge not a mere intellectual fancy, but—entirely in the spirit of both Bruno and Heraclitus—a philosophical commitment dictated by the nature of reality. Thus, under the title

[7]Giordano Bruno, *Dialoghi italiani* . . . , with notes by Giovanni Gentile, 3d ed. by Giovanni Aquilecchia (Florence: Sansoni, 1958), p. 573.

"extremes meet," he frequently noted empirical evidences of polarity. For instance, on shipboard to Malta in 1804 he writes: "Extremes meet. The Captains of a fastest-sailing Vessel & the obstinately Laggardmost of a Convoy, equally vexed, and restless" (*N,* II, 2066). In December 1803 he collected a number of examples of the coincidence of contraries: "I have repeatedly said, that I could have made a Volume, if only I had noted down, as they occurred to my Recollection or Observations, the instances of the Proverb, Extremes Meet/—This Night, Sunday, Dec. 11, 1803, ½ past 11, I have determined to devote the last 9 pages of my Pocket[book] to the collection of the same." He then produces the heading, in large capitals, "EXTREMES MEET." Immediately underneath he supplies, from Milton, a motto for the enterprise:

> The parching Air
> Burns frore, and Cold performs the Effect of Fire.
> Par. Lost, Book 2. 594.

There follow ten instances, differing widely, of how extremes meet:

Insects by their smallness, the Mammoth by its hugeness, terrible.

Sameness in a Waterfall, in the foam Islands of a fiercely boiling Pool at the bottom of the Waterfall, from infinite Change.

The excess of Humanity & Disinterestedness in polite Society, not to give Pain, e.g. not to talk of your own Diseases or misfortunes, & to introduce nothing but what will give pleasure, destroys all Humanity & Disinterestedness by making it intolerable thro' Desuetude, to listen to the Complaints of our Equals or of any where the Listening does not gratify or excite some vicious Pride, & sense of Superiority.

A perfectly unheard of Subject, & a crambe bis cocta, chosen by a man of Genius—difficult to say, which would excite in the higher degree the sense of Novelty. E.g. the Orestes of Sotheby.

[61]

Dark with excess of Light.

Self-absorption & Worldly-mindedness N.B. The latter a most philosophical word

The dim Intellect *sees* an absolute Oneness, the perfectly clear Intellect *knowingly perceives* it. Distinction & Plurality lie in the Betwixt.

    9. The naked Savage, & the Gymnosophist.

    10. Nothing & intensest absolutest Being.

    11. Despotism and ochlocracy. [*N*, I, 1725]

The examples are Heraclitean enough in their obscurity as well as in their reliance on common observation. Two, however, differ somewhat from this characterization. The fourth from the last, about dim intellect seeing oneness, and clear intellect knowingly perceiving it, and the penultimate example, about the coincidence of "Nothing & intensest absolutest Being," are metaphysically abstract rather than gnomically empirical observations.

Indeed, they are virtually Hegelian in their abstraction. The statement that "Nothing & intensest absolutest Being" coincide is in fact almost identical with the first triad of Hegel's larger *Logik: "Das reine Seyn und das reine Nichts ist also dasselbe.* Was die Wahrheit ist, ist weder das Seyn, noch das Nichts, sondern daß das Seyn in Nichts, und das Nichts in Seyn,—nicht übergeht,— sonder übergegangen ist"—pure being and pure nothing are therefore the same; truth is neither being nor nothing, but the fact that being—not passes over—but has passed over into nothing, and nothing into being.[8]

The close similarity of these formulations, however, can be

---

[8]*Georg Wilhelm Friedrich Hegel's Werke,* complete edition by a group of friends of the late author: Ph[ilipp] Marheineke, J[ohannes] Schulze, Ed[uard] Gans, L[eo]p[old] v[on] Henning, H[einrich] Hotho, C[arl] Michelet, F[riedrich] Förs-

misleading if taken as an indication of a generalized congruence in the mental styles of Coleridge and Hegel. To step into that "maelstrom of thought" (the description is Geoffrey Hartman's) that constitutes Hegelian philosophy is to be swept into a dialectic of opposites pouring forth in the most stringent abstraction and fullness of philosophical formulation. The "primary concepts or starting-points of logic" are for Hegel "being and nothing, and as that which contains the two previous determinations as moments, becoming" (III, 23). In his first great treatise, *Die Phänomenologie des Geistes,* he intended to

> set out an example of the true method of philosophical science as applied to ... consciousness. We have here modes of consciousness each of which in realizing itself abolishes itself, has its own negation as its result, and thus passes over into a higher mode. The one and only thing *for securing scientific progress* ... is knowledge of the logical precept that negation is just as much affirmation as negation, or that what is self-contradictory resolves itself not into nullity, into abstract nothingness, but essentially only into the negation of its *particular* content, that such negation is not an all-embracing negation, but is *the negation of a definite somewhat* that abolishes itself, and thus is a definite negation; and that thus the result contains in essence that from which it results—which is indeed a tautology, for otherwise it would be something immediate and not a result. Since what results, the negation, is a *definite* negation, it has a *content*. It is a new concept, but a higher, richer concept than that which preceded; for it has been enriched by the negation or opposite of that preceding concept, and thus contains it, but contains also more than it, and is the unity of it and its opposite. [III, 41]

In general, for Hegel "it is in this dialectic ... and in the comprehension of the unity of opposites, or of the positive in the negative, that *speculative knowledge consists*" (III, 44).

---

ter (Berlin: Duncker and Humblot, 1832–45), III, 78–79. Again: "Das Seyn, das unbestimmte Unmittelbare ist in der That nichts, und nicht mehr noch weniger als Nichts"—being, the indeterminate immediacy, is in fact nothing, and neither more nor less than nothing (III, 78). Hegel is hereafter quoted from these volumes, unless otherwise indicated.

Hegel differed from Coleridge, and from his own contemporaries and immediate predecessors, in the dynamic or progressive emphasis of his logic—the restless movement from thesis to antithesis to synthesis, and the continual reinstitution of the process (or, if we heed Kojève's observation that "The expressions 'Thesis', 'Antithesis', 'Synthesis' almost never appear" in Hegel's writing, we may substitute "the 'dialectical' expressions he commonly uses," that is, " 'Immediacy', 'Mediation', 'Overcoming' [and their derivatives]."[9] Such logical movement was certainly implied, and frequently stated, in other theories of contrariety, as, for instance, in Blake's formula: "Without Contraries is no progression";[10] or again, in Oken's statement that "the revelation of polarity is movement."[11] It is also inherent in Coleridge's conception that "Distinction & Plurality" lie between "the dim Intellect" that sees an absolute oneness, and "the perfectly clear Intellect" that knowingly perceives it—an ideation not unlike the Hegelian progression from "notion" (*Begriff*) to "absolute knowledge" (*absolute Wissenschaft*); but the insistence and expansion of statement that accompany such formulations weave the distinctive fabric of Hegelian discourse. Coleridge's commitment to dialectical movement, though implied, is more tentative than that of Hegel.

Another difference between Hegel and Coleridge lies in the characteristic hiddenness of the latter's process of thought—what I have elsewhere referred to as the fact that Coleridge "customarily presents us with completed opinions based on unexpressed arguments rather than with the process of argument

[9]Alexandre Kojève, *Introduction to the Reading of Hegel,* trans. James H. Nichols, Jr. (New York: Basic Books, 1969), pp. 208–09, n14.

[10]*The Poetry and Prose of William Blake,* ed. David V. Erdman, with commentary by Harold Bloom, 3rd printing, with revisions (Garden City, N.Y.: Doubleday, 1968), p. 34.

[11]*Lehrbuch der Naturphilosophie,* by Dr. [Lorenz] Oken, Professor in Jena, member of several learned societies (Jena: Friedrich Frommann, 1809–11), I, 23.

[64]

itself."[12] Hegel, on the other hand, explicates his arguments in relentlessly abstract accumulation; this powerful idiosyncrasy, indeed, is largely what guarantees him inclusion among the half dozen or so greatest philosophers of our cultural history. We may compare Coleridge's Heraclitean terseness in "Nothing & intensest absolutest Being" with Hegel's pile-driving specification of the thought process involved in such a formula. Discussing the concept of "contradiction," toward the conclusion that "positive and negative are the same," Hegel writes:

> If we consider the two independent determinations of reflection for themselves, we see that the positive is positedness as reflected into self-equality; positedness which is not relation to an other, and thus persistence in so far as positedness is transcended and excluded. But hereby the positive converts itself into the relation of a not-being—into a positedness.—It is thus contradiction: it is the positing of self-identity, and, by excluding the negative, it makes itself into the negative of something, that is, into that other which it excludes from itself. This, as excluded, is posited as free from the excluding term, and consequently as intro-reflected and itself excluding. Thus exclusive reflection is the positing of the positive as excluding the other in such a manner that this positing is immediately the positing of its other, which excludes it. [IV, 58]

Although the principle of the reconciliation of opposites received its most varied and systematic exposition in Hegel's dialectical construction of the world, it was a principle that also pervaded Romantic thought in general. Under the name of *Polarität,* and conceived on the analogy of the positive and negative poles of magnetism, it dominated that whole spectrum of German scientific speculation called *Naturphilosophie.* As Hegel said, in his *Enzyklopädie*:

> Positive and negative are supposed to express an absolute difference. The two, however, are at bottom the same: the name of

[12]Thomas McFarland, *Coleridge and the Pantheist Tradition* (Oxford: Clarendon Press, 1969), p. 236.

either might be transferred to the other. Thus, for example, debts and assets are not two particular self-subsisting species of property. What is negative to the debtor, is positive to the creditor. A way to the east is also a way to the west. Positive and negative are therefore intrinsically conditioned by one another, and exist only in relation to each other. The north pole of the magnet cannot be without the south pole, and *vice versa*. If we cut a magnet in two, we do not have a north pole in one piece, and a south pole in the other.... The other is seen to stand over against *its* other. Thus, for example, inorganic nature is not to be considered merely something else than organic nature, but the necessary antithesis of it.... Nature in like manner is not without mind, nor mind without nature.... In modern physical science the opposition, first observed to exist in magnetism as polarity, has come to be regarded as a universal law pervading the whole of nature. [VI, 240-41]

Hegel's phrasing here indicates that "polarity" is the cultural property of an age and intellectual community rather than his own distinctive formulation. Indeed, the actual word *Polarität* is not very Hegelian in its occurrence, but is associated more usually with Goethe and Schelling.[13] Furthermore, despite Hegel's own ambitious scientific schematizings, *Naturphilosophie* as such is customarily thought of as the peculiar domain of Schelling and his followers (though Hegel too used the name);[14] and in their treatises the doctrine of polarity assumes a kind of absolute centrality. As Schopenhauer said, looking backward from an

[13]Cf., e.g., Hermann Zeltner, *Schelling* (Stuttgart: Friedrich Frommann, 1954), p. 123: "The two fundamental premises of Schelling's explanation of nature are *Polarität* and *Steigerung,* and here he is especially close to Goethe."

[14]Hegel, in fact, sharply rejected *Naturphilosophie* as presented by the school of Schelling. For instance, he writes to a correspondent in 1814: "You know that I have had too much to do not merely with ancient literature, but even with mathematics, more recently with the higher analysis, differential calculus, physics, natural history, chemistry, to let myself be taken in by the humbug of *Naturphilosophie,* philosophizing without knowledge of facts and by mere force of imagination, and treating mere fancies, even imbecile fancies, as ideas" (*Briefe von und an Hegel,* ed. Johannes Hoffmeister [Hamburg: Felix Meiner, 1952-61], II, 31).

unsurpassed command of all the intricacies of German Romantic thought, a chief characteristic of the "Naturphilosophen der Schellingischen Schule" was their emphasis on the fact that "*polarity*, that is, the splitting of a force into two qualitatively different and opposite activities striving for reunion . . . , is a basic type of almost all the phenomena of nature, from the magnet and crystal up to man."[15] To bring forward a striking example, Oken, one of the most ardent of the "Naturphilosophen der Schellingischen Schule," enunciated the sweeping dictum: "Keine Welt ohne polare Kraft"—there would be no world without polar force. "There is therefore no simple force in the world," said Oken further: "each is an appearance of itself, a position of $+ -$, or a *polarity*." Yet again: "The cosmic entelechy is itself polarity, is the primal polarity [*Urpolarität*]. Polarity breaks out in the moment where the world creation stirs itself. . . . Every individual thing is a doubleness" (I, 22-23).

Oken was here writing in 1809, in a three-volume work dedicated to "his friends Schelling and Steffens from Oken." He was proceeding confidently along a broad thoroughfare laid down more than a decade before by the first of the three friends. For Schelling, earlier than Hegel, and in no way less fully or insistently, had in the late 1790s projected a comprehensive philosophy of polar oppositions and their reconciliations. His imagination fired by the practical experiments of Franklin, Galvani, Volta, and other pioneer investigators of electrical phenomena,[16] Schelling turned to electricity and its laws as the model for an entire metaphysic of existence. "God as dyad is

[15]Arthur Schopenhauer, *Sämtliche Werke,* ed. Arthur Hübscher, 3d ed. (Wiesbaden: F. A. Brockhaus, 1972), II, 171.

[16]A single instance may help to illustrate the excitement generated by these investigators. Johann Wilhelm Ritter's *Beweis, dass ein beständiger Galvanismus den Lebensprocess in dem Thierreich begleite* (Weimar, 1798), was dedicated to "the great men F. A. v. Humboldt and A. Volta." For Volta and Galvani see further Rudolf Haym, *Die romantische Schule: Ein Beitrag zur Geschichte des deutschen Geistes* (Hildesheim: Georg Olms, 1961), pp. 578-79.

electricism," said his disciple Oken in witness to the radical fascination of electrical discovery (I, 112). "Galvanism is the principle of life," said Oken again. "There is no other life force than galvanic polarity" (II, 10).

Permeating as it does almost all the work of Schelling's most vital period, the theory of electrical polarity receives especially full discussion in a treatise of 1798 called *Von der Weltseele; eine Hypothese der höheren Physic zur Erklärung des allgemeinen Organismus*, which was an extension and documentation of emphases sketched in the programmatic *Ideen zu einer Philosophie der Natur* of the preceding year. For instance, in the first-named work, following a discussion of "the universal dualism of nature," Schelling says that electricity "is no form of combustion, which even Lavoisier had supposed; electrical activity belongs to a higher sphere of nature's operations than does combustion." He then sets forth "as the first fundamental of the doctrine of electricity, that no electricity without the Other exists—is there—or can exist," and that this empirical fact allows us to "deduce the concept of positive and negative forces. Neither positive nor negative principles are something in themselves or *absolutely real*. That they are called positive or negative is proof that they exist only in a definite *reciprocal relation*."[17]

When Schelling later in the same treatise proceeds to "define more exactly the concept of polarity," he observes that "it is certain *a priori* that in the whole of nature there are divided— truly opposed—principles at work; these opposed principles united in one body impart to it polarity; through the phenomena of polarity we become acquainted with, so to speak,

---

[17]*Friedrich Wilhelm Joseph von Schellings sämmtliche Werke*, ed. K. F. A. Schelling (Stuttgart and Augsburg: J. G. Cotta, 1856–61), II, 430, 432. The edition is in two *Abtheilungen*, the first consisting of volumes numbered 1–10, the second of volumes numbered 1–4. To avoid cumbersome identifications of *Abtheilungen*, references to the first *Abtheilung* are cited as volumes I–X, to the second as volumes XI–XIV.

only the *narrower* and more *defined* sphere within which the universal dualism operates" (II, 476).

The conception of a universal dualism in nature, based on the phenomena of magnetic polarity, is central to Schelling's thought. To take another instance, in his *Erster Entwurf eines Systems der Naturphilosophie* of 1799, he speaks of "Franklin's idea" that "the differentiation of the world is probably not merely mathematical, but is founded on a *universally operative physical cause*. This physical cause can be nothing else than magnetism" (III, 122 n1). The universe, says Schelling, is "one self-maintaining system" that "has formed all things from one pulsating point" (III, 125). Although we "must think of the continuing of the universe as organic," and "the continuing of a system is nothing other than a reciprocity of expansion and contraction—an eternal metamorphosis" (III, 126 n2); nevertheless, says Schelling, there is "no doubt that the organism first contracts and then expands itself through the same mechanism by which two electricities attract and then repel one another" (III, 167, n3). It is "*one and the same universal dualism that extends from magnetic polarity through electrical phenomena, loses itself in chemical heterogeneities, and finally reappears in organic nature.*" He continues: "If magnetism has brought about the first opposition in nature, there was thereby simultaneously planted the seed of an infinite evolution, the seed of that infinite splitting into ever new products in the universe" (III, 258). And Schelling concludes that there "*is therefore* ONE *cause, which has brought about the original opposition in nature; this cause we can denote by the* (unknown) *cause of the primal magnetism*" (III, 260).

Hegel, too, devoted close attention to the phenomena of magnetic polarity, and in his own *Naturphilosophie* as expressed in the second part of the first edition of his *Enzyklopädie* he produces a discussion based on the understanding that

> the magnet represents in a simple, naive fashion the nature of the notion [*Begriff*], namely in its developed form as conclusion

[*Schluss*]. The poles are the materially existing ends of a real line (of a rod, or also in a body extended in all dimensions): as poles they possess, however, not a mechanically material reality, but an ideal one; they are absolutely inseparable. The *point of indifference,* in which they have their substance, is the unity in which they are as determinations of the notion; so that they have meaning and existence in this unity alone, and *polarity* is the relation solely of such moments. [VII, i, 246]

In an expanded version of this discussion in the revised *Enzyklopädie,* Hegel further observes that

If the magnet is cut in two, then each piece is again a whole magnet; the North pole arises again immediately in the broken piece. Each is the positing and excluding of the other from itself; the termini of the conclusion [*Schluss*] can exist not for themselves, but only in combination. [VII, i, 249]

Hegel's appeal to magnetic polarity, however, is on the whole less resonant than that of Schelling and his *naturphilosophische Anhänger*—metaphysically more cautious, one might say. As Haering has stressed, "people have probably been all too hasty in allowing themselves to be carried along, through the outer similarity of the Schellingian concept of 'Polarität' and the Hegelian concept of 'Negativität', opposition, dialectical unity etc. to a simple identification of the two standpoints—primarily for the reason that Hegel himself adduces the Schellingian examples, and especially magnetic polarity, as illustration for his own meaning. But when two do the same thing, then it is not the same thing."[18]

---

[18]Theodor Haering, *Hegel: Sein Wollen und sein Werke. Eine chronologische Entwicklungsgeschichte der Gedanken und der Sprache Hegels* (Aalen: Scientia Verlag, 1963), I, 690. Pursuing this contention, Haering provides lengthy discussion of the ways in which the two men were in fact not doing "the same thing." But briefer illustration may suffice here. We may take a passage from each man as comparative example. First Hegel, then Schelling. "Das Seyn," says the former, "ist zuerst gegen Anderes überhaupt bestimmt"—being is in the first place de-

Doubtless some of the difference in Hegel's tone and emphasis from that of Schelling—and the commentator just cited provides an extended discussion of that difference—was attendant upon his psychological position as "latecomer" (I use Harold Bloom's redaction of Nietzsche's term) with respect to Schelling's formulations. As Rudolf Haym notes, one of the most remarkable facts about Schelling was his extraordinary quickness in seeing the metaphysical possibilities of the discoveries made in late eighteenth-century physics and chemistry (p. 578): he was preeminently an early formulator ("Schelling," wrote Novalis in about 1798, "is the *philosopher of modern chemistry*").[19] Nonetheless I should urge, even if paradoxically, that chronological gradations are only schematically, not substantively, important for the understanding of the doctrines of polarity and the harmony of opposites.

Far more important than chronological awareness is the realization that the various enunciations of such doctrines in this period, like Romanticism itself, constitute a kind of cultural flood, one in which divisions into "before" or "after" have little relevance, and where creeks and branches of individual discovery or originality, though arising at different points along the banks, all flow inevitably to a common mingling in the larger current of the age. Indeed, the very idea of "an age" or "a time" tends to repudiate the importance of smaller temporalities and priorities within the larger entity. For instance, Coleridge's "extremes meet" notation in which he sees the coincidence of

---

termined as opposed to other in general (III, 74). "Das Universum," says the latter, is "ein selbständiges System" that has "alle von Einem pulsirenden Punkt aus sich gebildet"—the universe is one self-maintaining system that has formed all things out of itself from one pulsating point (III, 125). The characteristic abstractness of Hegel, and on the other hand the metaphorical dynamism of Schelling—what has been called his "dithyrambic" quality—are here fairly apparent.

[19] *Novalis Schriften: Die Werke Friedrich von Hardenbergs*, ed. Paul Kluckhohn and Richard Samuel, 2d ed., prepared from manuscripts, enlarged and improved, in 4 vols. and an accompanying vol. (Stuttgart: W. Kohlhammer, 1960-), III, 26.

"Nothing & intensest absolutest Being" precedes by about a decade the first triad of Hegel's *Logik;* on the other hand, since both Coleridge and Hegel had long been thinking about such topics, and continued to think about them much later, the special formulations should be seen as more or less arbitrary emergences from the deeper currents of the time. Although Schelling began serious publication earlier than did Hegel (the latter's *Phänomenologie des Geistes* did not appear until 1807, whereas Schelling's *System des transzendentalen Idealismus* not only appeared as early as 1800 but also marked the close of Schelling's most dynamic phase), it would be difficult to say that either of the erstwhile friends and youthful roommates carried on the *process of thought* in chronological befores and afters.

In this respect, to attach honorific significance to Schelling's prior publication is like saying that upstream is somehow better than downstream. After all, as Richard Kroner emphasizes, Hegel's *Enzyklopädie* is

> the richest and most complete presentation that German idealism found; it is the form of that system that idealism was everywhere striving toward in its development, that Schelling in 1802 termed the "first task to be solved in the future," and of which he had prophetically said that if the system be "once presented and perceived in its entirety, the absolute harmony of the universe and the divinity of all natures in the thoughts of man will be established forever."[20]

In that perspective, surely, Hegel's "latecomer" status is a virtue rather than a defect; he becomes, as it were, the sea into which Schelling's river flows. And such, mutatis mutandis, is the ambivalent truth about the chronological befores and afters of Coleridge and of others in the Romantic community of thought.

Of more significance than chronological fixations is the ap-

---

[20]Richard Kroner, *Von Kant bis Hegel,* 2d ed. (Tübingen: J. C. B. Mohr [Paul Siebeck], 1961), II, 502–03.

prehending of—to vary the metaphor—the *texture* of the Romantic involvement in polarity: the closeness of weave in the common emphasis no less than the differing threads in the historical transmission and the idiosyncratic patternings of individual commitment. Chronology in and of itself brings us little light. Goethe, for instance, was as profoundly involved with polarity as were Schelling and Hegel, and became so earlier than either; but he was also involved contemporaneously with them, and continued in deep commitment perhaps even later than Schelling. Thus in 1810, in his *Farbenlehre,* he hails the doctrine of polar oppositions; he had, however, as a commentator emphasizes, been devoting "intensive work" to that treatise since 1790, and had begun thinking about the theory of color as early as 1777.[21]

Moreover, Goethe's tone is one that welcomes the agreement of other minds rather than insisting on his own priority (or indebtedness). As he says in the *Farbenlehre:*

> True observers of nature, however they otherwise consider themselves as differing, will nonetheless agree with one another that everything that appears, everything that is to meet us as a phenomenon, must indicate and in some way represent itself as either an original separation that is capable of being made one, or an original unity, which can attain to a division into two. To divide into two that which is united into one, to make into one that which is sundered into two, is the life of nature; this is the eternal systole and diastole, the eternal syncresis and diacresis, the breathing in and out of the world in which we live, move, and have our being.[22]

One of the "true observers of nature" who agreed with Goethe was Schelling, who, quite in accord with the emphasis of

[21]Rike Wankmüller, in *Goethes Werke,* Hamburg ed., XIII (Hamburg: Christian Wegner, 1955), 605.
[22]Johann Wolfgang Goethe, *Gedenkausgabe der Werke, Briefe und Gespräche,* ed. Ernst Beutler (Zurich: Artemis Verlag, 1948–71), XVI, 199. Goethe is hereafter quoted from these volumes.

Goethe's passage, wrote that "where appearances are, there are already opposed forces. The theory of nature therefore supposes as immediate principle a universal heterogeneity of matter, and, in order to be able to conceive this, a universal homogeneity. Neither the principle of absolute heterogeneity nor that of absolute homogeneity is the true one; the truth lies in the union of both" (II, 390).

Even where Goethe speaks of his own particular contribution, he connects his invocation of polarity with the laws of reality itself:

> It would be most highly to be desired, however, that the language by which the particularities of a certain sphere of investigation are designated be taken from the sphere itself; the simplest appearance treated as a basic formula and the manifold deduced and developed from that.
>
> The necessity and propriety of such a language of signs, where the basic sign expresses the appearance itself, has been quite well sensed in the extending of the formula of polarity, borrowed from the magnet, to electricity and further matters. The plus and minus that can be posited in this situation have found a proper application in many other phenomena; indeed, the musical artist, probably without troubling himself about those other subjects, has been prompted by nature to express the main difference of musical tones by major and minor.
>
> Thus we have for a long time wished to introduce the term polarity into the theory of colors; with what right and in what sense, let the present work reveal. [XVI, 205]

The conception of polarity, as such quotations suggest, was never far from Goethe's mind; in truth, it was for him, possibly even more than for Romanticism in general, one of the most central of all propositions that made possible a world. The "two great drive wheels of all nature," he wrote in 1828, are "the concept of polarity and that of evolution [*Steigerung*], the former belonging to matter insofar as we think it material, the latter, on the contrary, belonging to it insofar as we think it spiritual; the former is in a state of ever-continuing attraction and repulsion, the latter in one of ever-striving ascent" (XVI, 925). On one occasion, Goethe compiles—somewhat in the manner of Coleridge's "extremes meet" notations—a random list of examples of the "duality of the appearance as contrast":

> Ourselves and objects
> Light and dark
> Body and soul
> Two souls
> Mind and matter
> God and the world
> Thought and extension
> Ideal and real
> Sensuousness and reason
> Imagination and understanding
> Being and longing
> Two halves of a body
> Right and left
> Breathing
>   Physical experience:
> Magnet
>
> [XVI, 863-64]

In Goethe's constant musings on the principle of polarity, however, personal reverie was not the sole preoccupation. On the contrary, he, like others in the Romantic era, participated in that frequent and varied interchange—that intense interweaving of thought—that raised certain matters, and polarity was importantly one of them, beyond the conception of source and influence to the status of being "in the air." For a single instance, on a visit to Tübingen in September 1797, he casually records a meeting with Karl Friedrich von Kielmeyer, professor of chemistry and medicine, and an important authority on organic and dynamic topics:[23]

---

[23]See Karl Friedrich von Kielmeyer, *Ueber die Verhältnisse der organischen Kräfte unter einander in der Reihe der verschiedenen Organisationen, die Gesetze und Folgen dieser Verhältnisse* (Tübingen: Osiander, 1793).

Early this morning with Professor Kielmeyer, who visited me, various things about anatomy and physiology of organic natures. His
program will be printed very soon for the purpose of his lectures.
He harangued me with various thoughts as to how he is inclined to
join the laws of organic nature to general physical laws—for example, to polarity, to the reciprocal modification and correlation of
extremes, to the extendable force of expansible fluids. [XII, 151]

Such peripheral influence, as it were, may well to some extent
have set up its own little harmonic eddy of opposites between
Goethe and his interlocutor; that it could have "influenced"
Goethe in the sense of placing hitherto unknown principles in
his head, however, is surely not the case. For example, some five
years earlier than this interview he writes to a correspondent as
follows: "Since our excellent Kant says in plain words that there
can be no material without attraction and repulsion (that is,
without polarity), I am much reassured to be able, under this
authority, to proceed with my view of the world according to my
own earliest convictions, in which I have never lost confidence"
(XIX, 732).

The statement to which Goethe refers had appeared in the
course of a discussion of the dynamic in Kant's *Metaphysische
Anfangsgründe der Naturwissenschaft,* which was published in
1786. In that treatise Kant had argued that the conception of
matter depended entirely upon that of a tension of attracting
and repelling forces.[24] His argument was of great importance to
thinkers of the Romantic era.[25] Hegel refers to it repeatedly; for

[24]*Kant's gesammelte Schriften,* ed. by the Royal Prussian Academy of Sciences
(Berlin: Georg Reimer; continued to the present by Walter de Gruyter, 1902–),
IV, 511.

[25]For Coleridge's knowledge of and admiration for the *Metaphysische Anfangsgründe der Naturwissenschaft,* see, e.g., *BL,* I, 99. Cf. Barfield: "This relatively
brief treatise is more thickly annotated than any other volume I have come
across, and the marginalia make it obvious that it was ardently studied and
pondered by Coleridge" (p. 248). See further W. Schrickx, "Coleridge Marginalia in Kant's *Metaphysische Anfangsgründe der Naturwissenschaft,*" *Studia Ger-
manica,* 1 (Ghent, Belgium, 1959), 161–87.

instance, in the *Wissenschaft der Logik:* "Kant, as is well known, has *constructed matter from repulsive and attractive force,* or, at least, he has erected (as he calls it) the metaphysical elements of this construction." But, objects Hegel in an extended discussion designed to validate his own thought against that of his predecessor, "at bottom Kant's method is *analytical* and not constructive" (III, 201–02). As another example, taken almost at random, Carl August Eschenmayer, in a treatise of 1797 that attempts to apply Fichte's *Wissensschaftslehre* to natural science, and which was carefully studied by Novalis, explicitly summons the Kantian conception that "the dynamic teaches us that the existence of matter can be conceived only under the assumption of the concurrence of two elemental forces";[26] "in the metaphysics of nature the concept of matter in general is taken apart and deduced from two opposed forces, namely those of repulsion and attraction."[27]

Goethe himself refers on still another occasion in 1792 to Kant's analysis as a major presentation of the doctrine of polarity: "I had not allowed it to escape me, in Kant's *Naturwissenschaft,* that attractive and repelling force belongs to the nature of matter, and neither can be separated from the other in the concept of matter; hence there became clear to me the primal polarity of all natures, a polarity that interpenetrates and animates the infinite manifoldness of all appearances" (XII, 373).

Such statements by Goethe, occurring throughout a continuous course of thirty-six years, and with direct assurance that they pertain to his "earliest convictions," demonstrate an enormously personal involvement in the doctrine of polarity.[28] They also demonstrate, however, paradox though it may be, participation

---

[26]As copied by Novalis, in *Novalis,* II, 381.

[27]C. A. Eschenmayer, *Säze aus der Natur-Metaphysik auf chemische und medicinische Gegenstände angewandt* (Tübingen: J. F. Heerbrandt, 1797), p. 88.

[28]For additional discussion and illustration of Goethe's commitment to polarity see, e.g., Werner Danckert, *Goethe: Der mythische Urgrund seiner Weltschau* (Berlin: Walter de Gruyter, 1951), pp. 371–400.

in what can accurately be described as the spirit of the age. The same double structure, I suggest, marks the involvement of Coleridge as well.

It seems desirable and even rather necessary, indeed, to dwell upon this double character of Coleridge's own preoccupation with polarity and the reconciliation of opposites; for Barfield, in his otherwise useful and important study, largely neglects to present either the fact or the significance of the communal dimension of Coleridge's thought. Eschewing "the comparative approach," Barfield takes as "a fair description of what I myself should actually be trying to do" a statement from J. A. Appleyard's *Coleridge's Philosophy of Literature:*

> What is wanting in the sizable bibliography of literature on Coleridge is a full-scale study of the development of his philosophy which will consider him on his own terms and not as a representative of something else, whether it be German idealism, English Platonism, pantheistic mysticism, semantic analysis, or depth psychology. The idea or organizing insight ought to be internal to his thought, so as to see what that thought is and not merely what it is like or unlike.[29]

Despite the seeming reasonableness of such an approach, however, I find myself in disagreement with it, and indeed, I think it leads to misunderstandings as to the real nature of Coleridge's thinking. Strictly speaking, neither Coleridge nor any other philosopher can be said "on his own terms" to have thought anything at all. Not only the philosophical language he uses, but the formulation of the very problems he confronts, are given him by his intellectual culture. If there were no culture, there would be no thought. Dull and speechless tribes have no tradition of philosophy, and having no tradition, they have no

[29]Barfield, p. 4; and J. A. Appleyard, *Coleridge's Philosophy of Literature: The Development of a Concept of Poetry 1791–1819* (Cambridge: Harvard University Press, 1965), p. ix.

philosophers. One can only speculate how many mute, inglorious Miltons, alike of poetry, of science, and of philosophy, have been born, grown to adulthood in vain, and then vanished for want of a nurturing tradition. Texts are possible only in contexts.

In other words I should argue, in direct contravention of Appleyard's call, that it is exactly in the understanding of "something else" that philosophical meaning inheres; that to understand what a philosopheme is "like or unlike" is the very process of understanding "what that thought is." Cassirer insists that the chief contribution of Socrates was the transforming of philosophy from "an intellectual monologue" into a "dialogue": "Truth is by nature the offspring of dialectic thought. It cannot be gained, therefore, except through a constant coöperation of the subjects in mutual interrogation and reply. It is not therefore like an empirical object; it must be understood as the outgrowth of a social act."[30] Coleridge's thought, like that of other philosophers, is "the outgrowth of a social act." Only if it is heard as a voice in a complex dialogue with his forebears and contemporaries can its meaning be ascertained. There are no Robinson Crusoes of the intellect.

Indeed, in a cultural ambiance dominated by the vision of the reconciliation of polar oppositions, the largest of those oppositions suspended in the cultural act is precisely the one indicated above for Goethe: the polarity of the individual talent and the tradition in which it functions.

The approach sponsored by Appleyard and Barfield can accordingly never be more than a heuristic device, a Vaihingerian *as if* plea. Its attractiveness is that it greatly simplifies the task of the interpreter, and to some extent that of the reader as well. But to simplify in this way can also be to distort. Barfield's special virtue as a commentator is the tenacity with which he confronts

[30]Ernst Cassirer, *An Essay on Man: An Introduction to a Philosophy of Human Culture* (New Haven: Yale University Press, 1944; rpt. 1970), p. 5.

passage after passage that has heretofore been ignored or dismissed as Coleridgean vaporing. But this very virtue of, so to speak, New Critical concentration on the passages at hand is also his main defect; for by taking everything at face value, without the safeguards of that "complex and allusive web of comparative philosophy" that he rejects (p. 4), Barfield does violence to two aspects of our understanding of Coleridge. First of all, he provides a system of Coleridge's thought that is really what Coleridge worked through and rejected rather than what he finally endorsed. Secondly, to treat Coleridge's profound interest in polarity without reference to the cultural situation on the continent is to destroy the historical ecology of his thought.

With regard to the first of these deficiencies, we may take a revealing instance. Barfield lays great stress on a clear understanding of the two chapters at the end of the first volume of the *Biographia Literaria:* "this is the place [he writes of Chapter XII] where, more than anywhere else, the dynamic philosophy is brought together in epitome. It is impossible to master the chapter without becoming substantially seised of what Coleridge thought. But that is difficult and is likely to be attempted by comparatively few. If it were otherwise, there would be the less need for such a book as this" (p. 63). But what Barfield's simplified approach does not allow him to take into account is, first, that Chapter XII is mostly the thought of Schelling and, secondly, that Coleridge, in explicit rejection of the importance placed on it by Barfield, at the end of his life dismissed "the metaphysical disquisition at the end of the first volume of the 'Biographia Literaria'" as "unformed and immature" (*TT,* 28 June 1834).

With regard to the other deficiency in Barfield's approach, that is, the lack of referential placement in an intellectual tradition and the attendant violence done to the historical ecology of Coleridge's mental activity, a single citation may suffice for illustration. Led on by a penchant for Rudolf Steiner, Barfield follows Steiner into the realm of Goethe's morphological speculations:

> Goethe's *Metamorphosenlehre* [writes Barfield] . . . was published in
> 1790. Not only is its method based on precisely what Coleridge
> demands, namely penetration from *natura naturata* into *natura
> naturans,* but its "archetypal plant" (*Urpflanze*) is the very embodi-
> ment of the idea of polarity as the basis of life. In some of the other
> writings Goethe's epistemology (so far as he develops it philosophi-
> cally) is thoroughly Coleridgean. [p. 242]

Barfield is here standing at a threshold opening onto vast
movements of European thought; but all he can say, constricted
as he is by a method that refers everything to Coleridge "on his
own terms," is that the Goethean endorsement of polarity is
"thoroughly Coleridgean." It is precisely this kind of Anglocen-
tric distortion of perspective that has fueled the wrath of learned
anti-Coleridgeans from Ferrier to Wellek.

In truth, the first of the examples opens out into larger
Romantic ideational currents no less than does the second. For
the twelfth chapter of the *Biographia Literaria* is concerned with
the logical polarity of ego and the external as represented by the
formal terms "subject" and "object." The opposition was of recurring urgency in Coleridge's thought, as is witnessed by Carlyle's wickedly hilarious recollection of his characteristic discourse: "He had knowledge about many things and topics, much
curious reading; but generally all topics led him, after a pass or
two, into the high seas of theosophic philosophy, the hazy in-
finitude of Kantean transcendentalism, with its 'sum-m-mjects'
and 'om-m-mjects.' "[31] "All knowledge rests on the coincidence of

---

[31] *The Works of Thomas Carlyle in Thirty Volumes,* Centenary Edition [ed. H. D.
Traill] (London: Chapman and Hall [1896–99]), XI, 56. Again: "I still recollect
his 'object' and 'subject', terms of continual recurrence in the Kantean province;
and how he sang and snuffled them into 'om-m-mject' and 'sum-m-mject', with a
kind of solemn shake or quaver, as he rolled along" (p. 55).

an object with a subject," confirms Coleridge himself in the twelfth chapter of the *Biographia* (I, 174).

But in so saying, Coleridge translates exactly the opening statement of Schelling's *System des transzendentalen Idealismus:* "Alles Wissen beruht auf der Übereinstimmung eines Objektiven mit einem Subjektiven" (III, 339). Coleridge subsequently—and for a considerable space in his larger argument he is following Schelling so closely as to be simply translating, or "plagiarizing," his German contemporary—produces ten theses having to do with the polarity of subject and object. "It must be remembered," he says, "that all these Theses refer solely to one of the two Polar Sciences, namely, to that which commences with, and rigidly confines itself within, the subjective, leaving the objective (as far as it is exclusively objective) to natural philosophy, which is its opposite pole." Still following Schelling, although not exactly translating, he then says that "the true system of natural philosophy places the sole reality of things in an ABSOLUTE, which is at once causa sui et effectus, . . . in the absolute identity of subject and object, which it calls nature, and which in its highest power is nothing else than self-conscious will or intelligence" (*BL,* I, 185, 187).

If Coleridge in these instances goes beyond the bounds of propriety in his unacknowledged use of Schelling, he at least demonstrates the critical acumen for which he is famous. For there is no fuller or more explicit statement of the doctrine of universal polarity in terms of subject and object than that provided by the opening pages of Schelling's treatise. "We can call the content of everything in our knowledge that is merely *objective, nature,*" says Schelling there: "the content of everything *subjective* on the other hand is called the *ego,* or the *intelligence.* Both concepts are opposed to one another. Intelligence is originally thought as the merely representing, nature as the merely representable, the former as the conscious, the latter as being without consciousness. There is however in each knowledge a reciprocal coincidence of both" (III, 339). "If all *knowledge* has as it were two poles, which reciprocally presuppose and demand one another," continues Schelling, "then they must seek themselves in all sciences; there must accordingly be two fundamental sciences, and it must be impossible to go out from the one pole without being driven onto the other" (III, 340). Since "both opposed entities are necessarily reciprocal," says Schelling further, then "to make the objective pole the first, and to deduce the subjective from it" is "the task of *Naturphilosophie*." If there is a "*Transzendental-Philosophie,* then there is left for it only the opposed direction—to go out from the subjective, as from the first and *absolute,* and to have the *objective* arise out of it." The "whole system of philosophy," concludes Schelling, is accordingly "completed by two fundamental sciences, which, opposed to one another in principle and in direction, reciprocally seek and supplement one another" (III, 342). In this sweeping formulation, surely, we encounter an apex of the doctrine of polarity.

Despite these emphatic polar schematisms, however, it would be a serious historical error to think that Schelling had any special property rights, terminological or substantive, to the examination and manipulation of the logic of subject and object.[32] To cite merely one counterclaim, Ernst Bloch argues that the "seminal idea" (*Kerngedanke*) of all Hegel's thought is "dialectic subject-object mediation."[33] As Goethe, who knew both Schelling and Schelling's philosophy so very well and sympathetically, remarked, "where object and subject touch one another, there is life; if Hegel in his identity-philosophy puts himself in the middle between *Objekt* and *Subjekt* and maintains this place, then we want to render him praise" (XXIII, 492).

Neither Schelling nor Hegel, moreover, was the originator of

[32]For instance, compare Novalis: "Objectiv und subjectiv nothwendige Zeichen, / welches im Grunde einerley ist / sind daher die Einzigen, wodurch sich ein Gedachtes mittheilen lässt" (II, 109).

[33]Ernst Bloch, *Subjekt-Objekt: Erläuterungen zu Hegel* (Berlin: Aufbau-Verlag, 1951), p. 31.

the German commitment to subject/object philosophizing. Rather, as in so many instances, it was to Kant, or possibly more precisely to Reinhold's presentation of Kant, that the Romantic preoccupation with subject/object logic owed its rise.[34] Thus in the same place where Goethe commends Hegel's position on the issue of *Subjekt* and *Objekt*, he also surveys the development of the topic from its beginning, with the observation that "Kant was the first who laid an orderly groundwork. On this foundation construction has proceeded in various directions" (XXIII, 492).

A single example should suffice to justify Goethe's contention as to Kant's direct priority. Schelling's initial proposition, quoted above, that "all knowledge (*Wissen*) rests on the agreement of an object (*Objektiven*) with a subject (*Subjektiven*)" is clearly a mere restatement of Kant's observation, in the course of distinguishing opinion (*Meinen*), belief (*Glauben*), and knowledge (*Wissen*), that "when the holding of a thing as true is sufficient both subjectively and objectively (*sowohl subjectiv als objectiv*), it is knowledge (*Wissen*)" (III, 533).

Goethe himself participated in subject/object conceivings, even if less insistently for such logical oppositions than for polarities in the natural sciences he so much loved. "Everything that is in the subject," he said, "is in the object—and still something more. Everything that is in the object, is in the subject—and still something more. We are in a double manner lost and made safe. By conceding the object its more and renouncing our subjective more. By exalting the subject with its more and not recognizing the other more." His "general confession of belief" was that

---

[34]See Karl Leonhard Reinhold, *Versuch einer neuen Theorie des menschlichen Vorstellungsvermögens* (Prague and Jena: C. Widtmann and I. M. Mauke, 1789), e.g., pp. 296-303. Cf. Kroner, I, 316-22, and Johann Eduard Erdmann, *A History of Philosophy*, trans. Williston S. Hough, II (London: Allen and Unwin; New York: Macmillan, 1915), 476. See further Alfred Klemmt, *Karl Leonhard Reinholds Elementarphilosophie: Eine Studie über den Ursprung des spekulativen deutschen Idealismus* (Hamburg: Felix Meiner, 1958), e.g., pp. 58-91.

a) In nature there is everything that is in the subject;
y) and something above it.
b) In the subject there is everything that is in nature;
z) and something above it.[35]

Of greater pertinence for judging the dissemination of subject/object preoccupation in Romantic thought, however, is a treatise of 1804 by the political theorist Adam Müller called *Die Lehre vom Gegensatze*—that is, *The Theory of Opposition*. The book presents such typically polar section headings as "Object and Subject," "Positive and Negative," "Nature and Art," "Man and Wife," and "Youth and Age"; and among these oppositions, that of subject and object receives explicit formulation:

> *Objekt* is that which stands in opposition to the *Subjekt*, and vice versa. Therefore a subject that might be opposed to no object is absolutely nothing; for of such a subject it would merely be affirmed that the *Gegenstand* [object] (*das Objekt, das Entgegenstehende*) does not stand opposite it—in short, that it is not a subject, which is a contradiction. . . . What would here be maintained of object and subject is valid for all possible applications of this formula, for all possible objects and subjects; and therefore something is only there (real) insofar as something is there standing against it (anti-real or ideal); force is there and functions only insofar as a counterforce stands against it, works against it; an activity, only insofar as opposite activity (passivity) stands against it; the I is only something insofar as the not-I (*Gegenich*) is there . . . . [36]

If we pause at this juncture to take stock, we realize that the Romantic doctrine of polarity has up to now been revealed in three different even if intertwined forms: firstly, as the preceding discussion illustrates, in the logical opposition of subject and

[35]Both statements quoted in Danckert, p. 231, in the course of a chapter entitled "Subjekt-Objekt" (pp. 222–32).

[36]Adam Müller, *Kritische, ästhetische, und philosophische Schriften*, critical ed., ed. Walter Schroeder and Werner Siebert (Neuwied and Berlin: Hermann Luchterhand, 1967), II, 219–20.

[85]

object derived from Kant's analysis of representability; secondly, as the physical opposition of attractive and repelling forces derived from Kant's discussion of the metaphysical fundamentals of the dynamic; and thirdly, as an analogy of the phenomenon of magnetic polarity, made popular by eighteenth-century empirical investigations of electrical laws.

Coleridge's awareness and commitment, perhaps predictably, extended to all three of these major forms. For instance, in addition to his subject/object preoccupation in the twelfth chapter of the *Biographia* and elsewhere, he speaks of polarity in the form of attractive and repelling forces: "If we pass to the construction of matter, we find it as the product, or *tertium aliud,* of antagonist powers of repulsion and attraction." Coleridge says again, invoking the same distinction, "That nothing real does or can exist corresponding to either pole *exclusively,* is involved in the very definition of a THING as the synthesis of opposing energies."[37]

It was the third form of polarity, however, the one analogized from electrical phenomena, that especially stimulated Coleridge's imagination, as, by its connection with new horizons of scientific possibility, it stimulated also that of Schelling and his school. "A new light," Coleridge recognizes, "was struck by the discovery of electricity, and, in every sense of the word, both playful and serious, both for good and for evil, it may be affirmed to have electrified the whole frame of natural philosophy" (*TL*, p. 31). Defining life as the "tendency to individuate," Coleridge says that "this tendency to individuate cannot be conceived without the opposite tendency to connect, even as the centrifugal power supposes the centripetal, or as the two opposite poles constitute each other, and are the constituent acts of one and the same power in the magnet" (*TL*, pp. 49–50).

As with Schelling and Hegel, Coleridge's commitment to total

[37]*Hints Towards the Formation of a More Comprehensive Theory of Life*, ed. Seth B. Watson (London: John Churchill, 1848), pp. 55, 69. Hereafter cited as *TL*.

system in philosophy led him necessarily to account for—or to attempt to account for—the relationship of nature to mind, of the inanimate to the animate. Accordingly, his own version of *Naturphilosophie*, although one of the three necessary realms addressed by the putative *magnum opus* (as was also true for the parallel but quite independent organization of Hegel's *Enzyklopädie*) finds its fullest sketch in the posthumously published treatise from which we have just been quoting, *Hints Towards the Formation of a More Comprehensive Theory of Life*. In that essay, the principle of polarity became the key to the understanding of natural reality, as it was for the Schellingian school. "What is the most general law," queries Coleridge, for the tendency to individuation?

> I answer—*polarity*, or the essential dualism of Nature, arising out of its productive unity, and still tending to reaffirm it, either as equilibrium, indifference, or identity. [*TL*, p. 50]

His sense of systolic and diastolic flux is similar both to that of Goethe and to that of Schelling and his followers:

> Thus, in the identity of the two counter-powers, Life *sub*sists; in their strife it *con*sists: and in their reconciliation it at once dies and is born again into a new form, either falling back into the life of the whole, or starting anew in the process of individuation. [*TL*, pp. 51–52]

Again:

> the whole *actual* life of Nature originates in the existence, and consists in the perpetual reconciliation, and as perpetual resurgency of the primary contradiction, of which universal polarity is the result and the exponent. [*TL*, p. 70]

He links *Polarität* and *Steigerung* as emphatically as do any of his continental compeers:

[87]

my opinions will be best explained by a rapid exemplification in the processes of Nature, from the first rudiments of individualized life in the lowest classes of its two great poles, the vegetable and animal creation, to its crown and consummation in the human body; thus illustrating at once the unceasing *polarity of life, as the form of its process, and its tendency to progressive individuation as the law of its direction.* [*TL,* p. 67]

As such quotations indicate, Coleridge was working in the spirit of his time no less wholeheartedly than were his German contemporaries. Indeed, if the Romantic era was in some fundamental sense inaugurated and characterized by the French Revolution and its reverberations, then it could also be complementarily defined as an allegiance to new theories of dynamic process, and in particular to those associated with the phenomena of electrical polarity; and it is entirely typical of Coleridge's unusual cultural sensitivity that he was able to see this twin truth with an accuracy usually afforded only by a much later historical perspective. "Henceforward," he writes of the emergence of electrical conceptions onto the intellectual scene, "the new path, thus brilliantly opened, became the common road to all departments of knowledge; and, to this moment, it has been pursued with an eagerness and almost epidemic enthusiasm which, scarcely less than its political revolutions, characterise the spirit of the age" (*TL,* p. 32).

A revealing illustration of the "eagerness and almost epidemic enthusiasm" with which electrical polarity was pursued is supplied by a treatise published at Giessen in 1819 by a minor investigator named Johann Bernhard Wilbrand. Called—I cite the title at length in order to indicate the comprehensiveness of the treatment—*Das Gesetz des polaren Verhaltens in der Natur; dargestellt in den magnetischen, electrischen und chemischen Naturerscheinungen; in dem Verhalten der unorganischen Natur zur organischen Schöpfung; in den Erscheinungen des Pflanzen- und Thierlebens; in dem Verhalten unsers Weltkörpers zu dem umgebenden*

Planetensystem, it plods with Teutonic thoroughness through almost every conceivable variation of polar relationship.[38] Part of the volume's interest lies in its fullness; a still larger part, at least in terms of the contextual interrelationships addressed by this essay, lies in the fact that it is not, as one might suspect, an offshoot of Schellingian *Naturphilosophie;* nor again of Hegelian systematizing; nor yet again of Goethe's morphological speculations. Indeed, Schelling, Hegel, and Goethe are not even mentioned; the book instead is a contribution to "the founding of a scientific physiology," and is dedicated to "physicists, physiologists, and scientific physicians." Its reference is to scientific writers all over Europe—Galvani, Volta, Alexander von Humboldt—and a host of other empirical investigators.

And yet, though the treatise acknowledges no debt to the figures with whom we have been most concerned, it takes up, in explicit fullness, most of the emphases—excepting those exclusively philosophical—that we have encountered. For instance, after an introduction tracing the "development of the concept of polarity," it begins, predictably enough, with a first chapter entitled "Polar Relation in the Phenomena of Magnetism." The second chapter is called "Polar Relation in the Phenomena of Electricity." The third is "Polar Relation in the Phenomena of the Chemical Process," while the succeeding chapter, "Reciprocal Relation of Magnetic, Electrical and Chemical Phenomena," is divided into three sections: "Comparison of Magnetic Polarity with Electrical Polarity"; "Comparison of Electrical Polarity with the Chemical"; and "Comparison of Magnetism with the Chemi-

---

[38]Wilbrand defines "the characteristics of the concept of polarity" by three related criteria: "(1) an opposition between two, which reciprocally presuppose one another, and where the one has a real meaning only in opposition to the other; (2) inner unity of this opposition in a third, which (3) as a unity of a peculiar kind owes its existence to the opposition and would not exist without the opposition" (*Das Gesetz des polaren Verhaltens in der Natur* [Giessen: C. G. Müller, 1819], p. 12).

cal Process."[39] By the eighth chapter, "Polar Relation in the
Functions of Animal Life in General," we encounter subhead-
ings such as "Nourishment, Respiration, Circulation"; and by
the tenth we are presented with the polar relation of seasonal
changes. In short, this is a work that in its preoccupation with
electrical science as a model for universal polarity truly incorporates "the spirit of the age" and amply justifies Coleridge's words
about "eagerness and epidemic enthusiasm."

As a defining component of the spirit of the age, polarity was
naturally enough conceived in varying forms and in differing
contexts. If we revert to our earlier metaphor of a textured
fabric, we may see the Romantic tapestry as one in which polarity's strands weave themselves not only into symmetrically repeated figures, but also as one in which certain patterns appear
but once; as one in which not only the three primary colorations,
so to speak, of subject/object logic, attraction/repulsion dynamic,
and—most important of all—magnetic analogy are evident, but
also as one in which secondary shadings and blendings occur.
Thus, to take an example of a special patterning, the "demonic,"
a conception that was among Goethe's most personal intellectual
emphases, rested on a unique version of the principle of polarity. "He thought," runs the passage in *Dichtung und Wahrheit,* "to
discover something in nature, both as animate and inanimate, as
souled and unsouled, that manifested itself only in contradictions and accordingly could be comprehended under no concept, still less under a word. It was not divine, for it seemed
irrational; not human, for it had no understanding; not devilish,
for it was beneficent. . . . This being [*Wesen*], that seemed to step

---

[39]With reference to the emphasis of these three divisions of Wilbrand's fourth
chapter, compare Coleridge: "We revert again to potentiated length in the
power of magnetism; to surface in the power of electricity; and to the synthesis
of both, or potentiated depth, in constructive, that is, chemical affinity"; ". . . in
the present state of science, the magnetic, electric, and chemical powers are the
last and highest of inorganic nature" (*TL,* pp. 56, 59).

in between all the rest, to part them, to combine them, I called demonic [*dämonisch*], after the example of the ancients" (X, 839-40).

No less idiosyncratic than Goethe's conception of the demonic was Coleridge's conception of the state as depending on a polarity of permanence and progression. "The two antagonist powers or opposite interests of the state, under which all other state interests are comprised," he writes in *On the Constitution of the Church and State*, "are those of Permanence and of Progression." To this declaration he appends a footnote in which with characteristic subtlety he attempts to discriminate different forms of a general theory of oppositions:

> Permit me to draw your attention to the essential difference between *opposite* and *contrary*. Opposite powers are always of the same kind, and tend to union, either by equipoise or by a common product. Thus the + and − poles of the magnet, thus positive and negative electricity are opposites. Sweet and sour are opposites; sweet and bitter are contraries. . . . Even so in the present instance, the interest of permanence is opposed to that of progressiveness; but so far from being contrary interests, they, like the magnetic forces, suppose and require each other. Even the most mobile of creatures, the serpent, makes a *rest* of its own body, and drawing up its voluminous train from behind on this fulcrum, propels itself onward. On the other hand, it is a proverb in all languages, that (relatively to man at least) what would stand still must retrograde. [*CS*, p. 24]

The doctrine of polarity runs all through Coleridge's political awareness. Indeed, not even Marx himself conceived political realities in a more insistently dialectic opposition than did Coleridge:

> We have thus divided the subjects of the state into two orders, the agricultural or possessors of land; and the merchant, manufacturer, the distributive, and the professional bodies, under the common name of citizens. [*CS*, p. 26]

And that polar archetype, the magnet, is repeatedly invoked as metaphorical underpinning of Coleridge's most fundamental political conceptions:

> In order to correct views respecting the constitution, in the more enlarged sense of the term, viz. the constitution of the *Nation*, we must, in addition to a grounded knowledge of the *State*, have the right idea of the *National Church*. These are the two poles of the same magnet; the magnet itself, which is constituted by them, is the CONSTITUTION of the nation. [*CS*, p. 31]

As with individual patterns of realization, so with subsidiary strands in the historical provenance of Romantic concern with polarity. To the three major derivations noted above, one may add two important but somewhat less culturally dispersed ones. The first reflects the single influence of Spinoza. That philosopher had observed that to define any object of thought, the conception of negativity must be invoked—that is to say, to recognize that anything is something, it must simultaneously be recognized that it is not something else—and he expressed this insight in the formula *determinatio negatio est*.[40] To Hegel, this was an insight of the most profound importance. "'Determinateness is negation posited affirmatively', is the meaning of Spinoza's *omnis determinatio est negatio*," he said: "this proposition is of infinite importance" (III, 117). "Determination is negation is the absolute principle of Spinoza's philosophy," he said again (IV, 194). It was also, in truth, the absolute principle of his own insight; for the realization that being (*Sein*) and nothing (*Nichts*) are one and the same is authenticated precisely by the conception of *determinatio negatio est,* and this both Hegel and his followers well understood. As Schopenhauer later remarked, with the sarcasm that was inevitable whenever he referred to Hegel,

[40]*Spinoza Opera*, commissioned by the Heidelberg Academy of Sciences, ed. Carl Gebhardt, 2d ed. (Heidelberg: Carl Winters Universitätsbuchhandlung, 1972), IV, 240.

the vagueness and ambiguity of Spinoza "did not prevent the Neo-Spinozists of our own day from taking all that he said as gospel. Of these the Hegelians, of whom there are actually still a few, are particularly amusing by their traditional reverence for his proposition *omnis determinatio est negatio.* At this, in accordance with the charlatan spirit of the school, they put on a face as if it were able to shake the world to its foundations" (III, 96). Whether or not it shook the world, the formula did manage to express in a single concept a necessary polarity as the condition of being.

The second of these subsidiary historical strands in the transmission of the doctrine of polarity descended from thinkers of the Renaissance, especially from a nucleus that included Bruno (and Schelling's title of 1802, *Bruno,* perhaps serves as a single adequate reminder of the Nolan philosopher's importance for Romanticism), Nicholas of Cusa, Paracelsus, and Boehme. As a commentator has said of their differing versions of polarity,

> the doctrine of the *coincidentia oppositorum* is as little a passing insight for Nicholas of Cusa as is the unity of microcosmos and macrocosmos, despite all opposition, for Paracelsus, or the unity of light and dark, good and bad, etc. for Boehme; rather their thought's whole nature and being is thoroughly interpenetrated and supported by the doctrine of contrariety, which is for them the root and the basic experience out of which all individual things arise.[41]

One example of how subtly and variously the emphases of these thinkers pervaded Romanticism may be supplied by noting a passage in Coleridge in which Paracelsus's microcosm/macrocosm polarity blooms once again. In his *Theory of Life,* Coleridge near the end comments that

---

[41]Theodor Haering, "Cusanus-Paracelsus-Böhme: Ein Beitrag zur geistigen Ahnenforschung unsrer Tage," *Zeitschrift für deutsche Kulturphilosophie,* 2 (1935), 19.

Man possesses the most perfect osseous structure, the least and most insignificant covering. The whole force of organic power has attained an inward and centripetal direction. He has the whole world in counterpoint to him, but he contains an entire world within himself. Now, for the first time at the apex of the living pyramid, it is Man and Nature, but Man himself is a syllepsis, a compendium of Nature—the Microcosm![42]

Despite the presumed lodgment of this discussion in the matrix of contemporary nineteenth-century biological argumentation, and especially in the *Naturphilosophie* of the speculative scientists of the Schellingian school, the passage is actually a restatement of the fundamentals of Paracelsus's position. Paracelsus—who considered himself "not an apostle or anything like an apostle, but a philosopher in the German manner [*ein philosophus nach der teutschen art*]"[43]—says, for instance:

> The Great World, the macrocosm, is closed in itself in such a way that nothing can leave it, but that everything that is of it and within it remains complete and undivided. Such is the Great World. Next to it subsists the Little World, that is to say, man. He is enclosed in a skin, to the end that his blood, his flesh, and everything he is as a man may not be mixed with that Great World.... For one would destroy the other. Therefore man has a skin; it delimits the shape of the human body, and through it he can distinguish the two worlds from each other—the Great World and the Little World, the macrocosm and man—and can keep separate that which must not mingle. [I, 9, 178]

For Paracelsus the opposition of macrocosm and microcosm is polar, that is to say, each member is necessary to a unity that exists only by their opposition: "The mysteries of the Great and the Little World are distinguished only by the form in which

---

[42] *TL,* p. 85. For Coleridge's knowledge of Paracelsus see, e.g., *CL,* IV, 973–74.
[43] *Paracelsus: Sämtliche Werke,* ed. Karl Sudhoff et al. (Munich: O. W. Barth, 1922–), II, 1, 76.

they manifest themselves; for they are only *one* thing, *one* being" (I, 8, 280). Likewise, Coleridge's opposition of "Man and Nature," in which "Man himself is a syllepsis, a compendium of Nature—the Microcosm," is virtually identical to Paracelsus's insistence that "No brain can fully encompass the structure of man's body and the extent of his virtues; he can be understood only as an image of the macrocosm. . . . For what is outside is also inside, and what is not outside man is not inside. The outer and the inner are *one* thing, *one* constellation" (I, 8, 180).

Although all the Renaissance figures mentioned above—and others as well—were known in the Romantic era, not all were equally familiar to each philosophical or literary expositor of polarity; and consequently, when isolating strands of influence, we should be aware of interstices of stitching. For instance, Goethe, despite his consuming preoccupation with polarity, does not seem to have known Nicholas of Cusa and the *coincidentia oppositorum* of that thinker;[44] he paid special attention, on the other hand, to Telesio's doctrine of contraries (XVI, 397-98). Again, Barron Field, Wordsworth's friend and commentator, in discoursing of "the real peculiarity of Mr. Wordsworth's poetical theory," cites "the philosophical dogma of Thomas Campanella, an Italian writer of the early part of the seventeenth century," and quotes Campanella as maintaining that "contrariety is necessary for the decay and reproduction of Nature; but all things strive against their contraries, which they could not do, if they did not perceive what is their contrary."[45]

It may be said in general, however, that such minor figures as Campanella and Telesio, and even major figures such as Nicholas of Cusa and Paracelsus, were less important in the provenance of the Romantic doctrine of polarity than was Jacob

---

[44]See Ernst Hoffmann, "Nikolaus von Cues und die deutsche Philosophie," *Neue Heidelberger Jahrbücher,* new series (1940), pp. 35-76, especially p. 52 n27.

[45]*Barron Field's Memoirs of Wordsworth,* ed. Geoffrey Little (Sydney: Sydney University Press, 1975), p. 120.

Boehme (who was himself, like Bruno, obligated both to Cusanus and to Paracelsus). Speaking of Boehme's "influence on romanticism and occultist currents," Berdyaev has said that "Boehme is the fountainhead of the dynamism of German philosophy, one might even say of the dynamism of the entire thought of the nineteenth century. He was the first to conceive cosmic life as an impassioned battle, as a movement, as a process, as an eternal genesis."[46] Indeed, it is to Boehme that Blake seems to have looked more or less exclusively for his own awareness of the principle of contrariety; and Coleridge too, through the same English translations that were available to Blake, was fully cognizant of Boehme's thought.[47] In that thought the principle of contrariety receives repeated emphasis, as, for instance:

[46]Nicolas Berdyaev, "Unground and Freedom," in *Six Theosophic Points and Other Writings by Jacob Boehme,* trans. John Rolleston Earle (Ann Arbor: University of Michigan Press, 1958), p. xxxiii. (The volume is hereafter cited as *Six Theosophic Points.*) One of the most intriguing aspects of Boehme's possible influence is the question of whether or not Newton derived from him the third law of motion, which is certainly the most important of all conceptions of polarity. Newton's third law states that "to every action there is always opposed an equal reaction, or the mutual actions of two bodies on each other are always equal and directed to contrary parts" (*Isaac Newton's Philosophiae Naturalis Principia Mathematica . . .* , ed. Alexandre Koyré and I. Bernard Cohen [Cambridge: Harvard University Press, 1972], I, 55). This of course provides the basis, among other realities, for all future exploration of outer space. In 1742, several years after Newton's death, William Law wrote in a letter to a friend that "when Sir Isaac Newton died, there was found among his papers large abstracts out of Behmen's works written in his own hand," and in another statement Law said flatly that "the illustrious Sir Isaac ploughed with Behmen's heifer." In the absence of confirming documentation, however, the matter has remained problematic. For the conclusion that Boehme did not influence Newton, see, e.g., Stephen Hobhouse, "Isaac Newton and Jacob Boehme," *Philosophia: philosophorum nostri temporis vox universa,* 2 (1937), 25–54. For the conclusion, on the other hand, that Boehme did influence Newton, see, e.g., Karl Popp, *Jakob Böhme und Isaac Newton* (Leipzig: Hirzel, 1935).

[47]The English translations were published as *The Works of Jacob Behmen, the Teutonic Theosopher . . . with Figures, illustrating his principles,* left by the Reverend William Law, M.A., 4 vols. (London, 1764–81). Coleridge annotated a set of these important and rather rare volumes, now in the British Museum, and the marginalia, which occupy approximately 150 pages, were apparently composed

"Nothing without contrariety can become manifest to itself; for if it has nothing to resist it, it goes continually of itself outwards, and returns not again into itself." Again, from the same treatise: ". . . were there no contrariety in life, there would be no sensibility, nor will, nor efficacy therein, also neither understanding nor science. For a thing that has only one will has no divisibility. If it finds not a contrary will, which gives occasion to its exercising motion, it stands still."[48] The similarity between the contention of this passage, and Blake's "without contraries there is no progression," is obvious.[49]

Just as the Renaissance traditions of contrariety and coinciding opposites, especially as vitalized by Boehme, became only slightly less important a stimulus to Romantic theories of polarity than those supplied by electrical experimenters or by Kant, so too were there in use illustrative images only scarcely less important than that supplied by the magnet. Chief among them was probably that of the division of human sexuality into male and female, and both Schelling and Hegel found in this phenomenon illustration for their respective conceptions of polarity and dialectic.[50] As Wilbrand observes,

> there exists between the two sexes, as far as reciprocal need is concerned, the same relation that obtains between magnetic or electrical polarity. Just as a magnetic polarity, as merely northern,

---

over a number of years—1808 to 1827 might be a reasonable supposition. See further Thomas McFarland, "Excursus Note XIX: Coleridge and Boehme," *Coleridge and the Pantheist Tradition,* pp. 325–32.

[48]*On the Divine Intuition,* I, pars. 8 and 9, in *Six Theosophic Points,* p. 167.

[49]Behind Boehme, however, lies Paracelsus, who also realizes that progression depends on polarity; e.g.: "But the seed of a single man does not yet make a complete man. God wills to make a man out of two, and not out of one; he wills man composed of two and not of one alone. For if man were born of the seed of one individual, he would not change in nature" (I, 1, 262–63).

[50]See, e.g., Haering, *Hegel,* I, 677 ff. But the illustration was so inevitable that it occurred everywhere—for instance, one of the section headings in the second chapter of the second book of Müller's *Die Lehre vom Gegensatze* is "Mann und Weib."

[97]

or merely southern, is actually unthinkable, but rather the two reciprocally presuppose each other, so is it certainly true that a merely male or merely female sex is not only contrary to appearance in the whole of nature, but also unthinkable, because the female is female only in contrast to the male, and *vice versa*. [pp. 269-70]

Wilbrand further argues that woman cannot be considered an inferior or incomplete man, because such an hypothesis violates the structure of polarity: that "just as a polar relation cannot fail to be recognized between male and female," by the same token "it cannot be doubted that in each sex human nature is given perfect in itself" (p. 269).

Among the variations of the sexual metaphor, two, that of the androgyne, and that of elective affinity, deserve special note. The former was part of the heritage of antiquity, and a *locus classicus* is of course the myth of Aristophanes in Plato's *Symposium*.[51] But among the Renaissance progenitors of Romantic polarity, androgyny was a specific and recurrent feature of the thought of Paracelsus. Thus he speaks of "the *rebis*—the bisexual creature—which transmutes silver and other metals into gold" (I, 3, 141); and his commentator, Yolande Jacobi, glosses the term as follows:

REBIS. The hermaphrodite, or bisexual being; in its unity, that is to say, by combining the two antitheses, the male and the female

[51]*Symposium* 189D-193D, especially 189D-E. In later aspects of ancient thought, the androgynous conception became essential to the cosmological speculations of Gnosticism; e.g.: "So there is a bisexual power and conception. . . . [B]eing one is found to be two, a male-and-female being having the female within it." "But after this they called themselves gnostics, alleging that they alone 'knew the deep things' . . . . These men, according to their own doctrine, reverence beyond all others Man and the Son of Man. Now this Man is bisexual and is called by them Adamas" (*Gnosis: A Selection of Gnostic Texts,* ed. Werner Foerster, trans. R. McL. Wilson [Oxford: Clarendon Press, 1972-74], I, 260, 263).

principle, it represents, in accordance with an old alchemistic idea, the highest and most desirable degree of the process of transmutation—totality.[52]

Such a polar variation was carried into Romanticism by the occultist currents so ably elucidated by scholars like Viatte; and perhaps its most recurrent appearance is in the work of Franz von Baader, Boehme's most devoted Romantic disciple.

To limit ourselves to perhaps the single most intriguing illustration of its currency, however, we must turn our attention to a curious late Romantic French cult called *Evadanistes*. The doctrine of *Evadisme* derived its name from an amalgam of Adam and Eve, and as a commentator says, "It was an androgynous religion composed of male and female elements, and, to compensate for the humble part she had hitherto played in the religions of the world, her name, Eve, came first. The leader—or prophet—of this new religion was a man called Ganneau who styled himself *Le Mapah*—a name made from the first syllable of *maman* and the first syllable of *papa*." In one of the *Mapah*'s "platras," or printed proclamations of religious androgeneity, it is said that "Mary is no longer the Mother. She is the wife. Jesus Christ is no longer the son. He is the husband." "Finally," continues the commentator,

the *Mapah* greets them both together as the great symbol, the personification of unity in duality, under one name *Androgyn-Evadam*.

'Humanity is now constituted for the great betrothal.
The hour of human virility has come.
The era of *Evadah* is at hand.
   Hosannah!'[53]

---

[52]Yolande Jacobi, ed., *Paracelsus: Selected Writings,* trans. Norbert Guterman (New York: Pantheon Books, 1951), p. 331.
[53]Enid Starkie, *Petrus Borel the Lycanthrope: His Life and Times* (Norwalk, Conn.: New Directions, 1954), pp. 50–54.

The sexual, and even the androgynous, illustration of polarity, though not a large factor in the thought of Coleridge and of Wordsworth, was not entirely absent even in their minds. Thus the *Mapah*'s "great betrothal" is to some extent analogous to the polar union of Wordsworth's "great consummation" of nature and the mind of man, for which the "spousal verse" of "The Recluse" would chant the celebration.[54] And *Christabel*'s Geraldine is sexually ambivalent (we recall Coleridge's indignation at Hazlitt's bruiting it about that Geraldine was in fact a man) (*CL*, IV, 918). On more than one occasion, moreover, Coleridge observed that the feminine was an important element in the finest masculine natures. "The truth is," he said at one point, "a great mind must be androgynous" (*TT*, 1 Sept. 1832).

But more widespread than the metaphor of androgyny was that of elective affinity. The interest in this latter conception stemmed from a work of 1775 by the Swedish chemist, Torbern Bergman, entitled *De attractionibus electivis*, which, Germanized, became the title of Goethe's novel of human relationships published in 1809 as *Die Wahlverwandtschaften*. As the author of the latter work told Riemer, "the moral symbols in the natural sciences (for example that of elective affinity discovered and used by the great Bergmann [*sic*]) are more spiritual, and allow themselves to be combined with poetry, indeed with society, above all others."[55]

Goethe was by no means the only Romantic figure to be intrigued by the scientific affinities of acids and alkalis. Hegel devoted philosophical consideration to elective affinity (*Wahlverwandtschaft*) in both the *Enzyklopädie* (VII, i, 405–10) and the *Wissenschaft der Logik*. In the latter, after arguing that musical harmonies are forms of elective affinity (III, 430–31), he

[54]*The Poetical Works of William Wordsworth*, ed. Ernest de Selincourt and Helen Darbishire (Oxford: Clarendon Press, 1940–49), V. 4–5 (lines 57–68).

[55]*Gedenkausgabe*, XXII, 565. Bergman's work was translated into English in 1785, under the title *A Dissertation on Elective Attractions*, and the translator, Dr. Thomas Beddoes, was later to become a friend of Coleridge.

proceeds to a lengthy discussion of chemical affinities, based on the then recent investigations of Berthollet, Johann Wilhelm Ritter, and Berzelius. Significantly for our interests in this essay, he entertains the possibility not only that "every chemical effect is ultimately an electrical phenomenon, but also that what appears to be the effect of so-called elective affinity is really brought about only by an electrical polarity which is stronger in some bodies than in others" (III, 443). Wilbrand, working independently of Hegel, is more positive: "the doctrine of chemical affinity, and elective affinity [*chemischen Verwandtschaft, und Wahlverwandtschaft*] rests solely and singly on a polar relationship between the substances" (p. 56).

How widely disseminated the interest in this version of polarity was may be indicated by a single example: the unforgettable scene in *Madame Bovary* where Rodolphe conducts a seduction of Emma while both are listening from within the town hall to the speech of an official outside. In high Romantic fashion, Rodolphe discourses to Emma of "dreams, presentiments, magnetism"; and then he proceeds to "the affinities": "Du magnétisme, peu à peu, Rodolphe, en était venu aux affinités, et, tandis que M. le président citait Cincinnatus à sa charrue, Dioclétien plantant ses choux et les empereurs de la Chine inaugurant l'année par des semailles, le jeune homme expliquait à la jeune femme que ces attractions irrésistibles tiraient leur cause de quelque existence antérieure."[56]

The "magnétisme" invoked by Rodolphe's sexual design encompassed not only the electrical phenomenon with which the era was so fascinated, but also the all but equal fascination with Mesmerism, or "animal magnetism." The importance of this latter vogue for the late eighteenth and nineteenth centuries can hardly be overestimated;[57] and animal magnetism, like the af-

---

[56]Flaubert, *Madame Bovary,* Part 2, Chapter 8.
[57]See, e.g., Fred Kaplan, *Dickens and Mesmerism: The Hidden Springs of Fiction* (Princeton: Princeton University Press, 1975), especially "The Mesmeric Mania," pp. 3–33.

finities, seemed to be still another of the reasons for thinking, in the speculative intoxication of early Romanticism, that nature and spirit were but polar aspects of a common unity. Indeed, as a recent commentator has said,

> Of the many systems for bringing the world into focus, mesmerism had most in common with the vitalistic theories that had multiplied since the time of Paracelsus. Indeed, Mesmer's opponents spotted his scientific ancestry almost immediately. They showed that, far from revealing any new discoveries or ideas, his system descended directly from those of Paracelsus, J. B. van Helmont, Robert Fludd, and William Maxwell, who presented health as a state of harmony between the individual microcosm and the celestial macrocosm, involving fluids, human magnets, and occult influences of all sorts.

Furthermore, as the same commentator notes, Mesmer himself explicitly made use of the conception of magnetic polarity in his own practice: "Mesmer and his followers put on fascinating performances: they sat with the patient's knees enclosed between their own and ran their fingers all over the patient's body, seeking the poles of the small magnets that composed the great magnet of the body as a whole."[58] Wilbrand, for his part, though unwilling as a scientist to speak too confidently about the inner truth of Mesmerism—and awake also to the possibilities that Mesmerism presented to the charlatan—observes that

> rapport occurs only between the magnetiser and the magnetised person, and it is established with a third person only when he enters into contact with the magnetiser, which points, as it were, to a linear relation similar to that which obtains in genuine magnetic phenomena. Likewise, the inner blending of the magnetised person with the magnetiser is similar to the inner blending of the two polar directions of a real magnet. [pp. 276-77]

[58]Robert Darnton, *Mesmerism and the End of the Enlightenment in France* (Cambridge: Harvard University Press, 1968), pp. 14, 4.

Another major invocation of polarity and the coincidence of opposites in the Romantic period, but this one having to do with literary rather than with scientific issues, was constituted by the adoption of the reconciliation of opposites as a guiding principle of art. Although both Schelling and Hegel adopted polarity as a principle of their aesthetic theories, it is perhaps true that no single German thinker applied it as unequivocally to literary definition as did Victor Hugo. In his *Préface de Cromwell* of 1827, a document that lies at the very heart of the French Romantic sensibility, Hugo incorporated the spirit of the age into a manifesto that proclaimed that "la poésie vraie, la poésie complète, est dans l'harmonie des contraires."[59]

The necessity for the "harmonie des contraires" arises, in Hugo's view, out of the fragmented nature of our reality and experience, as witnessed and influenced by Christianity: "Nous venons de voir comme . . . le christianisme sépare profondément le souffle de la matière. Il met un abîme entre l'âme et le corps, un abîme entre l'homme et Dieu" (I, 414). Because our experience is one of separation and sundering, the role of art, following Christianity, is to rejoin the original elements: "Le christianisme amène la poésie à la vérité. Comme lui, la muse moderne verra les choses d'un coup d'oeil plus haut et plus large. Elle sentira que tout dans la création n'est pas humainement *beau*, que le laid y existe à côté du beau, la difforme près du gracieux, le grotesque au revers du sublime, le mal avec le bien, l'ombre avec la lumière" (I, 416). Again: "Elle se mettra à faire comme la nature, à mêler dans ses créations, sans pourtant les confondre, l'ombre à la lumière, le grotesque au sublime, en d'autres termes, le corps à l'âme, la bête à l'esprit; car le point de départ de la religion est toujours le point de départ de la poésie.

[59]Victor Hugo, *Théâtre complet,* Preface by Roland Purnal, Notices and notes by Jean-Jacques Thierry and Josette Mélèze, Bibliothèque de la Pléiade, 66 (Paris: Gallimard, 1963-64), I, 425.

Tout se tient" (I, 416). We live as the heirs of Christianity, says Hugo, and Christianity assumes that man is double, composed of two beings, one mortal and one immortal: "Du jour où le christianisme a dit à l'homme: 'Tu es double, tu es composé de deux êtres...'; de ce jour le drame a été créé" (I, 425).

Drama is therefore the necessary form of modern art: "the poetry born of Christianity, the poetry of our time, is therefore drama; the character of the drama is the real; the real results from the natural combination of two types, the sublime and the grotesque" (I, 425). Having erected this arch of theory, Hugo—in true Romantic fashion—finds Shakespeare the keystone and completion. Shakespeare, he says, united the genius of Homer and the sublime with that of Dante and the grotesque: "We have here arrived at the poetic summit of modern times. Shakespeare is drama, and drama incorporates in the same breath the grotesque and the sublime, the terrible and the ridiculous, tragedy and comedy" (I, 422).

The "harmonie des contraires" that for Hugo is so perfectly exemplified by Shakespeare is the same motif that Coleridge—the greatest Shakespearean critic of the day—describes as constituting the poetic imagination itself:

> The poet, described in *ideal* perfection, brings the whole soul of man into activity, with the subordination of its faculties to each other, according to their relative worth and dignity. He diffuses a tone and spirit of unity, that blends, and (as it were) *fuses,* each into each, by that synthetic and magical power, to which we have exclusively appropriated the name of imagination. This power ... reveals itself in the balance or reconciliation of opposite or discordant qualities: of sameness, with difference; of the general, with the concrete; the idea, with the image; the individual, with the representative; the sense of novelty and freshness, with old and familiar objects; a more than usual state of emotion, with more than usual order; judgement ever awake and steady self-possession, with enthusiasm and feeling profound or vehement; and while it blends and harmonizes the natural and the artificial, still subordinates art

to nature; the manner to the matter; and our admiration of the poet to our sympathy with the poetry.[60]

The comprehensiveness of this justly famous passage in its deployment of the principle of polarity cannot readily be matched by any single *locus* in either French or German literature. But it was written entirely in the spirit of the time, and other poets than Coleridge and Hugo saw the "reconciliation of opposite or discordant qualities" and the "harmonie des contraires" as the first task of successful poetry. Hölderlin, to restrict ourselves to a single illustration, reveals, in some turbulent notes connected with *Empedokles,* how constantly the principle of polarity was working in his conception of what he was doing as a poet:

> ... thus it is necessary that the poetic spirit in its concord and harmonic progress also provide itself an infinite point of view, ... a unity, where in harmonic progress and alternation everything may go forward and backward, and by its thoroughly characteristic relation to this unity may win not merely objective connection, for the onlooker, but also felt and tangible connection and identity in the alternation of the opposites, and it is its final task, to have a thread, a memory in the harmonic alternation, by which the spirit may remain present to itself, never in a single moment, and again in a single moment, but continuing in one moment as in another, and in differing moods ....

Further down in this same seamless outpouring, which is entitled *Über die Verfahrungsweise des poetischen Geistes,* Hölderlin

---

[60]*BL,* II, 12. The doctrine of reconciled oppositions figures no less prominently in Coleridge's conceptions of drama and of Shakespeare than it does in those of Hugo. Shakespeare is characterized by "signal adherence to the great law of nature that opposites tend to attract and temper each other." The one great principle of dramatic illusion is "that ever-varying balance, or balancing, of images, notions, or feelings ... conceived as in opposition to each other" (*Shakespearean Criticism,* ed. T. M. Raysor, 2d ed. [London: Dent; New York: Dutton, 1960], I, 199, 181).

strikes off a veritable *glissando* of invocations of opposites and their reconciliation: ". . . *in der unendlichen Einheit,* welche einmal Scheidepunct des Einigen als Einigen, dann aber auch Vereinigungspunct des Einigen als Entgegengesezten, endlich auch beedes zugleich ist, so daß in ihr das Harmonischentgegengesezte weder als Einiges entgegengesezt, noch als Entgegengeseztes vereinigt, sondern als beedes in Einem als einig entgegengeseztes unzertrennlich gefühlt, und als gefühltes erfunden wird. Dieser Sinn ist eigentlich poetischer Karakter . . . ."[61]

The "Harmonischentgegengesezte," the "harmonie des contraires," the "reconciliation of opposite or discordant qualities," summoned as criteria of poetry and the poetic imagination, serve to conclude this conspectus—where much has been necessarily shortened or omitted—of the major appearances of the doctrine of polarity in the Romantic era. There has throughout been no attempt to observe nominal distinctions between doctrines of contrariety and those of polarity, or other supposedly significant differentiations of formulation, none of which to my mind has a real basis in the ontology of the problem.

Rather than develop this contention, however (which I would like to think self-evident), I shall devote the remaining space, before venturing briefly to assess the deeper significance of polar commitments in the Romantic era, to marking three minor but not unimportant historical points about the ramification of the nineteenth century's protean concern with contraries and oppositions.

First of all, it is necessary to realize that the polar commitment sometimes appeared in disguised or inexplicit forms. "The *naturphilosophisch*-romantic doctrine that life is an oscillation between two poles," says Ricarda Huch in an insight that isolates

---

[61]Hölderlin, *Sämtliche Werke,* Stuttgart Hölderlin Edition, commissioned by the Kultusministerium of Baden-Württemberg, ed. Friedrich Beissner (Stuttgart: W. Kohlhammer, 1946–), IV, 251.

the point, "is to be applied literally to the vacillating wanderlust and longing of the Romantics between the geographical poles."[62] One thinks here not only of the actual voyagings of Romantic authors such as Byron, Nerval, or Lenau, but even more directly of Coleridge's Mariner, journeying specifically to and from the polar region, with contrarieties of sun and moon, the dead and the living, as *basso ostinato* of his progress.

Secondly, it is necessary to realize that the concern with a dialectic of oppositions did not suddenly disappear with the demise, whenever that may supposedly have been, of Romanticism proper. For instance, J. J. Bachofen, who despite his sobriquet of "Mythologe der Romantiker" actually wrote in the middle decades of the nineteenth century, based both his mythological exegeses and his anthropological conjectures squarely upon the conception of dialectical oppositions and their synthesis. To cite a single example from his essay on mortuary symbolism:

> We shall now attempt to elucidate the original idea underlying the connection between eggs and circus games. . . . Material life moves between two poles. Its realm is not that of being but that of becoming and passing away, the eternal alternation of two colors, the white of life and the black of death. Only through the equal mixture of the two is the survival of the material world assured. . . . Indeed, the positive power cannot for one moment exist without the negative power. Death, then, is not the opposite but the helper of life, just as the negative pole of magnetism is not the adversary of the positive pole but its necessary complement, without which the positive pole would vanish immediately, and life give way to nothingness.[63]

Bachofen, though active in the middle of the century, might still be considered a Romantic. Other invocations of the doctrine

---

[62]Ricarda Huch, *Die Romantik: Ausbreitung, Blütezeit und Verfall* (Tübingen: Rainer Wunderlich Verlag Hermann Leins, 1951), p. 383.

[63]*Myth, Religion, and Mother Right: Selected Writings of J. J. Bachofen*, trans. Ralph Manheim (Princeton: Princeton University Press, 1967), pp. 33–34.

of contraries, however, by figures clearly beyond any usual description as Romantics, exist in profusion. For instance, a recent commentator compares Ruskin with Hegel: "there can be no doubt that Ruskin was a dialectical thinker." "If one major theme has been the unity of Ruskin's thought, another has been its progression by opposites. . . . In practice Ruskin tended to use contrasting terms which acted as separate but parallel categories, each category containing polarities of an idea within it. . . . If Ruskin's terminology is thought of as a series of polarities . . . the apparent contradictions in what he says about art become comprehensible. . . . His critical theories depend upon a series of dynamic opposites."[64] Again, Browning not only adopted a thesis-antithesis-synthesis structure for *The Ring and the Book,* but also, in the view of a modern commentator, devotes one part of his poetic endeavor to arguing that "men fail when they do not admit the dual thrusts of their natures and recognize only one pole of the dialectic tension," and another part to depicting "man held in tension by a polarity of opposing thrusts."[65]

But the doctrine of oppositions persists with hardly less vigor in this century than it did in the nineteenth. Major figures like Yeats and minor ones like Eli Siegel provide familiar examples, and even Edwin Arlington Robinson on one occasion espoused a "system of 'opposites'," which consisted in "creating a fictitious life in direct opposition to a real life which I know."[66] More recently—indeed in 1976—a critic of Shakespeare, J. W. Lever, argues that modern scholarship has "grasped a latent dualism, an acceptance of multiple oppositions and polarities, at the root of Shakespeare's response to thought and experience," and that Shakespeare is characterized by "an artistic philosophy and a

[64]Robert Hewison, *John Ruskin: The Argument of the Eye* (Princeton: Princeton University Press, 1976), pp. 208, 202–03.

[65]Clyde de L. Ryals, *Browning's Later Poetry, 1871–1889* (Ithaca: Cornell University Press, 1975), pp. 115, 64.

[66]James G. Hepburn, "E. A. Robinson's System of Opposites," *PMLA,* 80 (1965), 266–74.

philosophical art, mutually interacting, alike sustained by the willing acceptance of contraries."[67]

Lever's contention, which is put forth in seeming oblivion of all that Shakespeare represented to the Romantic sensibility, illustrates the third of our concluding remarks about the historical ramification of concerns with polarity: that is, it illustrates the phenomenon of recurrence. The historical dimension becomes—such is the peculiar intermixture of cultural transmission in the group experience and logical inevitability for an individual's own process of thought—the serpent with its tail in its mouth. As a single instance, we may take the figure of Heraclitus with whom Coleridge conceives the polar tradition to have begun, and who has otherwise seemed only tangential to the historical appearances of polar awareness.

Now Marx, as we probably all know, adopted, with certain qualifications, the polar logic of Hegelian dialectic:

My dialectic method is not only different from the Hegelian, but is its direct opposite. To Hegel, the life-process of the human brain, i.e., the process of thinking, . . . is the demiurgos of the real world, and the real world is only the external, phenomenal form of "the Idea." With me, on the contrary, the ideal is nothing else than the material world reflected by the human mind, and translated into forms of thought.

The mystifying side of Hegelian dialectic I criticized nearly thirty years ago. . . . [Since then] I have openly avowed myself the pupil of that mighty thinker. . . . The mystification which dialectic suffers in Hegel's hands by no means prevents him from being the first to present its general form of working in a comprehensive and

---

[67] J. W. Lever, "Shakespeare and the Ideas of His Time," *Shakespeare Survey 29*, ed. Kenneth Muir (Cambridge: Cambridge University Press, 1976), pp. 89, 91. For perhaps the best of modern studies that conceives Shakespeare's art in terms of polarity or "complementarity," see Norman Rabkin, *Shakespeare and the Common Understanding* (New York: Free Press, 1967), e.g., p. 12: "Shakespeare tends to structure his imitations in terms of a pair of polar opposites. . . . The technique of presenting a pair of opposed ideals or groups of ideals and putting a double valuation on each is the basis of Shakespeare's comedy as well as his tragedy."

conscious manner. With him it is standing on its head. It must be turned right side up again.... [68]

Thus Marx. From him, the principles of dialectical materialism were transmitted to Lenin. Lenin, however, subsequently came across Heraclitus and rediscovered him as an exemplar of dialectical materialism: "A very good account of the elements of dialectical materialism," he wrote of one of Heraclitus's fragments.[69] Such circular confirmation seems peculiarly appropriate in its relationship to the theory of opposites, for the serpent with its tail in its mouth—or uroboros—has itself been elucidated at length as the Jungian archetype for the primal unity that precedes all separation and polar opposition.[70]

In truth, Heraclitus, though rarely at the cultural surface in the polar tradition, is everywhere just beneath that surface. "The only thinker to whom he is close," writes Berdyaev of Boehme, "is Heraclitus" (p. xxxvii). Coleridge, again, called a sketch of part of his own system "*Heraclitus redivivus*," and in that same sketch summoned insistently the doctrine of polarity; e.g.: "But observe that Poles imply a null punct or point which being both is neither, and neither only because it is the Identity of Both. The Life of Nature consists in the tendency of the Poles to re-unite, and to find themselves in the re-union" (*CL*, IV, 771). Yet again, Hegel—to adduce a final illustration before the conclusion of this essay—says, in his first observation to the first triad of the larger *Logik,* that "Heraclitus was profound enough to emphasize . . . the higher total concept of Becoming, saying: 'Being is not more than Nothing is', or 'All things flow', which means, everything is Becoming" (III, 80).

---

[68]*Karl Marx, Friedrich Engels, Werke* (Berlin: Dietz Verlag, 1961–68), XXIII, 27.
[69]Quoted in Guthrie, I, 403 n1.
[70]See Erich Neumann, *The Origins and History of Consciousness,* trans. R. F. C. Hull (Princeton: Princeton University Press, 1969), e.g., pp. 10–12, 15–17. The uroboros symbolizes the "time of the beginning, before the coming of the opposites" (p. 12).

So we arrive now at the necessity of attempting to formulate the deeper cultural significance of the efflorescence of the doctrine of polarity in the Romantic era. In part, one must agree with Alice D. Snyder's assessment, in her pioneering study of the principle of the reconciliation of opposites in Coleridge:

> A theoretical insistence upon inclusiveness, in all spheres, and a temperament that found in abstract metaphysical entities, in mere words, real emotional values of almost enervating ultimateness, made it natural that Coleridge should pin his faith to the principle of the Reconciliation of Opposites.... The principle... serves primarily to define that which is positively inclusive, and absolute; at the same time it gives room for all the negations, oppositions and double meanings that must arise in any fundamental dealing with words and metaphysical concepts.[71]

Yet this understanding is merely the reverse side, so to speak, of a truth whose obverse is more deeply etched and culturally more revealing. As Whitehead has noted, "In the earlier times the deep thinkers were the clear thinkers—Descartes, Spinoza, Locke, Leibniz. They knew exactly what they meant and said it. In the nineteenth century, some of the deeper thinkers among theologians and philosophers were muddled thinkers. Their assent was claimed by incompatible doctrines; and their efforts at reconciliation produced inevitable confusion."[72] The Romantic commitment to reconciled oppositions is, in largest description, an attempt to cope with the increasing incompatibility of the data that impinged on cultural consciousness. In all its varied patterns and emphases, such a commitment serves one overriding preoccupation: that of conceiving sundered entities as a reunited whole. Thus Coleridge speaks of "the *polarizing* property

---

[71] Alice D. Snyder, *The Critical Principle of the Reconciliation of Opposites as Employed by Coleridge* (Ann Arbor: The Graduate School of the University of Michigan, 1918), p. 17.
[72] Alfred North Whitehead, *Science and the Modern World* (Cambridge: Cambridge University Press, 1926), p. 115.

of all finite mind, for which Unity is manifested only by corre-spondent opposites" (*F*, I, 515n). In such a formulation the real witness is not to reconciliation but to fragmentation.

Incompleteness, fragmentation, and ruin, which I elsewhere call the diasparactive triad, constitute the deepest underlying truth of Romanticism's experience of reality. The normative awareness of the century as a whole was what Hegel termed "the unhappy consciousness," and the unhappy consciousness was a consciousness of irreconcilable conflict.[73] As a modern commen-tator has urged, "even a cursory examination of the writings of the major Romantic poets reveals that the traditional view is seriously oversimplified and misleading. . . . What seems at first glance triumphant affirmation, is revealed on closer observation as a desperate struggle for affirmation against increasingly pow-erful obstacles."[74]

Thus doctrines of contraries and oppositions flourished be-cause contraries and oppositions were ever more the stuff of cultural and psychological awareness. Although the image of the magnet provided a paradigm for conceiving plurality within a larger unity, the more frequent form of real experience was that of fragmentation. The "harmonie des contraires" was necessary to Hugo precisely because there is "un abîme entre l'âme et le

---

[73] *Hegel's Werke*, II, 158. Cf. Judith Shklar: "The aesthetic revolt of romanti-cism was . . . only part of a more general dissatisfaction with the entire age. If we look deeper, beyond even the conscious expressions of romantic thought, we discover a specific consciousness. . . . This is the 'alienated soul' that has lost all faith in the beliefs of the past, having been disillusioned by skepticism, but is unable to find a new home for its spiritual longings in the present or future. Hopelessly tossed back and forth between memory and yearning, it can neither accept the present nor face the new world. . . . It was not only that 'God is dead', but that culture had perished. . . . The sense of lostness in the 'real' world that marks the unhappy consciousness, and that lies at the root of the romantic revival, is also what gives the movement its continuity" (*After Utopia: The Decline of Political Faith* [Princeton: Princeton University Press, 1969], pp. 15–16).

[74] Edward E. Bostetter, *The Romantic Ventriloquists: Wordsworth, Coleridge, Keats, Shelley, Byron* (Seattle: University of Washington Press, 1963), p. 5.

corps, un abîme entre l'homme et Dieu." And Novalis understood that "polarity is an imperfection—there shall one day be no polarity. It enters a system before it is perfect.... With polarity there arises a separation of that which is necessarily united" (III, 342).

The conception of reconciled opposites is in this perspective nothing less than an attempt to overcome the ruptured awareness of existence; to the extent that it dominates modes of thought, to that same extent will the desire for unity, and the concomitant reality of incompleteness and fragmentation, be necessarily apparent.

Coleridge's own polar schematisms are, typically for him, but also generically for a wider definition of Romantic activity, almost invariably inconclusive or fragmentary. For a single instance, we may note the opening of a letter that contains some of his scientific speculations: "In my literary Life you will find a sketch of the *subjective* Pole of the Dynamic Philosophy; the rudiments of *Self*-construction, barely enough to let a thinking mind see *what it is like* ... while the inclosed Scrawl contains a very, *very* rude and fragmentary delineation of the *Objective* Pole, or the Science of the Construction of *Nature*" (*CL*, IV, 767).

To the degree, however, that diasparactive awareness is a major criterion of Romantic consciousness, Coleridge's incompleteness as a practicing polar schematist becomes a badge of honor; and by the same paradox, Hegel's triumphant filterings of world and mind through the net of dialectical polarity into completed system are exercises in the mechanism of denial no less than they are completed wholes. Indeed, it was exactly because reality was not to be so easily tamed by *a priori* networks of logic that German idealism was historically discredited and gave way to positivism. For as Sir Francis Bacon, an honored figure in Coleridge's intellectual background, early and accurately realized, "The human understanding is of its own nature prone to suppose the existence of more order and regularity in the world than it finds. And though there be many things in nature which are singular and unmatched, yet it devises for them parallels and conjugates and relatives which do not exist."[75]

From this standpoint, the fact that Coleridge's own use of polarity is both less systematic and less complete than that of Hegel or Schelling perhaps testifies as much to the larger hegemony of diasparactive awareness in his life and work as it does to a less responsible reporting of reality. In any case, Nietzsche—for whom too Heraclitus was honored as an "incredible man" ("Unter Menschen war Heraklit als Mensch unglaublich")—subjected the polar logic so lauded by his German predecessors to a sardonically skeptical scrutiny. Although he refers to the "*Gegensatz-Charakter*" of existence and says that the "fundamental belief of metaphysicians is *belief in the antitheses of values (Gegensätze der Werte),*" he actually had little respect either for metaphysicians or for their fundamental beliefs. Speaking of the subject/object relationship, he says: "There are no oppositions: only from the oppositions of logic do we have the concept of polarity (*Begriff des Gegensatzes*)—and it is falsely carried from there over into the observation of things." The doctrine of polarity was for Nietzsche based on an "error of reason." It "may be doubted whether polarities (*Gegensätze*) exist at all." "General, imprecise observation sees everywhere in nature polarities (as, for instance, 'warm and cold'), where there are no polarities (*Gegensätze*), but only variations of degree (*Gradverschiedenheiten*)."[76]

The recognition of "variations of degree" was a hallmark of

[75]*The Works of Francis Bacon,* ed. James Spedding, Robert Leslie Ellis, and Douglas Denon Heath, New Edition (London: Longmans & Co., 1870), I, 165. Several sections later (No. LIV) Bacon notes disparagingly that "Gilbert also, after he had employed himself most laboriously in the study and observation of the magnet, proceeded at once to construct an entire system in accordance with his favorite subject."

[76]*Friedrich Nietzsche: Werke in drei Bänden,* ed. Karl Schlechta (Munich: Carl Hanser, 1954-56), III, 269, 595; II, 568; III, 541; I, 447; II, 568; I, 907.

Coleridge's nuanced observation of the particularities of nature and experience; and although such attention to degree was undoubtedly one of the reasons for his eminence as a literary critic, it worked against the completion of a system based on polar reconciliations. His intellectual activity, as House has noted, was "grounded in a minute analysis of the phenomena of sense. He is far more alert and sensitive to the modes in which sense-experience conditions the life of the mind than most technical philosophers.... His quivering alertness to every stimulus of sense was ... the ground of his strengths and weaknesses."[77] The principle of reconciled opposites held out hope for unifying this mass of discrete data. But the diasparactive form of Coleridge's thought and experience was too pervasive. We are left finally not with a Coleridgean system, but with repeated testimonies to a mighty split in his allegiance and concern: reason and understanding, imagination and fancy, the head and the heart, "I am" and "it is," subject and object—these and other characteristic dichotomies testify to the ineradicable presence of diasparactive process in Coleridge's deepest awareness. The principle of polarity that aligns these sunderings was treasured, by him and by his Romantic contemporaries, as a path to an ultimate wholeness. But for Coleridge, even more strikingly than for his contemporaries, the actual experience from which such treasuring arose was one of fragmentation and splitting apart, and those wounds the doctrine of polar reconciliations was never satisfactorily able to heal.

[77]Humphry House, *Coleridge: The Clark Lectures 1951-52* (London: Rupert Hart-Davis, 1953), p. 14.

]3[

Coleridge and the Enchantments
of Earthly Paradise

Max F. Schulz

To solve both private and public problems, Coleridge characteristically fell back upon the "purus putus Metaphysicus." Like
the other Romantic poets, however, he was constrained at times
to adopt strategies for confronting reality that were multiform,
drawing indiscriminately on psychology, myth, and theology, as
well as metaphysics. Always, though, the object of Coleridge's
concern was spiritual and aesthetic, the wedding of man's soul,
as well as of his mind, to "this goodly universe / In love and holy
passion" (to use the apt words of Wordsworth in the Introduction to *The Excursion,* 53-54, 57-58), and the giving of artistic
form to "the spousal verse / Of this great consummation"
through the reduction of "multitude to unity" and "succession to
an instant" (*BL,* II, 16).

One of the most insistent forms this myth of integration took
in the Romantic period was a harking back to paradise, to a time
when man lived in a golden age of harmony with himself, his
fellow man, and God. Coleridge was a sophisticated heir of a
tradition stretching in English back to the Renaissance and in
Latin and Greek back almost to the beginnings of Western culture. And in that tradition the earthly paradise is identified with
a *genius loci* where man and nature occupied a magic, expressive

space, and formed a whole mythically associated with a garden.[1] For him, as two hundred years earlier for Shakespeare, England's "valleys, fair as Eden's bowers" ("Ode to the Departing Year," 123), provided this secluded and enclosed holy place, "this other Eden, demi-paradise" (*Richard II*, II.i). In part, Coleridge's awe for his "Mother Isle" has its patriotic side, with his country in a war of survival against a rapacious France. His praise of the sanctified island, in "Fears in Solitude" (1798), originates in such sentiments:

> O native Britain! O my Mother Isle!
> How shouldst thou prove aught else but dear and holy
> To me, who from thy lakes and mountain-hills,
> Thy clouds, thy quiet dales, thy rocks and seas,
> Have drunk in all my intellectual life,
> All sweet sensations, all ennobling thoughts,
> All adoration of the God in nature,
> All lovely and all honourable things,
> Whatever makes this mortal spirit feel
> The joy and greatness of its future being?
> There lives nor form nor feeling in my soul
> Unborrowed from my country! O divine
> And beauteous island! thou hast been my sole
> And most magnificent temple, in the which
> I walk with awe, and sing my stately songs,
> Loving the God that made me!
>
> [182–97]

At other times, however, his soul, dilating with paradisal fervor, soared abroad, escaping England's shores. When he gazed on a sunset over the ocean, all seemed

---

[1]I am paraphrasing John Vernon's fine definition of the garden as it figures in man's mythic and cultural structuring of reality, in *The Garden and the Map: Schizophrenia in Twentieth-Century Literature and Culture* (Urbana: University of Illinois Press, 1973), especially pp. xii–xv and 5–6.

> Less gross than bodily; and of such hues
> As veil the Almighty Spirit, when yet he makes
> Spirits perceive his presence.
>
> ["This Lime-tree Bower," 41-43]

And there in the empyrean sublime his soul momently took up its paradisal abode.

Toward the conclusion of her monumental two-volume history of the theme of the Happy Man in seventeenth- and eighteenth-century English poetry, Maren-Sofie Røstvig summarizes the transformations that had occurred to the classical conception of golden groves and the Christian conception of Eden, and to the concomitant dimensions of space and place. By the end of the first quarter of the eighteenth century, she says, space had

> become the new *hortus conclusus* of the meditating Christian. What had begun in the seventeenth century as a belief in a small, charmed circle inside a world pervaded by death and corruption, was carried over into the eighteenth century as an ever widening sphere of perfection. After the seventeenth-century garden came the open landscape of the early eighteenth century, and, hard upon the heels of this event, the whole terrestrial scene and, finally, space itself. By 1728 the belief had triumphed that *all* was perfect, and the process of extending the limits of the landscape of retirement could go no further. The magic grove of the Hortulan Saint had become an "undistinguish'd void" penetrated by a "universal smile."[2]

The traditional view of paradise as a garden enclave had restricted Eden historically to moments at the beginning and end of time and geographically to a narrow plot of ground. Residual in Romantic definitions of the space-time continuum was the

[2]Maren-Sofie Røstvig, *The Happy Man: Studies in the Metamorphoses of a Classical Ideal,* 2 vols. (Oslo: Akademisk Forlag; Oxford: Basil Blackwell, 1954, 1958), II, 287-88.

notion of an extended Eden, which not only included the whole earth, but incorporated the cosmos, and which was realizable in the here and now. "The earth is all before me" (*Prelude,* I, 15), Wordsworth exults in a reversal of Milton's view of Adam and Eve's exile from Eden. Not the wilderness it struck first man but an all-encompassing paradise, so the terrestrial world stretching away to the horizon appeared to Wordsworth's eyes:

> —Beauty—a living Presence of the earth
> Surpassing the most fair ideal Forms
> Which Craft of delicate Spirits hath composed
> From Earth's materials—waits upon my steps;
> . . . Paradise, and groves
> Elysian, Fortunate Fields—. . . why should they be
> A history only of departed things,
> Or a mere fiction of what never was?
> For the discerning intellect of Man . . . shall find these
> A simple produce of the common day.
>
> [Introduction to *The Excursion,* 42-55]

The extended Eden, both terrestrially and cosmically, was a millennial possibility that Coleridge sought both poetically and philosophically. Yet by neither route was he able to realize unalloyed paradisal bliss. Despite his enjoyment of the Quantock Hills and of the Borrowdale Fells, and despite his Romantic proclivity to identify "a new Earth and new Heaven" ("Dejection," 69) with the spirit genius lurking in every "green and silent spot, amid the hills" ("Fears in Solitude," 1) and in every "roaring dell, o'erwooded, narrow, deep" ("This Lime-tree Bower," 10), Coleridge like Milton's Satan looked longingly on the verdant terrestrial scene of Eden but hesitated to enter and claim it as his birthright. As for the larger world beyond the firmament, despite his intellectual ache "to behold and know something great—something *one* and *indivisible,*" he could not entirely rid his mind of the suspicion that metaphysically he was counterfeiting infinity.[3] Whether Coleridge's personal and philosophical inhibitions as regards paradise are also characteristic of his contemporaries is problematical, although as the age "progressed" wearily into the first decades of the nineteenth century faced with the Napoleonic juggernaut year after year, the advent of leafy paradise in the public consciousness retreated back into the myths of the past. From our perspective in time, his personal hesitancies seem to prefigure the public disillusionment of the Victorians, looking out on the brick wastes of their cities. Paradise was no longer attainable simply by stepping into some rural bower.

In the last quarter of the century, then, at least some heirs to the legacy of cosmic perfection, and of cosmic voyages such as that on which Akenside takes the reader in *The Pleasures of the Imagination,* found the bequest from their ancestors less than an enrichment of their lives. One problem was that the "universal smile" permeating space added up to less a plenum than a spiritual vacuum. It can be said with some accuracy that the first generation of Romantics expended much intellectual energy in extricating the mind from their embryo existential situation—in reuniting lived duration with eternity, *locus mundus* with infinity, and time with space. "If I do not greatly delude myself," the irrepressible Coleridge, not yet thirty, informs Tom Poole in a letter of 16 March 1801,

> I have not only completely extricated the notions of Time and Space; but have overthrown the doctrine of Association, as taught by Hartley, and with it all the irreligious metaphysics of modern Infidels—especially, the Doctrine of Necessity—This I have done; but I trust, that I am about to do more—namely, that I shall be able

[3]*CL,* I, 349. I admit that in Coleridge's use of the striking phrase "*all things* counterfeit infinity!" he probably did not intend the negative sense with which I have used it here; but I have few doubts that Coleridge was not unaware of the negative meaning residual in *counterfeit* even as he wrote it.

to evolve all the five senses, that is, to deduce them from *one sense,* and to state their growth, & the cause of their differences—& in this envolement to solve the process of life & Consciousness. [*CL*, II, 706]

This follows by one month a February letter in which he had proudly cited his being in deep philosophic pursuit of the subject: "Change of Ministry interests *me* not—I turn at times half reluctantly from Leibnitz or Kant even to read a smoking new newspaper" (*CL*, II, 676).

That was 1801. Interestingly, back in 1797–98 Coleridge had enjoyed for a brief year or so "by way of his poetry" leaps of imagination which freed him from those isolated instants of sensation without discernible connectives, instants to which the psychology of his day otherwise condemned him. And one of his insights in those years is the ultimate derivation of all qualitative diversity of phenomena, all exponential forms, including such comprehensive categories as time and space, from an elemental and active Power self-divisible into perceptible contrary forces. It would be another fifteen years before he could begin to define this philosophy of nature in formal terms; but "Frost at Midnight" contains an early poetic expression of his intuitions of a dynamic (as opposed to empirical/associationist) resolution of "the process of Life & Consciousness."

At the start of the poem, Coleridge is vexed by the calm, "its strange / And extreme silentness" (9–10). In a real sense, physically as well as mentally, he is isolated from the other inhabitants of his house and from the "numberless goings-on of life" (12) in the village and beyond. Confined not only by the four walls of his room but also by the limited horizon of his irritable thoughts, he remains imaginatively blind and deaf (in "the hush of nature" [17]) to the invisible creative operation of the frost. By the end of the poem, in the famous and oft-quoted final stanza, his understanding has expanded to comprehend that the imperceptible processes of the "secret ministry of frost" (72), of the gentle breathings of his child Hartley, and of the meditation of his mind are parts of the same single creative process of life, participants in the original divine act that continues inexhaustibly. He arrives at this insight by connecting his lonely boyhood at Christ's Hospital, where "pent mid cloisters dim, / [He] saw naught lovely but the sky and stars" (52–53), to the far different childhood he envisions for Hartley, who shall "wander like a breeze / By lakes and sandy shores, beneath the crags / Of ancient mountain, and beneath the clouds" (54–56). With these spatial and temporal projections of his memorial and prophetic imagination, Coleridge breaks out of his sterile confinement-to-isolated-moments, the "vacancies / And momentary pauses" of his thought (46–47), in which he finds himself trapped at the beginning of the poem; and breaking out he communes not only with an observable world of nature, of summer and winter, icicles, owls, and apple trees, but also with "the numberless goings-on of life" by which these objects come into being, as well as with past and future through the conjoinment of generations. In the interface of two childhoods in Coleridge (his own and his son's), two kinds of time interlock: the poet's ruminative sense of human time, past and future, comes into synchrony with eternal time, without loss, indeed with extension, of grounding in the spatial parameters of two places and two persons. It is a unity comprehending all seasons, all generations, and all distances between heaven and earth, both mental and actual, that is realized in the final lines of the poem when Coleridge imagines Hartley's future in language descriptive of the present winter scene outside his cottage. Its multifaceted polar configurations of inner/outer, past/future, time/space, summer/winter, creative/created, and light/sound receive concentrated expression in the image of the formative icicle "quietly shining to the quiet Moon" (74).

Synesthetic fusion of light and sound is one of Coleridge's most persistent conceptual forms for conveying his vision of "the one Life within us and abroad." References to this union appear everywhere in his thought and writing, in his intimate notebook efforts to come to terms with his life as well as in his attempts to formulate a philosophy of nature. The disjunction of light and sound established the figurative polarities of his psychic life in such poems as "Dejection: An Ode" (1802) and "To William Wordsworth" (1807); and the fusion of their properties symbolized his refusal to accept a relativistic knowledge tied to sense data, such as the description of the universe provided by science.

That Coleridge was responsive, however, to the imperatives of the new empirical models of reality is discernible even at subliminal levels of his thought. He was painfully aware of how one's susceptibility to events keeps forcing one to break out of a fixed perspective on things to a relative view that takes into account the possibility that when we change any unit in a complex of parts we create a new set of relationships. The use of multiple perspectives to the events of the wondrous voyage related in "The Ancient Mariner"—the Wedding Guest's, the old mariner's, the marginal glossist's, and finally the minstrel narrator's—is an aesthetic acknowledgment by Coleridge of an existential situation of which he is philosophically only half conscious. A similar multiplicity of viewpoint is intrinsic to the historical and visionary versions of Xanadu presented in "Kubla Khan." But Coleridge refused to give his wholehearted philosophical allegiance to this limited and relativistic sensory world. All his life he struggled to formulate an absolute and holistic version of reality. He does not deny the Newtonian universe; he impatiently dismisses it for mistaking material effects for ontological explanations—in short, for not getting at the means by which the universe operates. Between the great years of bardic vision (1796-98) and the equally great years of metaphysical conception (1815-19), Coleridge reaches for a metascientific world in which clock time and paced-off space of the phenomenal scene yield to a plenum of elemental creative energies that find their primal and ideal source in God.[4] His preoccupation with the problem is revealed in a remarkable series of moon-and-skyscapes he records in his notebooks in the autumn and winter of 1803.

One of the most illuminating is recorded on "Wednesday Morning, 20 minutes past 2 o'clock. November 2nd. 1803."

The Voice of the Greta, and the Cock-crowing: the Voice seems to grow, like a Flower on or about the water beyond the Bridge, while the Cock crowing is nowhere particular, it is at any place I imagine & do not distinctly see. A most remarkable Sky! The Moon, now waned to a perfect Ostrich's Egg, hangs over our House almost— only so much beyond it, garden-ward that I can see it, holding my Head out of the smaller Study window. The Sky is covered with whitish, & with dingy *Cloudage*, thin dingiest Scud close under the moon & one side of it moving, all else Moveless: but there are two great Breaks of Blue Sky—the one stretching over our House, & away toward Castlerigg, & this is speckled & blotched with white Cloud—the other hangs over the road . . . —this is unspeckled, all blue—3 Stars in it/more in the former Break—all unmoving. The water leaden white, even as the grey gleam of Water is in latest Twilight.—Now while I have been writing this & gazing between whiles (it is 40 M. past Two) the Break over the road is swallowed up, & the Stars gone, the Break over the House is narrowed into a rude Circle, & on the edge of its circumference one very bright Star—see! already the white mass thinning at its edge *fights* with its Brilliance—see! it has bedimmed it—& now it is gone—& the Moon is gone. The Cock-crowing too has ceased. The Greta sounds on, for ever. But I hear only the Ticking of my Watch, in the Pen-place

[4]For illuminating expositions of Coleridge's philosophy of nature, to which I am everywhere indebted, see M. H. Abrams' two detailed and near-exhaustive articles (hereafter cited as Abrams 1974 and 1972 respectively) on "Coleridge and the Romantic Vision of the World," *Coleridge's Variety: Bicentenary Studies*, ed. John Beer (London: Macmillan; Pittsburgh: University of Pittsburgh Press, 1974), pp. 101-33; and "Coleridge's 'A Light in Sound': Science, Metascience, and Poetic Imagination," *Proceedings of the American Philosophical Society*, 116 (1972), 458-76; Owen Barfield's *What Coleridge Thought* (Middletown, Conn.: Wesleyan University Press, 1971); Richard Haven's *Patterns of Consciousness: An Essay on Coleridge* (Amherst: University of Massachusetts Press, 1969); and Craig W. Miller's "Coleridge's Concept of Nature," *JHI*, 25 (1964), 77-96.

of my Writing Desk, & the far lower note of the noise of the Fire—perpetual, yet seeming uncertain/it is the low voice of quiet change, of Destruction doing its work by little & little. [*N*, I, 1635]

Coleridge is clearly intrigued here by the polarities of motion/stasis, light/dark, and sound/silence exhibited in nature—by what at first appears to be an anomaly of "cloudage" moving in a sky otherwise dominated by motionlessness, an observation which is disputed even as he watches by two breaks of blue sky closing. Equally fascinating to Coleridge is the luminescent tug-of-war between the dingy white scud of cloud, echoed in the leaden white of the river, and the brilliant light of moon and stars. And even as he is concentrating on these spatial phenomena, there sounds persistently on the periphery of his consciousness the constant ("for ever") voice of the river in conjunction with the localized and temporal crow of the cock, and as undersong of both (but unobserved) the persistent ticking of his watch. For a few brief moments of total absorption in the scene, Coleridge experiences the synchronization of eternal and chronometrical times. But as the stars fade behind the cloud and the moon disappears behind the house, the cock-crowing also ceases, leaving him aware for the first time since his vigil began of the noise of the fire in the grate, "the low voice of quiet . . . Destruction doing its work by little and little."

Several of Coleridge's observations here foreshadow his subsequent development of a dynamic philosophy of nature. Empirically, he remarks that the constant alterations of light in the sky have aural analogues in the terrestrial notes of change; hypothetically, he ascertains a vital union of light and sound, which is paradoxically revealed in the measurable motion of heavenly objects in space and in the recordable passage of earthly intervals of time. (The parallel of leaden-white color in river and cloud, while not contradictory of subsequent theorizing, does not prove to be a fruitful observation.) Equal in significance to his linking of the separate sounds of watch, cock, and fire to the chiaroscuro of moon and stars is his effort to isolate not only a permanence of form and essence in the skyscape but also to discern a continuous process in the natural landscape. He longs to discern a causal succession leading from observation of earthly and meteorological fact to apprehension of cosmic design and its divine intentions. A dozen years later, in the last chapter of *Biographia Literaria,* he will write an explicit confession of his hope that in temporal events he can glimpse intimations of eternity:

> The sense of Before and After becomes both intelligible and intellectual when, and *only* when, we contemplate the succession in the relations of Cause and Effect, which, like the two poles of the magnet manifest the being and unity of the one power by relative opposites, and give, as it were, a substratum of permanence, of identity, and therefore of reality, to the shadowy flux of Time. It is Eternity revealing itself in the phenomena of Time: and the perception and acknowledgment of the proportionality and appropriateness of the Present to the Past, prove to the afflicted Soul, that it has not yet been deprived of the sight of God . . . . [*BL*, II, 207]

In 1803, Coleridge has an intimation that the voice of the Greta, as opposed to the ticking of his watch, has provided him with just such a nexus between mundane and ideal worlds.

Almost twenty years after the icicle and moon lines of "Frost at Midnight," his conceptualization of such light and sound concatenations are given their most memorable poetic phrasing in the 1816–17 addition to "The Eolian Harp":[5]

> O! the one Life within us and abroad
> Which meets all motion and becomes its soul,
> A light in sound, a sound-like power in light,
> Rhythm in all thought, and joyance everywhere—

[5]As noted by Abrams (1972), pp. 461–62 and n, the "one Life" passage inserted as errata in the 1817 *Sibylline Leaves* was sent to the printer on paper that makes almost certain its composition between spring 1816 and spring 1817.

Methinks, it should have been impossible
Not to love all things in a world so fill'd;
Where the breeze warbles, and the mute still air
Is Music slumbering on her instrument.

[26-33]

The "one-Life" lines, written at a time when Coleridge had just completed the *Biographia Literaria,* are an instance of his successful transmutation of philosophical thought into poetic expression; for embedded in the lines is a well-defined religio-scientific world picture, in which the divine act of creation through the interpenetration and synthesis of the primary powers of light and gravity continuously generates and gives rise to all properties of matter, all forms and degrees, of the phenomenal world. In a brilliant exegesis of the "one/Life" passage, M. H. Abrams shows that the conception of life propounded there derives from Jacob Boehme's *Aurora,* Friedrich Schelling's *Naturphilosophie,* and Humphry Davy's chemical-electrical theories—all of which Coleridge had managed by 1816-17 to integrate into a metaphysical confirmation of his brave claims made in 1801 to Poole of having extricated the notions of time and space from Hartleian determinism (1972, pp. 458-76).

In any formulation of the basic premises of Coleridge's intellectual system, however, one must go beyond the poetic density of "The Eolian Harp" and the metaphysical shorthand of *Biographia Literaria.* As with such earlier cosmological speculators as Johann Kepler (1571-1630) and Henry More (1614-87), Coleridge in his eclectic search after truth about the universe is intent on assimilating a metaphysical-theological paradigm to a quantitative-scientific universe, on fitting a Christian schema to the cosmic model of his day. Each man offered a metaphysic based historically on earlier speculations, but carefully accommodated to new scientific data; and each plumbed for a mathematical harmony underlying, and in causal relationship to, the world of the senses. The problem for these men, as likewise for Ralph Cudworth (1617-1688), Isaac Barrow

(1630–1677), and Descartes (1596–1650), was where to locate God and how to define spirit in relation to matter. While stopping short of complete identification of God with space, More repeatedly, albeit uneasily, looks upon space as an immense and omnipresent potentiality of the divine essence, if not actually identical with God's presence.

Like More, Coleridge sees the terrestrial world as a spatially defined materialization of the Unitrine "omnipresence" of God.[6] That is, he sees space as a metaphysically independent entity, the ground of an infinite God whose existence beyond the world involves space. Uneasily aware like another Cambridge Platonist, Isaac Barrow, that God's "continued life before the creation of things in motion involved time,"[7] Coleridge does not rule time out of his considerations; but he has a tendency to associate it with the particular and the phenomenal (it is what he feels on his pulse), while reserving the ideal and transcendent to space. By mid-1818, in notebook and letters, Coleridge was pushing toward the conceptualization of a Deity whose "Unitrine" essence is more than actuality and yet in whose omnipresence originates the powers that are the source of the phenomenal world. In this seamless development from the ineluctable to the mundane, paradise logically follows as an ever-present possibility of the earth we tread and the space we occupy. Thus, space rather than time occupies the most important place in Coleridge's theogony.

[6]Coleridge's ponderings on the nature of reality, as he veers away from *Naturphilosophie*, are extended and torturous, but intellectually consistent, in 1817–19. See especially *N*, III, 4418–56, Aug.–Nov. 1818; and letters to James Gillman, Ludwig Tieck, Lord Liverpool, and C. A. Tulk from Nov. 1816 to Jan. 1818, *CL*, IV, 688–809. Since I am making no special claims for the intellectual status of Coleridge's ideas of paradise, I see no need to raise the question of his use of others' writings. His purview of paradise consists both of the enclosed garden and the cosmic extension of that enchanted plot of ground. There is little question that his response to the millennialism of his age partakes of the centuries-long development of a tradition, to which he brings his peculiar personal needs and unique penchant for clear-headed hard thought.

[7]Edwin Arthur Burtt, *The Metaphysical Foundations of Modern Physical Science* (New York: Harcourt, Brace, 1925), pp. 137, 153.

Still, their exact relationship worried him, and he was forever trying to fix it in various typically Coleridgean formulations of contraries. In one such formulation, time is seen to be concomitant with the willed act of the individual, and space with that of the Divine Will which is the ground of all acts. In this counterpoise of a personalized time to a transcendentalized space, Coleridge chose to emphasize the Logos, the substance of the word, in God's command, "Let there be Light"—hence the space through which the light was suffused—rather than the act of utterance, as had Jacob Boehme, when sound, hence time, would be primary.

Coleridge's ontological concern with the relative functions of time and space is everywhere evident in his attempts to formulate a philosophy of nature which, in Abrams's words, "is a sustained evangel" (1974, p. 122). With almost breathless inclusiveness he pushes beyond Kant's formal disposition of the categories, identifying time and space as "the symbola generalissima of all physical Science." By making them "common measures each of the other," he deduces from them "the Genesis of Length, Breadth, and Depth" (*CL*, IV, 768). From this equation it is only a step to the experiments of Sir Humphry Davy and further analogies in confirmation of the ladder of creation "per descensum" from the divine Unitrine presence to the lowest material form. Hence also Coleridge's admiration for Davy, the one contemporary chemist who, he believed, was most likely to prove the "mutual penetration & inter-susception" of physical and divine energies in "the natura rerum—i.e., the birth of things" (*CL*, IV, 760–61), until disappointment in Davy's acceptance of Dalton's atomic theory separated them philosophically.

Coleridge is trying to restate an older quantitative definition of time-space in new organic terms, and to link the divine nature of eternity-infinity to the transitory earth. At times, in his profound effort to reduce the facts of empirical observation and the facts of mind to the one "visible organismus of the whole *silent* or *elementary* life of nature" (*SM*, p. 72), as in *The Theory of Life* and in his Royal Society lecture of 1825 "On the *Prometheus* of Aeschylus," he resorts to a geometric shorthand that can appear unworthy of his thoughts. Yet, when he engages in a game of correspondences, as he often did in the last twenty years of his life, he had serious ends in mind: "when I take what is Length in the first Power, Breadth in the second, & Depth in the third . . . I take these . . . as corresponded to by Attraction, Repulsion, & Gravitation, and these again by Magnetism, Electricity, and Galvanism or Chemismus" (*CL*, IV, 768–69). The movement of mind from the natural scene to the symbolized universe in Appendix C of *The Statesman's Manual* is yet another of the many instances of his constant desire to realize a world of values sustained by a world of phenomena. Through his study window he sees the sun shine on the landscape. In the communion of sun and vegetation, "each in its own cast" and "all . . . co-existing in the unity of a higher form, the Crown and Completion of the Earthly, and the Mediator of a new and heavenly series," he conjectures, is to be found "the record and chronicle of . . . ministerial acts, and inchase[d] the vast unfolded volume of the earth with the hieroglyphics of her history" (*SM*, pp. 72–73). By way of such contemplation of the spiritual oneness of the universe did Coleridge entertain hopes of locating and surveying the earthly paradise, a demiparadise he might know cognitively and convert into his own through the intellectual experience of his system-making.

There was, unfortunately for Coleridge, however, a dark underside to his willed philosophy of belief in the once infinite, now quantified, distances of the heavens, which he desperately strove to respiritualize, an underside of self-misgiving that was always castrating his imaginative desire to bring "the whole soul of man into activity" (*BL*, II, 12). If Coleridge could give lodging in his mind and in his *Logosophical* theory to the far reaches of space, he was unable in a lifetime of effort to accord its "phantoms of sublimity" (*N*, I, 791) the same warm hospitality in his heart and in his poetical practice. On the pulses of his sensibility space was less a reassuring plenum and repository of divine extension than an infinite unbounded landscape "barren and soundless as the measuring sands" ("Limbo," 16). It is negation, the "darkness, and blackness, and . . . empty space," which Cain yearns for as surcease from this life ("The Wanderings of Cain," 40–41). It is the terrifying emptiness of the "wide wide sea" (*AM*, 233), according to the gloss, that led the guilt-ridden solitary figure of the Ancient Mariner to project onto the moon and stars a sociable yearning for his "own natural home." Similarly, in "Constancy to an Ideal Object" when Coleridge imagines a cottage inhabited by himself alone, unshared, he thinks of

> a becalmed bark,
> Whose Helmsman on an ocean waste and wide
> Sits mute and pale his mouldering helm beside.
>
> [22–24].

Recoiling from the limbo of lonely space, Coleridge sought solace in the domestic grove of "This Lime-tree Bower," the backyard of "The Nightingale," or the cottage doorway of "The Eolian Harp"; so he oscillated fretfully between expansive desire to encompass all and fearful recoil from "Vacancy and formlessness,"[8] between sallying forth in the loving comfort of "a goodly company" (*AM*, 604) and enclosing himself within the secure walls of Xanadu. His neurotic sensitivity to the unbounded was even afflicted at times by the multiplicity of "goings-on" in the world, as in "Frost at Midnight," leaving him unaccountably disquieted in the security of his cottage. Only when multeity was reconciled into unity did Coleridge's disquiet resolve into contemplative serenity.

Perhaps it was his *horror vacui* as much as anything else which drove him at times to crowd words at the beginning and end of

---

[8]Cf. Michael G. Cooke, "The Manipulation of Space in Coleridge's Poetry," *New Perspectives on Coleridge and Wordsworth,* ed. Geoffrey Hartman (New York: Columbia University Press, 1972), p. 176.

books and in the margins of pages already comfortingly printed and which contradictorily left him at other times paralyzed before a blank sheet of paper. Almost up to his death his poetry bears testament to his psychological terror of vacancy, whether of cosmic dimension or of personal inner intensity. Like a sleepless astronomer searching the barren night skies for signs of planetary life, Coleridge probed his feelings of emptiness. "I sate alone," he begins "The Garden of Boccaccio" (1828), "Cow'r'd o'er my own vacancy! / And . . . watch'd the dull continuous ache, / Which, all else slumb'ring, seem'd alone to wake" (4, 8–10). In "Love's Apparition and Evanishment" (1833) he likens his "vacant mood" and the "sickly calm" of his heart to a "ruin'd well" beside which "a lone Arab, old and blind," sits and vainly plumbs for some "human sound." His fear was of an emotional limbo from which his normally teeming mind shrunk.

The adjectives he applied to space reveal again and again his dread of emptiness. In that strange poem "Limbo" (1811) the "horror of blank Naught-at-all" (33) is equated with the oxymorons of "Lank Space" (15) and "weary Space / Fettered from flight, with night-mare sense of fleeing" (12–13). One is claustrophobic in its dimensionlessness and the other paralytic in its directionless motion.[9] The terror expressed here is of imprisonment in a cosmic vacuum of sorts, of sequestration in "a spirit jail secure" (32) of uninterrupted nothingness stretching to infinity on all sides.

His *horror vacui* recoils from the immeasurable, from an endless extension that in effect may as well be nowhere. In a notebook entry of 1814 he despairs because "Angels, Devils, Saints, Blessed Spirits, with none or indefinite Forms," open up to him "the Enormous and the Immeasurable . . . fearful Depths" instead of "resolving into finite Beauty, as the balance

---

[9]For an analysis of the complex verbalization of "Limbo," and allied poems "Ne Plus Ultra" and "On Donne's First Poem," and their subsequent complicated history of publication, see *N*, III, 4073n.

of the whole and the component parts, and the union of the opposite qualities of Distinctness and Comprehension in the mid point of Clearness." Faced with this yawning incorporeality, this absence of reticulated parts, Coleridge finds that the ethereal vagueness of spirits instills in him a "boundless yearning" that is a "negation of Life" instead of a "Serene Complacency or cheerful Pleasure" (*N*, III, 4213). The location of objects in space was necessary to define his sense not only of self but also of time. "I remember," he writes in the 1820s in one of his notebooks,

> when first I saw the connection between Time, and the being resisted: Space and non-resistance—or unresisted Action—that if no object met, stopped, or opposed itself to my sight, ear, touch, or sensitive power, tho' it were but my own pulse rising up against my own thumb, I could have no sense of Time; & but for these, or the repetition of these in the reproductive Memory or Imagination, should have no Time.... For in truth, Time and Self are in a certain sense one and the same thing: since only by meeting with, so as to be resisted by, *Another*, does the Soul become a *Self*. What is Self-consciousness but to know myself at the same moment that I know another, and to know myself by means of knowing another, and vice-versa, an other by means of & at the moment of knowing my Self. Self and others are as necessarily interdependent as Right and Left, North and South.[10]

Hence Coleridge's imagination desperately fixed on objects, landmarks, and anchorings that steady and orient the mind in defining the self in relation to the outside world. Moon, stars, and clouds in the otherwise blank sky accordingly drew his attention throughout his life. Skyscapes fill his notebooks and punctuate intense moments in his poems. They concentrate the Ancient Mariner's consciousness. The inability to orient oneself by their sight becomes in "Limbo" a haunting image of "growthless, dull Privation":

[10]Notebook 23, ff. 31v–32; quoted by Kathleen Coburn, *The Self Conscious Imagination: A Study of the Coleridge Notebooks in Celebration of the Bicentenary of His Birth 21 October 1772* (London: Oxford University Press, 1974), pp. 31–32.

> An Old Man with a steady look sublime,
> That stops his earthly task to watch the skies;
> But he is blind—a Statue hath such eyes;—
> Yet having moonward turn'd his face by chance,
> Gazes the orb with moon-like countenance,
> With scant white hairs, with foretop bald and high,
> He gazes still,—his eyeless face all eye;—
> As 'twere an organ full of silent sight,
> His whole face seemeth to rejoice in light!
> Lip touching lip, all moveless, bust and limb—
> He seems to gaze at that which seems to gaze on him!
>
> [20-30]

The lines seemingly convey the gestalt of man and nature, in contrast to the definitiveless circumambience of limbo.

> No such sweet sights doth Limbo den immure,
> Wall'd round, and made a spirit-jail secure,
> By the mere horror of blank Naught-at-all,
> Whose circumambience doth these ghosts enthral.
>
> [31-34]

But the sight of man defined in time by the otherness of the moon's light is contaminated by the disquieting circumstances of the situation. Inadvertently, and contrary to Coleridge's explicit intentions, the image offers yet another instance of limbo, man reduced to lifeless statue in a stance of intense yearning for nexus by way of light with a celestial body it can neither see nor feel nor measure.

Clearly, for Coleridge the divine plenum had not turned out as perfect as the *beatus vir* of 1728 had believed when he extended the *hortus conclusus* to include first the open landscape and then "the whole terrestrial scene" (Røstvig, II, 287–88). It is significant that Coleridge characterized limbo as the opposite of place, "Not a Place, / Yet name it so" (11–12). For assuagement of the *horror vacui* instilled by the "undistinguish'd void" that had become the *hortus conclusus,* Coleridge turned back to the *locus amoenus;* but the lime-tree bower, the sunny dell, the earthly garden presented him with literary and ethical problems, which compromised his resolve to create and his capacity to take pleasure in an English version of "Eden's bowers" where "dwelt the first husband and his sinless mate" ("The Improvisatore," 51–52). Moral scruples replaced ontological and metaphysical anxieties, inhibiting his contentment in a private and aesthetic solution to the desire for "the peacefull'st cot"—"a home, an English home, and thee" in some corner of the country ("Constancy to an Ideal Object," 18, 20).

The *locus amoenus* was no more free of ambivalences and hesitancies for Coleridge than was for him the identification of the endless reaches of the heavens with the *hortus conclusus.* By the time of the Renaissance it had acquired sinister connotations. Whereas the Greeks had kept the Blessed Isles distinct from the bewitched island of Circe, the late medieval and Renaissance man pictured the garden as both the place of ultimate redemption and of destructive temptation. If it was the Garden of Adonis, it was also the Bower of Bliss. The earthly paradise was easily transformed into an enchanted garden whenever the tree of life was ignored for the tree of knowledge, the sacred spring abandoned for a Narcissan fountain, agape jilted for eros. A. Bartlett Giamatti characterizes the enchanted garden as a "beautiful-seeming earthly paradise which in reality is a dangerous and deceptive place where man's will is softened, his moral fibre unraveled, and his soul ensnared. It is the garden where insidious luxury and sensual love overcome duty and true devotion."[11]

Coleridge's verse celebrations of the secluded bower and enclosed garden are tinged more often than not with the ambiva-

---

[11]A. Bartlett Giamatti, *The Earthly Paradise and the Renaissance Epic* (Princeton: Princeton University Press, 1966), p. 126.

lence of this literary heritage, which he complicates with his personal self-doubts. The results are poems that exhibit mixed feelings of elation and of guilt, either repudiating themselves or oscillating between contrary impulses. "The Eolian Harp" (1795) fits the first definition, "Reflections on Having Left a Place of Retirement" (1796) the second.

Critics have made much of Coleridge's unexpected recantation at the end of "The Eolian Harp" of what he characterizes as a momentary succumbing to speculation about false principles. Two schools of thought have developed about this critical problem. There are those who take for granted that he is denying in the last verse paragraph less the whole of the preceding part of the poem than the immediately preceding paragraph, in which he broaches the "vain Philosophy" that "all animated nature" may respond like "organic Harps" to "one intellectual breeze, / At once the Soul of each, and God of all" (44-48). And there are those who consider the poem to be lacking in thematic unity, because nothing in earlier lines prepares us for the ending.[12]

In their concentration on Coleridge's metaphysical "maunderings," the critics have neglected his equally wholehearted submission to luxuriant feeling when he likens the aeolian harp to a coy maid:

[12] I am familiar with the many critical arguments demonstrating the unity of the poem on the basis of a narrow interpretation of the grammatical reference of this or that word, thus limiting the range of Coleridge's repudiation. And when I read some of them I wish to believe the persuasive arguments; but when one places Coleridge's hesitancies in "The Eolian Harp" in the context of the other poems where like compunctions occur, one cannot ignore what is a recurrent pattern of thought. Within such a context the reading of "The Eolian Harp" with grammatical fastidiousness and push-pin pedantry appears wrong-headed when the poem is otherwise calling for a reading that embraces its whole statement. See, for example, William H. Scheuerle, "A Reexamination of Coleridge's 'The Eolian Harp,'" SEL, 15 (1975), 591-99; and Ronald C. Wendling, "Coleridge and the Consistency of 'The Eolian Harp,'" SIR, 8 (1968), 26-42. For other opinions see Humphry House, Coleridge: The Clark Lectures 1951-52 (London: Hart-Davis, 1952), and Albert Gérard, English Romantic Poetry (Berkeley: University of California Press, 1968).

How by the desultory breeze caress'd,
Like some coy maid half yielding to her lover,
It pours such sweet upbraiding, as must needs
Tempt to repeat the wrong! And now, its strings
Boldier swept, the long sequacious notes
Over delicious surges sink and rise,
Such a soft floating witchery of sound
As twilight Elfins make, when they at eve
Voyage on gentle gales from Fairy-Land
Where Melodies round honey-dropping flowers,
Footless and wild, like birds of Paradise,
Nor pause, nor perch, hovering on untam'd wing!

[14–25]

It is possible that mixed with his remorse felt for momentarily giving way to pantheistic "shapings of the unregenerate mind" is his shamed recoil from the sensual fantasies that animated the first half of the poem (the second verse paragraph), which would explain his abashed return at the end of his poetic fantasizing to the real presence of the woman beside him. If so, Coleridge would have us believe then that Sara is admonishing him on two scores. As a "Meek Daughter in the Family of Christ," she mildly reproves his heretical digressions; and as a "heart-honour'd Maid" she recalls him also from his erotic daydreams.

Although the final version of the poem seems to emphasize the metaphysical theme, it is significant that an early draft (MS. R., 1797) devoted more space to the sybaritic topic. In an extension of the analogy of harp and "coy maid," the seductive harmonies of the lute conjure up a further image of voluptuous lotus land:

> Music such as erst
> Round rosy bowers (so Legendaries tell)
> To sleeping Maids came floating witchingly
> By wand'ring West winds stoln from Faery land.

In the final version the allusion to luxuriant bowers of "sleeping Maids," where one softly sinks into bewitched repose, was ex-

cised in favor of neutral reference to "twilight Elfins" voyaging
"on gentle gales from Fairy-Land." One should not forget, in
this context, that the "white-flower'd Jasmin" (4) and the myrtle
(Venus's flower), which grow unpruned in licentious profusion
about the cottage, are ambiguously associated with both paradisal innocence (cf. also *CL*, VI, 678) and earthly Eros ("Meet
emblems they of Innocence and Love," 5). Similarly, "the star of
eve" is linked by Coleridge to wisdom (7–8); yet we also know it
as the planet Venus, on which point Coleridge is suspiciously
reticent. In short, just as Coleridge ostensibly turns away in the
final lines from the "idle flitting phantasies" (40) of atheistical
"vain Philosophy," so he had previously shied away through revisions from the attractiveness of the Bower of Bliss.

Thus does Coleridge ambivalently cope with a subject whose
sere flowers reach back to Renaissance poetry and whose roots
extend even farther into antiquity, a subject that can yet touch
the nerve ends of a foster child of the French Revolution, an
idealistic young man with a turn for ratiocination and apocalyptic dreams neurotically facing an undesired marriage. He may
momentarily have succumbed to premarital desires, which he
quickly rejected as unworthy of his betrothed's better nature. If
so, such desires were self-generated. As their subsequent connu-
bial history suggests, Sara Fricker was no Acrasia tempting
Samuel into sensual, and hence moral, corruption. If he was
enticed into marriage, the tempter was more Southey than Sara,
with an assist from Coleridge's own overwrought moral sensibility, both men believing that Coleridge had "compromised" Sara
with his courtship promises. We have equal difficulty in visualiz-
ing intellectually timid Sara and her "governessy" Christianity
(Humphry House's witty label) as a poetic emblem of Mary,
whom Christian tradition placed in the garden as a Second Eve
to confirm the promise of man's return to Eden. In this poem of
complex antecedents the traditions of *locus amoenus* and of *hortus
conclusus* lurk in the background; the ubiquitous scent of
"honey-dropping flowers" and the melodies of "birds of
Paradise" (here submerged in the image of the lute and its "de-

licious surges" of sound sinking and rising) hint alike at Hesperidean and Miltonic presences. Yet we cannot categorize the poem as one or the other, no more than we can identify it unequivocally as a nuptial poem, or a pastoral poem, or a meditative-descriptive poem, or a millenarian poem. In "The Eolian Harp" the paradisal subtheme of blissful retirement and the teleological theme of pantheism are kept as chastely separate as Coleridge's subtle verbal powers and his not altogether consciously controlled psyche could manage.

In "Reflections," written in the following year, but commemorating the same place, Coleridge more unequivocally identifies his theme with the Edenic tradition of paradise won for a brief spell and then lost indefinitely.[13] Unlike his unhappy ancestors Adam and Eve, who were expelled from Eden, he and his bride elect to leave their "Blessed Place," a "green and woody . . . Valley of Seclusion," because he guiltily rejects its "insidious luxury and sensual love" (6–16). But not unmixed in the voluntary decision is the religious recognition stemming from the Fall that conjugal serenity may translate fearfully into sexual enchantment. Rather than "dream away the entrusted hours / On roseleaf beds, pampering the coward heart / With feelings all too delicate for use" (46–48), he re-enters the world of work on behalf of his fellow men:

> I therefore go, and join head, heart, and hand,
> Active and firm, to fight the bloodless fight
> Of Science, Freedom, and the Truth in Christ.
>
> [60–62]

Coleridge has been goaded into this action by his puritanical conscience reacting to the "slothful loves and dainty sympathies"

---

[13]Cf. Max F. Schulz, "Coleridge, Milton and Lost Paradise," *N&Q,* 6 (1959), 143-44; William H. Marshall, "The Structure of Coleridge's 'Reflections on Having Left a Place of Retirement,'" *N&Q,* 6 (1959), 319-21; and Albert Gérard, "Clevedon Revisited: Further Reflections on Coleridge's 'Reflections on Having Left a Place of Retirement,'" *N&Q,* 7 (1960), 101-02.

of the garden bower. From atop the "stony Mount" overlooking his cottage, he has had a vision of God's ominipresence. The reminder of Eden, and of the reason for its loss, dashes his enjoyment of the Valley of Seclusion. Spread before his sight, mountain, sheep, clouds, fields, river, landscaped parks, woods, cottages, and city spires stretch to the channel with its islands, sailboats, coasts, and "shoreless Ocean." "It seem'd like Omnipresence!" Coleridge exclaims:

> God, methought,
> Had built him there a Temple: the whole World
> Seem'd *imag'd* in its vast circumference.
>
> [29–40]

But the attractiveness of the scene for Coleridge echoes a hilltop prospect glimpsed by Jesus, in *Paradise Regained* (II, 285–97), of what appears to be a new Golden Age but proves to be the false setting for Satan's banquet temptation (II, 338–65). Because of the discrepancy of his "Blest hour!" in comparison with the fate of his "brother man," he cannot rid himself of the suspicion that he is being tried, like Jesus, with temptations destructive of his peace.

The ambivalence of Coleridge's attitude toward his secluded dell is revealed in the successive titles of the poem, "Reflections on Entering into Active Life" and "Reflections on Having Left a Place of Retirement"; in his return at the end of the poem to nostalgic recollection of his "dear Cot" with its jasmin, myrtles, and roses; and in his millenarian prayer that all men might share in such bliss through the Second Coming's restitution of Eden on earth: "Speed it, O Father! Let thy Kingdom come!"

It is interesting in this context to recognize how second nature is millenarian language to the age. Anthony John Harding, paraphrasing John Passmore's distinction between two kinds of expectations of the creation of a perfected society, writes that the millennialist "looks to Christ's Second Coming as the condition of such a society's coming into being, whereas for Augustine and his followers the City of God is a historical reality, the glory of which is that it represents and foreshadows on earth the true Eternal City." In his late political thinking, Harding adds, Coleridge "is close to the spirit of Augustinianism."[14] In the mid-1790s, although his language at times sounds millenarian, and he numbered then among his philosophical-theological enthusiasms the Christian millenarians Joseph Priestley and Ralph Cudworth, only in a playfully fanciful way can Coleridge, even in his cautiously militant Watchman guise, be considered a millenarian himself. It is just as likely that the prayer concluding "Reflections" is his indirect way of asserting that no remedy can come to England without a change in its present government, a conviction which the Test Acts forebade his expressing openly and categorically.

Coleridge's complex response to the ethical question of retirement versus active do-goodism has literary and cultural sides to it as well as personal and political sides. In the second quarter of the eighteenth century, as Røstvig demonstrates, the *beatus vir* aspired to the ideal of moral benevolence and public virtues, a radical departure from the practice of the classical figure, who historically had retired to a rural backwater for self-centered reasons. Self-imposed exile was justified now by its assumption of duty to one's fellow men, "so as to share with them that feeling of joyous benevolence with which nature had inspired him in his solitary moments" (II, 291–92). For the Romantics a life of solitary communion with nature for selfish reasons once again held irresistible attraction, but the convention of moral benevolence and public virtues that animated the *beatus vir* the previous fifty years still exerted its influence. One hears the two voices in Wordsworth, in the visionary raptures prompted by nature (his

[14]Anthony John Harding, *Coleridge and the Idea of Love: Aspects of Relationship in Coleridge's Thought and Writing* (Cambridge: Cambridge University Press, 1974), p. 260. Harding is paraphrasing from John Passmore's *The Perfectibility of Man* (London: Duckworth, 1970), p. 145.

[141]

spots of time) and in the "still sad music of humanity" infiltrating his consciousness at such moments. The social contradictions inherent in the dichotomy are given comic expression when Coleridge reverses the pattern of private benefit leading to public benevolence by inviting the beneficiary, in the form of a hardworked ass ("I hail thee Brother"), into "the Dell / Of Peace and mild Equality to dwell" ("To a Young Ass" [1794], 26–28).

A tension between paradisal seclusion and workaday world informs "The Eolian Harp" and "Reflections." The garden becomes the setting for an inner struggle between succumbing to sensual ease and pursuing the arduous Christian way. Pleasure is "a Sorceress," Coleridge asserts in a notebook entry of 1803, who pitches "her Tent on enchanted ground." She is a fata morgana "born of Delusion." "Happiness can be built on Virtue only," he concludes, "must of necessity [have] Truth for its foundation" (*N*, I 1375).

In two other of the Conversation poems—"This Lime-tree Bower" and "Frost at Midnight"—the situation of the poet is contrived to let him minimize the risk of aspiring to full direct participation in the joy of "A new Earth and new Heaven" ("Dejection," 69). That happiness (or illusion of happiness) is awarded to others. Charles Lamb and Hartley Coleridge are blessed with seeing and hearing "the lovely shapes and sounds intelligible / Of that eternal language" of the "great universal Teacher" ("Frost at Midnight," 59–60, 62), while Coleridge faintheartedly occupies the borderland of paradise, imprisoned in a lime-tree bower or isolated in his midnight study, condemned as if for some crime like the Ancient Mariner's to dwell apart from the pious company of men and the holy presence of nature. And when, as recorded in "Reflections," he finds himself partaking of the bliss of earthly paradise, his conscience is constrained to expel from it the Adam in him.

The ambiguity of Coleridge's response to Eden *redivivus* as recorded in the Conversation poems contains a variety of intellectual forces, which he is striving not always successfully to assimilate into poetic unity. First, there is the thrust of his age to realize paradise in actual form. The Romantics continued to hope like their fathers and grandfathers that it was possible to institutionalize paradise on earth in their own time, principally either by political fiat or by rural retreat. Yet, we can see with hindsight how the world even by the end of the eighteenth century was growing in many ways more complicated for them than it had been for their ancestors. There were the counterforces of a nation at war, in the throes of industrial and agricultural dislocation, and under alternately mad and capricious rule, all working to mitigate, to qualify, and to deny their millennial optimism. For Coleridge, once the bloom of political and social optimism had wilted, such as his hopes for Pantisocracy, the spiritual dimensions of nature seemed to supply the most viable possibility. True freedom, "spirit of divinest Liberty" (21), is to be found in nature's rhythms, in the imperious swing of tree branches, the flight of clouds, the song of birds, the roll of ocean waves, which "yield homage only to eternal laws" (4). So he extolls nature in the first and last stanzas of "France: An Ode." Second, there is the eighteenth- and nineteenth-century emphasis on utility, which enlisted in its philosophical wake sundry varieties of do-good societies, socially conscious forms of muscular Christianity, and institutions based on the pleasure-pain stimulus. Although private happiness was held to be a natural goal and a public aim, the theorists of utility were not sympathetic in practice with what they considered to be the self-indulgence of solitary nature worship or of exclusive utopian communities. Third, there is the Miltonic literary tradition, which describes paradise in a mixture of classical and Christian terms, emphasizing its appearance as an idyllic but divinely disciplined garden. Contrariwise, as a warning to the incautious Christian who would seize on the garden bower as proof of his election to grace, there is the counter-tradition of the garden as enchanted rather than holy, a place insidiously seductive in its sensual luxury and ultimately destructive of man's moral will. Fourth, there are Coleridge's feelings of unworthiness, of having misused his talents and consequently of having lost the chance to enter celestial Jerusalem except by the grace of God's divine intervention.

It is interesting in the context of these contending influences on Coleridge's thought that while his evocations of garden enclosures ordinarily echo Edenic harmonies, intermingled with them are also heard the overtones of sensuality. If sex was not inimical to the Miltonic prelapsarian paradise, still it inevitably carried a connotation of shame and guilt into the postlapsarian garden. Latent always in Coleridge's mind is the worry that such joy is not conducive to man's future welfare. "The Eolian Harp" and "Reflections," even though ostensibly one anticipates and the other recalls his honeymoon idyll, contain consciously contrived earthly paradises which he is constrained to repudiate wholly or in part. Another, "Fears in Solitude," describes "a green and silent dell" (1–2, 228) in which he luxuriantly lapses into "half sleep" and "dreams of better worlds" (26–27), until, lulled "by nature's quietness / And solitary musings," his "heart / Is softened, and made worthy to indulge / Love" (229–31). Although the frame of reference of his emotion here is social and political, a humanitarian protest against war and human exploitation, the words that creep into his statement—softening heart, indulgent love, enervated half sleep, world of dreams— have residual meanings critical of the senses and even sinister in connotation when read in the context of his fears of the enchanted garden. Hence it is not surprising to learn that he is obliged to leave the green and "low dell" after having succumbed a few hours to self-indulgent desires of surcease from the active struggle against wickedness. Two later poems—"A Day-dream" (*ca.* 1802) and "Recollections of Love" (*ca.* 1807)— associate his love of Sara Hutchinson with the green peacefulness of woodland bower. In each instance the beloved appears as a phantom in a daydream:

You stood before me like a Thought,
A dream remembered in a dream.
["Recollections," 21–22]

The censoring mind of the poet will not have any more corporeal presence in the garden than might be made by the
"brooding warmth" that lies heavily on his breast and adds to the
"depth of [his] tranquil bliss" ("A Day-dream," 21–22). The
ardor inherent in the situation is transferred to the "woodland
wild Recess," the "sweet bed of heath" swelling up, then sinking
with "faint caress," as if the beloved were there ("Recollections,"
3–5). Two poems written toward the end of his life—"The Garden of Boccaccio" (1828) and "Love's Apparition and Evanishment" (1833)—indicate that Coleridge continued to equate the
garden bower with erotic enchantment, tremulous warmth of
feeling in the region of the heart, dreamy indolence and (in
"Love's Apparition," 9–16) "vacant mood," "sickly calm," and
"idle brain," all attesting to the difficulty encountered by the
soul's power to draw sustenance from the "secret ministry"
("Frost at Midnight") of nature, or to take comfort in the sacred
void of space.

The psychological breaching of the garden enclosure by the
sensual heat of Coleridge's desires had both its cultural antecedents and its worldly correlatives. The walled garden as allegori-
cal of the regenerated soul protected from the wilderness outside by wall and from the sun of divine justice inside by trees had
a long literary tradition, as Stanley Stewart shows in *The Enclosed
Garden.*[15] Milton's Eden was walled against the wilderness and
further protected by a forest of trees and by the steep sides of
the mountain whose top it occupied. Sixteenth- and
seventeenth-century gardens are shown in prints and paintings,
like Jan Sieberechts' depiction of *The Gardens of Chatsworth (ca.*

[15]Stanley Stewart, *The Enclosed Garden: The Tradition and the Image in
Seventeenth-Century Poetry* (Madison: University of Wisconsin Press, 1966).

1710, Lord Sandys),[16] to be similarly walled against the uncouth countryside very much like moated and bastioned castles built to withstand siege.

An interesting example of this conventional separation of the "ideal enclave" from the threatening energies of the untamed and unchaste world is presented in Bellini's painting *Sacred Allegory* (*ca.* 1488, Uffizi Gallery, Florence). The foreground contains a geometrically perfect square surrounded by a balustrade and paved in a pattern of alternating colors of diamond-shaped marble. At the center of the enclosure the diamond pattern translates into the square motif. The severely geometric scene is enlivened by a tree in a pot placed at the mathematical center, its trunk clasped by a child. Standing and sitting on the periphery are St. Paul, St. Joseph, St. Sebastian, Job, and the Virgin flanked by two saints, all either (with the exception of St. Paul) "sunk in contemplative melancholia . . . as if they found it inexhaustibly satisfying," or gazing in rapt attention on the child. The scene, as John H. Armstrong further notes, "is now thought to be a landscape-fantasy organized around the idea of paradise; and the design of the enclosure in the foreground is based on the traditional paradise-garden." Contrasted with the foreground scene of Christian piety and ordered harmony, and separated by a body of water, is a landscape of rocky coast and hills, a shepherd sitting in a cave surrounded with his sheep, a centaur pacing the shore, a man descending rough-hewn steps to the water's edge, and a village with people and animals standing about—all this stretching from middle to far distance. Armstrong finds in the landscape "an unmistakable Hesperidean atmosphere"; and if he is right, then the painting presents us with two balanced versions of the "ideal enclave," the pagan

---

[16]Conveniently reproduced by Christopher Hussey in *English Gardens and Landscapes 1700–1750* (London: Country Life, 1967), plate 2; and by John Dixon Hunt and Peter Willis in *The Genius of the Place: The English Landscape Garden 1620–1820* (London: Elek, 1975), plate 51.

and the Christian, the fearsome world of nature reduced imaginatively by the one to a golden age (although I do not know how Armstrong assimilates into it the centaur) and by the other to an emergent world picture reassuring in its mathematical regularity. But for the mood of midday torpor, however, the scene contains few details specifically Hesperidean—and there is that disturbingly intrusive figure of the centaur. Except for the tone of "'touching Chastity' which marks all Bellini's incursions into material which even borders on the profane,"[17] the two scenes are more contrastive than complementary, the foreground paradisal tableau representing the Renaissance ideal of an ordered and harmonious world, the middle distance depicting the fallen world of nature, rough, irregular, and only partly tamed by the agencies of society and religion. How else explain the figures of boys holding apples shaken down from a tree by another in the center middle ground? Is not the picture reminding us at once of the circumstances surrounding the Fall and of the reversal of that act through Christ's birth? A confirmation of this reading appears in Bellini's *Blood of the Redeemer* (1460-65, National Gallery, London) where there occurs an identical contrast between a similar geometrically ordered world in the foreground identified with Christ's redemptive promise of the eventual return of paradise, and a natural world in the middle ground that is uncultivated, barren, and wild.

By Coleridge's day the latter had become the necessary transition to the natural sublime, by way of the evolving nature and garden aesthetic of the eighteenth century; but given Coleridge's metaphysical hesitancies it is not surprising to find in "Kubla Khan" a mixed bag of garden styles: an old-fashioned prospect with formal gardens and park of "forests ancient as the hills" intermixed with the new taste for "sinuous rills" and "deep romantic chasm." The poem ostensibly celebrates in the "walls

[17]John H. Armstrong, *The Paradise Myth* (London: Oxford University Press, 1969), p. 102.

and towers . . . girdled" Xanadu what the seventeenth century *in situ,* and what Bellini in Renaissance Venice, had followed as horticultural and architectural ideal. With one important difference in degree. Of supreme focus in the Khan's paradisal grounds, and granted a position of commanding assertion, is an architectural fantasy given over to pleasure, which in Bellini's and even in the Whig aristocrat's worlds played a discreet and self-effacing secondary role to the greater imperative of moral didacticism. Charles I. Patterson, Jr., has called our attention to the essential divergence of Coleridge's aesthetic from that of Milton and the Old Testament poets. At the center of the Khan's landscape garden stands a pleasure dome, while at the center of Eden (in *medio paradisi* in the Vulgate Bible) stood the Tree of Life and the Tree of Knowledge of Good and Evil. The two trees exercise man's faculty for moral choice; the dome caters to his taste for the sensuous.[18] This shift of emphasis in Romantic aesthetics, while clinging to a spiritual base through its link with the divine expression of nature, did not displace an older Christian code of moral accountability. The two claimed equal allegiance in the minds of many Romantics and, in the instance of Coleridge, posed contradictory impulses which show up in his poetic paeans to paradise.

Like the earthly garden of biblical tradition, the rural Arcadia of Virgilian and Horatian song, and the lake country reality of Wordsworthian visionary experience, Xanadu is infiltrated with insidious temptations. In the mirrored reflection of its artistic order is imaged the disruptive impulses of the enchanted garden

---

[18]Charles I. Patterson, Jr., "The Daemonic in *Kubla Khan:* Toward an Interpretation," *PMLA,* 89 (1974), 1042n. House, p. 120, observes that the opening stanza presents a "conjunction of pleasure and sacredness." John B. Beer, *Coleridge the Visionary* (London: Chatto & Windus, 1959), and Carl Woodring, "Coleridge and the Khan," *EIC,* 9 (1959), 361–68, insist on the disjunction, Beer characterizing Xanadu as the contrived postlapsarian Eden of an oriental poet-king, and Woodring as the attempt of a profane potentate to appropriate the unencompassable sacred for his pleasure.

of Renaissance poems. If Xanadu has its serene glades, sunny hills, sacred river, and "gardens bright with sinuous rills," it also has its dark underside of sexual energy,

> that deep romantic chasm which slanted
> Down the green hill athwart a cedarn cover!
> A savage place! as holy and enchanted
> As e'er beneath a waning moon was haunted
> By woman wailing for her demon-lover!
>
> [12-16]

The wailing woman takes her place as the latest in the lineage of enchantresses that stretches from Circe and Eve to Alcina and Acrasia. Beneath the appearance of aesthetic harmony in the garden lurks a threat to the spiritual health of man. The pleasurable indolence of the place masks a savagery native to its cyclic rhythms of violent birth, sunny life, and icy death. Coleridge along with Byron and Shelley knew, as the eighteenth-century builders of landscape gardens seemed not to recognize, that the free run of paradise (witness the fates of Adam and Eve, and Satan) risks a compensatory retribution.

In a poem with the dense poetic texture of "Kubla Khan" there is, of course, a confluence of the personal, the literary, and the mythological. So much has already been written about the parallels between Coleridge's description of Xanadu and literary references to paradise, with special emphasis on Milton's description of Eden in *Paradise Lost*, that there is no need to repeat them here.[19] Most recently, E. S. Shaffer has extended the frame of reference of Xanadu to include the accumulated lore of the history of Eden, specifically the oriental versions of paradise that contributed their tributary streams of pre- and postlapsarian and pre- and postdiluvian times to the syncretic geography of Eden. In her eyes, "Kubla Khan" is the single most successful

---

[19]For a summary of these sources and parallels, see my chapter in *The English Romantic Poets,* ed. Frank Jordan (New York: MLA, 1972), pp. 135-208.

English Romantic expression of the new mythological syncretism, the new historicity of myth which guided the comparative mythologists of the late eighteenth century to treat the Christian story of human origins as one of the world-wide primitive myths, all telling the same truth under different guises. In "Kubla Khan" "all of Asia is present in one spot" (p. 165), a landscape "combining still-remembered paradise, wilderness, enclosed city, and cultivated court.... City and country, rural yet populous, idyllic yet threatening, holy yet secular, sacred yet fallen, court and cot—it is tempting to see the stereotypes of the eighteenth century merging into those that will dominate the nineteenth. Just for this moment, in this exotic setting, they exist simultaneously, and express a permanent condition of man."[20]

Besides the earthly paradise-enchanted garden design is an important paradise-Hades (or heaven-hell) configuration, examined by Maud Bodkin in *Archetypal Patterns in Poetry* as long ago as 1934. In a closely reasoned discussion which includes studies of analogues not only in "Kubla Khan" and *Paradise Lost* but also in the poetry of William Morris, especially *The Earthly Paradise;* in the *Aeneid* of Virgil, specifically Aeneas's descent to Hades; and in the *Commedia* of Dante, particularly Dante's toilsome ascent of Purgatory; Bodkin defines an archetypal rebirth pattern in which the soul moves from "the agony of hell, symbolized by blind darkness and cavern depths," to a vision of "the heavenly heights." "The image of the watered garden and the mountain height show some persistent affinity with the desire and imaginative enjoyment of supreme well-being, or divine bliss, while the cavern depth appears as the objectification of an imaginative fear."[21] The aspiration is to leave behind temporal bafflement and pain enroute to a plane of eternal illumination.

As regards "Kubla Khan," one controversial tradition would

[20]E. S. Shaffer, *"Kubla Khan" and The Fall of Jerusalem: The Mythological School in Biblical Criticism and Secular Literature 1770–1880* (Cambridge: University Press, 1975), p. 108. For the full discussion, see pp. 96–190.

[21]Maud Bodkin, *Archetypal Patterns in Poetry: Psychological Studies of Imagination* (London: Oxford University Press, 1934; rpt. New York, 1958), p. 143.

have it that Coleridge followed the negative route of poppy fumes to this goal. If Alethea Hayter[22] is right in her attribution of polar wastes, Northern lights, endless extensions of time and space, and boundless plains and seas as characteristic of opium dreams, then Coleridge's sensitivity to the reaches of the sky and his lifelong effort to fit the heavenly spaces into a teleological frame of reference is a startling instance of the massive coadunating power of his mind. In this instance, it struggled to give moral and metaphysical validity to the fragments of his drug-induced thoughts within the context of a Newtonian-Christian world picture. Reality resides in the act of unifying contraries, he was fond of asserting. What greater act of reconciliation than the incorporation of opium visions of chilly, lighted vaults of space, here confined to "caverns measureless to man," into the historical earthly garden, as an eighteenth-century extension of God's gift to man of the *hortus conclusus!*

Equally embedded in the literary-biographical undersong of the poem is the tradition of the divine guide. Dante is led by Beatrice in his ascent to paradise. Coleridge is helped in his "imaginative experience of transition from personal desire to ideal aspiration" by his vision of "an Abyssinian maid," a persona for the female inspiration who assumes the role of divine guide in his poetry.

The person who most often filled this role after 1800 was Sara Hutchinson.[23] But the intensity of Coleridge's longing, exacer-

---

[22]Alethea Hayter, *Opium and the Romantic Imagination* (London: Faber & Faber, 1968).

[23]Elisabeth Schneider's insistent arguments notwithstanding, it is probable that "Kubla Khan" was written before Coleridge met Sara Hutchinson at the end of October 1799, although interestingly Miss Schneider does link Sara in Coleridge's mind on other and subsequent grounds to the Abyssinian maid; see her *Coleridge, Opium and "Kubla Khan"* (Chicago: University of Chicago Press, 1953), pp. 233-36. For an extended discussion of the place of the Abyssinian maid in Coleridge's emotional as well as imaginative life, see Geoffrey Yarlott, *Coleridge and the Abyssinian Maid* (London: Methuen, 1967), especially pp. 152-53 and 310-12; and for a perceptive discussion of Coleridge's spiritualization of love, see Harding, *Coleridge and the Idea of Love,* especially pp. 79-124.

bated by his domestic situation, made him a treacherous pilgrim and her an untrustworthy divine guide. Her physical form kept materializing in his paradisal bower, deflecting his aspirant eyes to profane earth. As in "Kubla Khan," Coleridge was never quite able to separate his vision of the Abyssinian maid from that of the woman wailing for her demon-lover. In "The Picture" (1802), he ironically records one such failed resolution. Whereas Marvell sought, in "Upon Appleton's House," the solitary forest glades to escape the noisy distractions of social concourse, Coleridge's thinly disguised narrator-lover pushes deep into a "tangle wild of bush and brake" (14) to flee female enchantments, in search of "the spirit of unconscious life" (20) untouched by emotional agitation. Marvell is bent on meditative solitude, Coleridge on pure thoughts and guiltless feelings. In the "silent shade" of an oak tree he congratulates himself on being "safe and sacred from the step of man" (52–53), that is, woman, specifically his beloved: "these are no groves / Where Love dare loiter" (27–28). As the rest of the poem makes clear, Coleridge is scourging his paradise of the corporeal presence of his "Love" the better to inhabit it with her "form divine" (75). This idealized vision is intended to accompany him on his pilgrimage; but by the end of the poem the lure of the real woman has led him to forsake his hilly sacred grove for the pastoral vale where she lives.

After 1802 Coleridge's intellectual compulsion to free his earthly paradise of traditional temptation by idealizing Sara Hutchinson became psychologically urgent as he sought a resolution to his unrequited love for her. In a curious fragment possibly written at the time of his departure for Malta in 1804, he purifies away all Sara Hutchinson's earthly dross (see *N*, II, 2055n):

> All look and likeness caught from earth
> All accident of kin and birth,
> Had pass'd away. There was no trace

Of aught on that illumined face,
Uprais'd beneath the rifted stone
But of one spirit all her own;—
She, she herself, and only she,
Shone through her body visibly.

The need to spiritualize his passions leads him to identify the "pure Love of a good man to a good woman" (*N*, II, 2540) with his knowledge of the good, the true, and the beautiful.

> The best, the truly lovely, in each & all is God. Therefore the truly Beloved is the symbol of God to whomever it is truly beloved by!—but it may become perfect & maintained lovely by the function of the two / The Lover worships in his Beloved that final consummation of itself which is produced in his own soul by the action of the Soul of the Beloved upon it, and that final perfection of the Soul of the Beloved, which is in part the consequence of the reaction of his (so ammeliorated & regenerated) Soul upon the Soul of his Beloved / till each contemplates the Soul of the other as involving his own, both in its givings and its receivings, and thus still keeping alive its *outness*, its *self-oblivion* united with *Self-warmth*, and still approximates to God! [*N*, II, 2540]

By such contemplation, Coleridge hopes, he will win surcease from "reckless Despair" (*N*, II, 3148) and maybe even a modicum of "divine Joy" (*N*, II, 3092) with its glimpse of the heavenly plains.

If the twin images of "the high garden-land, sunlit, watered, blossoming, of the earthly Paradise, and . . . the heavenly heights beyond, infinitely remote, radiant, and commanding an infinitely far-ranging prospect"—with attainment in that order of progression—are for Coleridge "a recurring phase and permanent element of lived experience" (Bodkin, p. 146) and human expectation, it is equally a fact of the felt experience and the examined life that no man is fully armored against the haunting danger of a reverse movement from heaven to hell. The earliest myths contain the story of the fall of the rebel angels into hell and of the expulsion of our first parents from Eden. Coleridge is not unmindful of the obverse of human desires and divine promise. In "Kubla Khan" one "progresses" not upward but downward into "the caverns measureless to man." The sacred river Alph rises from a deep chasm to flow for a brief space through the high gardenland only to sink "in tumult to a lifeless ocean."

The emotional pattern of Coleridge's life confirmed the profane archetype, contra the heavenly one, as an ever-present threat to his aspirations. From childhood he had been accustomed to the possibility that he was undeserving of happiness. Last-born and the Benjamin of his father, he had been the object of his older brothers' jealousy. At nine he had been "orphaned" by his father's death, wrenched from the security of a large family and the familiarity of the market town Ottery St. Mary and "exiled" to the hellish competitiveness of Christ's Hospital and the alien din of London. Whether he suffered guilt feelings for his father's death is conjectural.[24] But that he believed his mother had abandoned him is evident in his subsequent alienation from her and his repeated references to surrogate mothers. Marriage to Sara Fricker culminated in unhappy separation from wife and children rather than in domestic bliss. Love for Sara Hutchinson and William and Dorothy Wordsworth caused more pain than joy over the years.

Is it any wonder that the history of "Kubla Khan" is one of ambiguity: the absence of explicit mention of it, the belated publication, the aborted ending! Coleridge's inclusion of the daemonic damsel in Xanadu is consistent with his ambivalence toward the garden's promise of supine refreshment of soul and with his flight from the earthly paradises celebrated in "The Eolian Harp" and "Reflections." In the only surviving autograph

---

[24] Cf. Norman Fruman, *Coleridge, The Damaged Archangel* (New York: Braziller, 1971), pp. 402-26.

of the poem, the Crewe manuscript,[25] Coleridge had given the name Amora to the holy mountain referred to by the Abyssinian maid in her song. It is intriguing, given the submerged pun on love in the word, that he changed it to Abora, which is identified in scriptural and literary commentary as one of the rivers of Eden.[26] The Abyssinian maid and her "symphony and song" of Mount Abora are further distanced by Coleridge to "a vision once I saw." And like the feat of Merlin fifty years later in Tennyson's *Idylls of the King*, Coleridge prefers to build his pleasure dome of song ("in air") rather than of mortar and stone. Psychologically, the shift from the opening laudatory description of Xanadu and the Khan's architectural achievement to the concluding celebration of the powers of the poetic imagination conforms to the pattern of emotion and imagery Maud Bodkin found in her study of Western literature. Coleridge longed to enjoy the supreme well-being of his paradisal vision, but he shrank in dread from a bliss that might prove to be sin temptingly disguised. In this sense the caves of ice objectify his fear of Xanadu as a potential Bower of Bliss, and his transformation of it in the last section of the poem into a "symphony and song" is his way of retaining the "experience of fascination" while alleviating the "pain of fear . . . in the relief of expression" (Bodkin, p. 110). The figments of the imagination pose less threat and are easier to control than the stench of the senses, whose imperatives assail one's will and lay siege to one's days.

[25]The date of the manuscript, conjectured to be as early as 1797, remains uncertain. See Alice D. Snyder, "The Manuscript of 'Kubla Khan,'" *TLS*, 1934, p. 541; and follow-up by E. H. W. Meyerstein, *TLS*, 1951, pp. 21, 85; Schneider, pp. 153-237; and John Shelton, "The Autograph Manuscript of *Kubla Khan* and an Interpretation," *REL*, 7, No. 1 (1966), 32-42. For summaries of the arguments on dating of the poem, see Schulz, "Coleridge," *The English Romantic Poets* (1972), pp. 158-59.
[26]See H. W. Piper, "The Two Paradises in *Kubla Khan*," *RES*, 27 (1976), 148; and "Mount Abora," *N&Q*, 20 (1973), 286-89.

Richard Mallette has recently shown how plant, journey, and opposition motifs give structural unity to the *Biographia Literaria.*[27] One can apply these *topoi* to the larger arena of Coleridge's life with equal fruitfulness. The natural earth in all its widespread formations represented for Coleridge an organic paradisal whole (plant). Unfortunately, his ability to enjoy the earthly Eden he literally was witness to in this life on all sides of him and the heavenly paradise he allegorically saw himself as a Grey-haired Passenger (*SM*, p. xxix) progressing toward in holy pilgrimage (journey) was constantly compromised by human disquiet and a feckless will (opposition). He was caught in an irresolvable contradiction. He lived in the garden and yet feared to stay there; he was of it but wished to be beyond it.

The simultaneous feelings of desire and dread Coleridge had for paradise infected other aspects of his psychic life. For most of his adult years he saw himself as a man sentenced to a tautological oscillation from unrequited yearning for joy to cowardly shrinking from pain. Nor did the pleasure-pain psychology of his day disabuse him of the meretriciousness of this dialectic. He is forever analyzing his "cowardice of pain" within a frame of reference of happiness (*N*, II, 2495). Out of the depth of his complex response to these twin reflexes, he jeers at Hume's "one *Moment,*" the simplistic reduction of his "whole being" to "an aggregate of successive single emotions" (*N*, II, 2370). "O friend!" he laments on Sunday, 23 December 1804, "I have never loved Evil for its own sake; no! nor ever sought pleasure for its own sake, but only as the means of escaping from pains that coiled round my mental powers, as a serpent around the body & wings of an Eagle! My sole sensuality was *not* to be in pain!" (*N*, II, 2368). Two weeks later he reviews his life, ticking off decisive actions—his hesitant courtship of Mary Evans, his marriage to Sara Fricker, his quarrel with Southey—as being

[27]Richard Mallette, "Narrative Technique in the 'Biographia Literaria,'" *MLR,* 70 (1975), 32-40.

always motivated negatively by dread rather than positively by hope. He wishes to yield himself up to joy; but an inner moral imperative maintains hard-core resistance. "I write melancholy, always melancholy," he jots in his notebook in 1803; "You will suspect that it is the fault of my natural Temper. Alas! no—This is the great Occasion that my Nature is made for Joy—impelling me to Joyance—and I never, never can yield to it.—I am a genuine *Tantalus*" (*N*, I, 1609). In 1808 he acknowledges a symbiotic relationship in his person of love, pain, joy, and the spiritual state of his being:

Love unutterable fills my whole Spirit, so that every fibre of my Heart, nay, of my whole frame seems to tremble under its perpetual touch and sweet pressure, like the string of a Lute—with a sense of vibratory Pain distinct from all other sensations, a Pain that seems to shiver and tremble on the threshold of some Joy, that cannot be entered into while I am embodied. [*N*, III, 3370]

The ground of his moral inhibition was the fear that if he should yield to joy he risked yielding also to all sorts of sensuous temptation.

In hypersensitive recoil from joy, and its correlative, pain, he longed at moments to give himself up to what John Armstrong calls "that seductive torpor" of the paradisal ideal, to float like the Indian Vishnu "along an infinite ocean cradled in the flower of the Lotus, and wake once in a million years for a few minutes—just to know that I was going to sleep a million years more" (*CL*, I, 350). In one of his most poignant, and duplicitous, entries in his notebooks, he describes the erotic relief of submitting to the inner urge for total indolence:

When in a state of pleasurable & balmy Quietness I feel my Cheek and Temple on the nicely made up Pillow in Caelibe Toro meo [on my celibate couch] the fire-gleam on my dear Books, that fill up one whole side from ceiling to floor of my Tall Study—& winds, perhaps are driving the rain, or whistling in frost, at my blessed Window, whence I see Borrodale, the Lake, Newlands—wood, water, mountains, omniform Beauty—O then as I first sink on the pillow, as if Sleep had indeed a material *realm*, as if when I sank on my pillow, I was entering that region & realized Faery Land of Sleep—O then what visions have I had, what dreams—the Bark, the Sea, all the Shapes & sounds and adventures made up of the Stuff of Sleep & Dreams, & yet my Reason at the Rudder/O what visions, ⟨μαστοι⟩ [breasts] as if my Cheek & Temple were lying on me gale o'mast on—[μεγαλόμαστον = large breasted]—Seele meines Lebens! [Soul of my life!]—& I sink down the waters, thro' Seas & Seas—yet warm, yet a Spirit—/

⟨οι⟩
Pillow = mast high [breasts]
[*N*, I, 1718 & n]

All his life Coleridge felt threatened by this tendency in his nature. Earthly paradise—a NEW PARADISE "Perdita" Robinson called Xanadu in her poem to Coleridge[28]—was not for him, he concluded in bleak self-judgment. As a son of fallen Adam he was heir to the need for work and striving. Only such activity would provide the necessary defense against the temptress Indolence and the sorceress Pleasure. The garden enclosure had for Coleridge an ambivalent meaning. He anxiously dreaded that Xanadu, removed from the regular course of life, isolated, rarefied, and exclusive, might be a fool's paradise, where a "dream of great internal activity" might lull him into sterility of spirit and imagination and "outward inefficience." "I found in my Books and my own meditations," he laments in 1809, "a sort of highwalled Garden, which excluded the very sound of the World without. But the Voice within could not be thrust out— the sense of Duty unperformed, and the pain of Self-dissatisfaction, aided and enforced by the sad and anxious looks of Southey, and Wordsworth, and some few others most beloved by me and most worthy of my regard and affections" (*CL*, III,

[28]Mary Robinson, "Mrs. Robinson to the Poet Colridge [sic]" (dated "Oct. 1800"), *Memoirs of the late Mrs. Robinson, written by Herself. With some posthumous pieces,* 4 vols. (London: R. Phillips, 1801), IV, 145-49.

216). Not "sunny spots of greenery" ("Kubla Khan") but desolation ("The Wanderings of Cain"), ocean desert ("The Ancient Mariner"), flinty soil ("Ode to the Departing Year"), "dark-brown gardens" and wintry winds ("Dejection"), and a dry well ("Love's Apparition and Evanishment") await the eager soul that would enter the sacred garden enclosure and by that action risk shutting itself off from life and the regenerative sense of duty fulfilled.

Given his pre-nineteenth-century sense of social activism and piety, and his personal guilt over his sloth, failed promise, and sensual addiction to drink and drugs, there is little wonder that Coleridge uneasily feared that every flowery bower was in reality an enchanted garden, and the paradisal breadth and depth of earth and sky a barren void.

]4[

Coleridge and Wordsworth:
The Vital and the Organic

JOHN BEER

The still-persisting tendency to separate Coleridge the "poet" from Coleridge the "philosopher" and to treat the two sides of his activity in separate compartments is nowhere more evident than in discussions of his view of the organic. Such discussions usually draw upon his theoretical comments on the subject, as found in philosophical works, critical comments, and notebook entries. Although one or two attempts have been made to use some of Coleridge's comments as a means of entry into the poetry,[1] the possibility that that poetry might throw light on the ideas has been less generally considered.

This is understandable enough: one does not normally look to

I have cited the following editions of Wordsworth's works by the abbreviations indicated:

Prelude   The Prelude, or, Growth of a Poet's Mind. Ed. Ernest de Selincourt, 2d ed. rev. Helen Darbishire. London: Oxford University Press, 1959. 1850 text unless cited as Prelude (1805). (Quoted by permission.)

WP   The Poetical Works of William Wordsworth. Ed. Ernest de Selincourt and Helen Darbishire. 5 vols. Oxford: Clarendon Press, 1940-49. (Quoted by permission.)

[1]Most notably, perhaps, by R. H. Fogle in The Idea of Coleridge's Criticism (Berkeley and Los Angeles: University of California Press, 1962), and particularly in Ch. 7, where he attempts to interpret "Christabel" in terms of the ideas he has discussed.

poetry as a source for philosophical theories. Recently, however, I have come to believe that the relationship between Coleridge's early poetry and his theories may be more intricate than has been supposed: that *all* his writings, particularly in the years when he was intimate with Wordsworth, grew from a common matrix of intellectual and poetic exploration which found its center in the need to rediscover for his age a significant relationship with nature, and that the poetry originally embodied a view of nature about which he later came to have reservations, and partly to disguise.[2]

That view of nature, I have further argued, was naturally shaped by forces which were at the time common to England and Germany, where the essential difference between mechanical views of the world and organic views, centering in the phenomenon of growth, had led to the assertion that the poet should align himself with the latter. But in Coleridge's case it was also, and to a much greater degree, concerned with the part played by energy in such growth. In general, theorists of the organic have taken for their model the growth of the vegetable, where the workings of vital energy simply contribute to its development. Whether that development realizes itself in simple expansion or in the outthrusting of tendrils, the energy is largely controlled by the pattern of growth implicit in the seed.

Coleridge, however, growing up in the England of the late eighteenth century, was unusually aware of certain implications of energy as they manifested themselves elsewhere. From the writings of men such as Priestley he could discover some of the current (and basically optimistic) scientific thinking on the subject; by other reading, particularly in mythology and romance, he was reminded that energy, whatever its role in the vegetable creation, was an ambiguous power, lending itself as easily to works of destruction as to those of creation.[3]

[2]I have developed this point of view at length in my book *Coleridge's Poetic Intelligence* (London: Macmillan, 1977)—hereafter cited as *CPI*.
[3]Ibid., especially Chs. 5 and 7.

Eventually, according to his account in *The Friend*,[4] his thoughts on the subject led him to make a radical distinction concerning the nature of organic life itself. In traditional early Renaissance terms, philosophers had traced four stages of creation: the inorganic or mineral, the vegetable, the animal, and the human. Each stage is there seen as containing and surpassing the previous one by introducing some further element. The rock simply is, the vegetable is and lives, the animal is, lives, and feels, the human being is, lives, feels, and has reason.[5]

This pattern still had a strong hold on the late eighteenth-century mind. When Erasmus Darwin looked at organic life in the 1790s and began to trace a possible pattern of its evolution, he suggested that a point of transition between vegetable and animal might exist in certain parts of the vegetable growth which had separated themselves from the parent body and taken wing, thus turning themselves into the insects which continued to return and feed on the flower.[6]

Coleridge, by contrast, argued (again, according to his own account) that this kind of theory was ignoring a fundamental distinction which must always be maintained between vegetables and those organisms which were to be described as "animated." The latter, he seems to have believed, had always been separate from the former and contained within themselves a different principle of life, since in them energy was to some extent free. Whereas the form of the vegetable must be essentially static, animals could make forms by their own movements; insects and birds could go further and also create dynamic forms by their interactions with one another, as in their patterns of flight.[7]

---

[4]Ibid., pp. 53–55, quoting *F*, I, 469–70.

[5]See, e.g., André Chastel, *The Age of Humanism, Europe 1480–1530*, tr. Katherine M. Delavenay and E. M. Gwyer (London: Thames and Hudson, 1963), p. 27, which reproduces a diagram from Bovillus' *Liber de Intellectu* showing the idea in schematic form.

[6]Erasmus Darwin, *The Botanic Garden* (London, 1791 [i]), p. 109; *Zoönomia; or, the Laws of Organic Life*, 2 vols. (London, 1794–96), I, 105.

[7]See, e.g., the account of bird-flight in *N*, I, 582 (revised 1589), quoted in *CPI*, p. 230.

Coleridge seems in fact to have believed that the existence of the vegetable still remained the best basic pattern for human emulation. The vegetable, unfolding itself in response to the vital energies provided by light, water, and moving air, offered itself as a model for the human psyche at its best. But one could not take over that model for humanity in any simple, naive manner, since it must also be seen that human nature partook of the animal as well, and was free to employ its energies for creation or destruction to a degree that the flower was not.

Since Coleridge himself liked to think in images, it may be useful at this point to illustrate the stages of the argument by means of some emblems and myths which appear in his writings. To begin with we may propose the simple image of the vegetable, realizing its own form through its own energies (or, as the Neoplatonists would prefer to say, "energizing" from the divine).[8] A slightly more complex version of this image is furnished by the interplay of vegetable organisms, as when a vine grows on an elm tree. The elm stands up strongly, the vine climbs round it. The elm might be said to have a bias toward the simple organic, the vine by the use of its climbing energy, toward the vital.[9]

A different picture emerges, however, when the energy manifested by the climbing vine is seen in separation, as in a serpent climbing round a tree. Here we are moving into the realm of mythological interpretation, for such motifs are particularly familiar in traditional iconography. In Christian myth, the motif usually appears as an emblem of evil: the serpent wreathes itself

---

[8]See, e.g., Iamblichus: "The energy of divine fire shines forth voluntarily, and in common, and being self-invoked and self-energetic, energizes through all things with invariable sameness, both through the natures which impart, and those that are able to receive, its light" (*The Mysteries of the Egyptians, Chaldeans and Assyrians*, tr. Thomas Taylor, 1821, p. 208). If Coleridge did not return to the Greek, the most available source for his *early* knowledge of the Neoplatonists was the long appendix, "The Restoration of the Platonic Theology," to Thomas Taylor's translation of Proclus' *Philosophical and Mathematical Commentaries* (1789–90). Cf. *CPI*, pp. 28–29.

[9]For later uses by Coleridge, see below.

down to tempt the woman to eat of the forbidden fruit, and when she yields, human energy is perverted toward evil. In the Greek myths and elsewhere, on the other hand, the serpent and tree are seen in a less sinister light. The serpent is sometimes a guardian of treasure, as in the garden of the Hesperides, where it guards the golden apples; there is an implication that the gaining of the treasure is a matter not of temptation but of adventure.[10] Elsewhere the serpent winding round the staff is an emblem of healing, as with the caduceus of Hermes—which again might suggest on a symbolic reading that health is associated with a right ordering of the relation between the vital energies and the organism.[11]

It is one of the more interesting features of the iconography as explored so far that it is also to be found in Blake, particularly in the illustrations to the *Songs of Innocence and of Experience* and the Lambeth prophetic books[12]—which must leave one asking whether we are dealing with a coincidental pair of reactions to common sources, or whether there might have been some oblique channel of communication by which the symbolic use of such images passed from one to the other.

When we turn to Coleridge's theories of animated life, on the other hand, the parallels still to be found are more likely to result from coincidence. The dominant images by which one might express the relation between the organic life of the vegetable and the vital energy of animated nature—those of the flower, and the bee that enters to feed upon it—would no doubt have appealed to Blake, who provides us with a fitting counter-

[10]For a detailed study of this tradition, relating it to both Sumerian and Greek myths, see John Armstrong, *The Paradise Myth* (London: Oxford University Press, 1969), especially Ch. 2.

[11]See *CPI*, p. 9.

[12]I have discussed some examples in my essay "Blake, Coleridge, and Wordsworth: Some Cross-currents and Parallels, 1789-1805," in *William Blake: Essays in Honour of Sir Geoffrey Keynes,* ed. Morton D. Paley and Michael Phillips (Oxford: Clarendon Press, 1973), pp. 236-37.

point in his image of the "invisible worm" that flies in the night and enters the rose to destroy it; but it is hard to find in Blake anything quite corresponding to the general account of the relationship between organic forms and vital energies that seems to be implicit in Coleridge's work. This leads Coleridge to more recherché images, such as that of the Temple of Memnon, where a musical string was reputedly set vibrating by the first light of the sun[13] (a neat image of the relationship between light and organism) and the Aeolian harp, fact rather than myth of the eighteenth-century world, since it was an actual instrument, which produced an extended music of nature when placed in a window where the breeze played over its strings.[14]

An image such as this allowed Coleridge to pursue his ideas concerning the relationship between the vegetative and animated nature (ideas for which there is no direct counterpart in Blake). These ideas come to a first point of fruition in his poem "The Eolian Harp" of 1795, describing how Coleridge, with the woman who is shortly to be his wife, visits their honeymoon cottage on a summer evening when the harmony of nature is impressive.[15] Everything moves together—the sound of the sea, the scent of the bean field, the peace of the sunset, and the feeling of love for his Sara—to give him the sense of a magical central process in nature, which is summed up by the sound of the Aeolian harp in the window, making a music of nature for them:

> And that simplest Lute,
> Plac'd length-ways in the clasping casement, hark!
> How by the desultory breeze caress'd,

[13]See *CPI,* p. 33 and n.

[14]For a full and detailed account of the Aeolian harp in England, see the title-essay in Geoffrey Grigson's *The Harp of Aeolus and Other Essays* (London: Routledge, 1947).

[15]Extracts from "The Eolian Harp" are given in the text of 1796, as reprinted in my Everyman edition of *Coleridge's Poems* (London: Dent; New York: Dutton, 1963, rev. 1974), pp. 52–53.

> Like some coy Maid half-yielding to her Lover,
> It pours such sweet upbraidings, as must needs
> Tempt to repeat the wrong! And now, its strings
> Boldlier swept, the long sequacious notes
> Over delicious surges sink and rise,
> Such a soft floating witchery of sound
> As twilight Elfins make, when they at eve
> Voyage on gentle gales from Faery Land,
> Where *Melodies* round honey-dropping flowers,
> Footless and wild, like birds of Paradise,
> Nor pause, nor perch, hovering on untam'd wing.

From this vision of a moment in nature when all her energies are perfectly harmonized, he moves, by a simple transition, to think of the fantasies which sometimes cross his mind when he is in a relaxed mood:

> Full many a thought uncall'd and undetain'd,
> And many idle flitting phantasies,
> Traverse my indolent and passive brain
> As wild and various, as the random gales
> That swell or flutter on this subject Lute!

Having thus guarded himself against possible charges of taking his own ideas too seriously, he records one of these fantasies—which turns out to be the suggestion that the very processes which he has been describing, both in nature and in his own mind, might be processes which subsist at the heart of all life:

> And what if all of animated nature
> Be but organic Harps diversely fram'd,
> That tremble into thought, as o'er them sweeps
> Plastic and vast, one intellectual Breeze,
> At once the Soul of each, and God of all?

No sooner has he set out this speculation than he breaks off, registering a reproof (real or imagined) from Sara and the reflection (already prepared for in the earlier lines) that such "shapings" are

> Bubbles that glitter as they rise and break
> On vain Philosophy's aye-babbling spring.

In one sense the movement looks like a simple turning away from the main argument, a reversion from near-pantheism to orthodox pietism. As such, it may appear artistically self-negating, an example of bad faith. But there is also a sense in which the argument of the poem is being subterraneanly continued. For when Coleridge spoke of his feelings of guilt, one of the things that he was recalling was the fate of some of his earlier attempts to express his emotions spontaneously, attempts which had led to his misdemeanors and debts at Cambridge. If that was what the promptings of the breeze had led to, it was not, in hindsight at least, desirable.

I have discussed this poem in detail because it seems to me to bring out one of the elements in Coleridge's thinking which I suggested was distinctive: his insistence that in any theory of organic form and vital energy it is necessary to recognize that vital energy may not necessarily work simply or benevolently: that energies can be destructive as well as constructive, so that no theory of simple genius will answer.

The two great poems which he wrote a couple of years later face the problem again, from a more radical point of view. Although "The Ancient Mariner" is often thought of as a Christian poem, that (as William Empson in particular has pointed out[16]) is partly due to the marginal glosses which were not added until twenty years later. The Mariner is religious, but he is superstitiously religious; and the religion which he recommends at the

---

[16]William Empson and David Pirie, eds., *Coleridge's Verse: A Selection* (London: Faber, 1972), pp. 42–44 etc.

end is more than a generalized religion of love. The events of the poem show the fate of a man who does not honor the vital play of life in a single creature, the albatross, and who subsequently finds himself exposed to the energies of the universe at their most destructive. What he then discovers in the roots of his being, when he contrives to bless the water-snakes as he delights in their energies, is that through such love the existence of an order of love in the universe at large can be discovered; but at the end of the poem he still hardly knows what to make of the experience. All that he can say for certain is that it is desperately important for human beings to show love to each other and to all creatures.[17]

"Kubla Khan," similarly, carries within itself a core of reservation concerning the nature of energy. Kubla, man of "natural" genius, creates his paradise garden and reduces it apparently to order, but the second stanza of the poem is full of images and events—the great disordered fountain, the woman wailing for her daemon lover, the ancestral voices prophesying war—that suggest the other, destructive side of energy. If there is such a thing as absolute genius it is rather to be found in a place transcending the normal forms of nature, as in the last stanza of the poem.[18]

In Coleridge's later development the impulse to emotional spontaneity is increasingly restrained, the fear of pantheism more marked. There is a great deal that is suggestive in the notebooks and letters, but he can find no way past his fear that spontaneous exercise of freedom might result in fearful anarchy. Energies spiraling in free play might appear beautiful, but the spiral could also turn into a vortex, whirling to destruction any hapless human being who might be caught up by it.[19] Coleridge gradually turns into the Conservative philosopher and

[17]An extended account on these lines is given in *CPI*, Ch. 7.
[18]Ibid., pp. 115–18.
[19]Ibid., pp. 57, 112, 166, 213–14.

theologian of his later years, who exercised a far-reaching influence over the Victorians. Yet I believe that it is possible to trace through all the movements of the later years a fascination with the ideas of his youth, which he tends still to put into footnotes or asides—and indeed the whole movement of his mind shows a resilience which actually lives out the interplay of form and energy: when one position fails him he becomes adept at moving to another, related one and trying again from there.

My present purpose, however, is not to pursue these matters, intricate and fascinating as they are, in Coleridge's own career, but to argue that although Coleridge himself found it difficult to make poetry from them after the year of his greatest poems, they did achieve their own poetic expression and monument elsewhere. At the time when Coleridge was writing "Kubla Khan," "The Ancient Mariner," and other poems, he was also in daily contact with the Wordsworths and expounding his ideas to them. (Even earlier, when the two poets met in 1795, Wordsworth read "Salisbury Plain" to Coleridge, and it is not impossible that Coleridge read "The Eolian Harp" in reply.[20]) And when one looks at Wordsworth's poetry of this time one sees many touches which suggest that he had been listening to, and excited by, speculations which Coleridge was indulging.

Sometimes the result of the stimulation is to be found in a short passage where Wordsworth pursues a speculation to an extreme. In some stanzas of the lyric poem beginning "Three years she grew,"[21] for instance, he imagines the ways in which nature might be thought to affect the growth of a young girl who was brought up in such proximity to nature as to allow its powers to influence her in a pure and direct manner:

> "Nor shall she fail to see
> Even in the motions of the Storm

[20]For Wordsworth's reading and Coleridge's response, see *BL*, I, 58; *WP*, I, 330; and *Prelude* (1805), xii, 356–65.
[21]*WP*, II, 214–16 (quoted from the 1800 version).

A beauty that shall mould her form
By silent sympathy.

"The stars of midnight shall be dear
To her; and she shall lean her ear
In many a secret place
Where rivulets dance their wayward round
And beauty born of murmuring sound
Shall pass into her face.

"And vital feelings of delight
Shall rear her form to stately height,
Her virgin bosom swell . . . . "

If the word "vital" suggests a reference to Coleridge's ideas, the words "stately" and "delight" encourage close reference to the account of the creative process in "Kubla Khan," where the "stately pleasure-dome" is finally thought to be realizable only if the poet is won to a "deep delight" by revival of the music of the Abyssinian maid. In Wordsworth's poem a similar process is seen as always available in nature to the human being exposed to its gentle influences and fierce energies—so that something in the energies even of the storm, as well as more directly in the playful eddies of dancing rivulets and murmuring sound or, more immediately still, the "vital feelings" of her own answering delight—will help to mold her growing form into beauty.

In a number of poems of this kind Wordsworth is trying to evaluate the benefits of living not in a rural community but in rural solitude. Village life in his eyes may be as corrupting to natural growth as life in the town, but to those who are preserved from both forms of social pressure, the organic and vital processes of nature may be free to work (as, in a more oblique fashion, he feels they worked upon himself).

He was even more exercised, perhaps, by the idea that this natural interplay of the vital and the organic could be hindered and thwarted by the workings of the civilization by which the growing human being was surrounded. In early draft lines (later to be used in *The Excursion*),[22] for instance, he speaks of the

> law severe of penury
> Which bends the cottage boy to early thought
> To thought whose premature necessity
> Blocks out the forms of nature, preconsumes
> The reason, famishes the heart, shuts up
> The infant being in itself & makes
> Its very spring a season of decay.

As a result the processes of natural growth are totally inhibited.

> The limbs increase but liberty of mind
> Is gone for ever, & the avenues
> Of sense impeded this organic frame,
> So joyful in its motions soon becomes
> Dull to the joy of its own motions dead
> And even the touch so exquisitely poured
> Through the whole body with a languid will
> Performs its functions, in the basking hour
>
> Scarce carrying to the brain a torpid sense
> Of what there is delightful in the breeze
> The sunshine, or the changeful elements

In following this line of thought through the same manuscript draft, we are reminded of another strand in Coleridge's thinking, related to his early enthusiasm for the Neoplatonists. At the center of the organic there is believed to exist a center of light and radiance corresponding to that in the sun which feeds it, so that when the organic and the vital are finely enough tuned in

[22]These lines are quoted from MS 18A at Dove Cottage, by kind permission of the Trustees. I am particularly grateful to Mr. E. P. Thompson, who used some of them in an unpublished lecture, thus drawing them to my attention, and who subsequently sent me a transcript which I have since been able to check against the original.

the human organism it becomes light-giving.[23] Elsewhere in the manuscript, Wordsworth exclaims:

> Oh never was this intellectual power
> This vital spirit in its essence free
> As the light of heaven, this mind that streams
> With emanations like the blessed sun
> Oh never was this [   ] existence formed
> For wishes that debilitate and die
> Of their own weakness. . . .

and the passage concludes with a declamation against the "feverish infirmities" which

> feed
> From day to day their never-ending life
> In the close prison-house of human laws.
>
> [*WP*, V, 473]

In the years that followed, Wordsworth also drew upon Coleridge's ideas in more subtle ways. Not only did he believe that the influx of vital forces in nature could help the growth of the child; he also suggested that one effect of being brought up among beautiful forms was to impress them so deeply at the organic level of being that they remained a firm resource, which could assist the psyche to maintain its integrity in less propitious surroundings. The assistance was not always totally effective: we may think of Poor Susan in the loveless world of London, to whom it is a relief when scenes of her childhood rise up before her eyes and "a river runs on through the Vale of Cheapside"; the vision must fade again, however, the relief be no more than temporary.[24] On the other hand, Wordsworth himself discovered a more reliable version of the resource in London when his sight of the crowd moving in and out at the fair, as if in some

---

[23]*CPI*, p. 29.
[24]"The Reverie of Poor Susan," *WP*, II, 217.

nightmare mill, was relieved as he superimposed upon the scene the remembered forms and energies of Lakeland landscape, which could contain it all and suggest that the world of mechanical death was sustained from beyond its limits by the world of organic life.[25] A striking use of this device is to be found in "The Brothers,"[26] where Leonard, yearning for the brother he has left behind him and finding that the energies of the ocean as they play around him are inducing a state of fever, is rescued by a work of his own inner nature which superimposes upon the restless seascape forms derived from the native country where they had grown up together:

> And, while the broad blue wave and sparkling foam
> Flashed round him images and hues that wrought
> In union with the employment of his heart,
> He, thus by feverish passion overcome,
> Even with the organs of his bodily eye,
> Below him, in the bosom of the deep,
> Saw mountains; saw the forms of sheep that grazed
> On verdant hills—with dwellings among trees,
> And shepherds clad in the same country grey
> Which he himself had worn.

Meanwhile, however, his brother, through a different working of that attachment, is suffering a tragic fate. The same desperate yearning, working in his inmost being, causes him to begin sleepwalking and is so powerful as to overcome his sense of place, so that when asleep on a pillar of rock on a summer's day, he rises and walks over the edge of it to his death.

Various ramifications of these ideas were, I would suggest, working in Wordsworth's mind throughout this period, helping to fertilize his poetic mind during a time of extraordinary fecundity. In "The Brothers" they help Wordsworth to gain some purchase on his major theme, that of the attachments that

[25]*Prelude* (1805), vii, 691–740.
[26]*WP*, II, 1–13.

can spring up between individuals brought up in close proximity to each other and to nature; in the Immortality Ode they play an intimate part in the total work of the poem, which is devoted, among other things, to an exposition of the way in which the child, originally so firm a part of the organic light and life of nature that it lives in a state of almost total vision and security, has to be weaned from that attachment and, as its own vision fades, to find a more lasting mode of living with nature, This is achieved partly by a dialectic of irritation and love between itself and its parents: its vital powers are stimulated by irritation ("Fretted by sallies of his mother's kisses") while its organic form is preserved in security by the steadfastness of the underlying relationship ("With light upon him from his father's eyes"). In the same way, the growth of its own powers of imitation enable it to mime many human roles, assisting it toward the sympathy it will later need, while the steadfastness of the original landscape keeps alive a sense of union with nature that may preserve a ground of attachment toward other human beings as well, the love of nature leading to love of man.

Perhaps the most striking reflection of Coleridge's ideas, however, is to be found in *The Prelude*—a poem which we have recently learned to appreciate in a new way through the rediscovery of the early, two-part version which Wordsworth composed, partly in Germany and partly in England, during the years 1798-99.[27]

Here again it would be wrong to suggest that Coleridge's ideas formed anything like a scaffolding for Wordsworth's construction. The process would seem more subtle and involved—as if

---

[27]Mr. Jonathan Wordsworth has kindly sent me a transcript which is to be the basis of the text in his forthcoming Norton edition of the poem and which, while adopting the same line-numbering as that in the Cornell Wordsworth (*The Prelude, 1798-1799*, ed. Stephen Parrish, Ithaca: Cornell University Press; Hassocks, Sussex: Harvester Press, 1977), differs from it in certain respects. I am grateful to Mr. Wordsworth for allowing me to use his text here—hereafter referred to as *1799*.

exposure to the terms of Coleridge's thinking gave Wordsworth a set of speculative instruments with which to probe the nature of his own early experience, sometimes resorting directly to Coleridgean terms, but also on many occasions being simply stimulated to record his experiences of youthful vitality as directly as possible.[28]

The chief of Coleridge's ideas which would seem to have stirred Wordsworth as he set to work on his recollections was that the process of natural growth, involving a minute cooperation between the unfolding organism and the vital powers, was mirrored in the human psyche itself. There also the maintenance and development of the creative power could be sustained only by a fruitful interplay between the organic and tbe vital.

The note is struck in a well-known early line of the poem: "Fair seed-time had my soul." That, however, though striking, might be no more than organic metaphor: it is as one looks at some subsequent passages that one sees how closely Wordsworth is looking at the process involved. As he shows us, for example, the simple vitality of the child in action, a vitality as yet untutored by long acquaintance with the forms of nature, we may recall Coleridge's image of the vital energy of the insect, which is led to find its natural food in the vegetable creation—an image which Wordsworth in fact uses explicitly to conclude his passage.

> The sands of Westmoreland, the creeks and bays
> Of Cumbria's rocky limits, they can tell
> How when the sea threw off his evening shade
> And to the Shepherd's hut beneath the crags
> Did send sweet notice of the rising moon
> How I have stood to images like these
> A stranger, linking with the spectacle
> No body of associated forms

---

[28]For further discussion of the relationship between Coleridge and Wordsworth during their time in Germany, see Ch. 4 of my *Wordsworth and the Human Heart* (1978).

And bringing with me no peculiar sense
Of quietness or peace, yet I have stood
Even while my eye has moved o'er three long leagues
Of shining water, gathering, as it seemed
Through the wide surface of that field of light
New pleasure, like a bee among the flowers.

[*1799*, i, 399-412]

As in "Three years she grew," Wordsworth suggests that there
are human beings who are so rewardingly passive to nature that
simple exposure to the vital powers of nature promotes their
growth into beautiful form. When he looks at his own experience, on the other hand, he believes that he can trace a more
vehement and oblique working of the same power, whereby the
energies of nature needed to work in a more violent way before
his nature was touched. It is through the "ministry of fear," for
example, that he traces many such workings, impressing the
landscape upon his mind:

. . . and thus
By the impressive agency of fear
By pleasure and repeated happiness
So frequently repeated, and by force
Of obscure feelings representative
Of joys that were forgotten these same scenes
So beauteous and majestic in themselves
Though yet the day was distant did at length
Become habitually dear, and all
Their hues and forms were by invisible links
Allied to the affections.

[*1799*, i, 432-42]

In the second part of the 1799 *Prelude* the discussion of the
interplay between the vital and the organic becomes still more
intricate. Here Wordsworth moves back behind the processes of
his boyhood education to consider the infant sensibility and the
way in which, under propitious conditions, it is sustained in its
full creative nature. In the womb, clearly, there is a full organic

union with the mother; as the baby learns to live in the outer world of sense it still needs a sense of connection with its mother to keep its vital powers alive. Unlike the "cottage boy" described in the fragment quoted earlier, in whom touch can scarcely carry to the brain "a torpid sense / Of what there is delightful in the breeze / The sunshine, or the changeful elements," this child, still free, is one

> who when his soul
> Claims manifest kindred with an earthly soul
> Doth gather passion from his Mother's eye
> Such feelings pass into his torpid life
> Like an awakening breeze....
>
> [*1799*, ii, 271-75]

In its physical union with the mother at its most intimate level, that of their common blood, the baby gains a sense of rapport with the inmost active powers of the world which it need never lose:

> Along his infant veins are interfused
> The gravitation and the filial bond
> Of nature, that connect him with the world.
> Emphatically such a being lives
> An inmate of this *active* universe....
>
> [*1799*, ii, 292-96]

(This theme of the security given to the child who enjoys a full and loving physical relationship with its mother is also to be found in Coleridge's writings, occurring tangentially in the Philosophical Lectures of 1819 and at length in the Opus Maximum.[29])

Wordsworth now makes it clear that what he has been talking about is the type of childhood which he believes he himself en-

---

[29]*The Philosophical Lectures,* ed. Kathleen Coburn (London: Pilot; New York: Philosophical Library, 1949), p. 115; OM, II, 64ff.

joyed, with the result that the creative power of the poet in him was properly nurtured:

> I have endeavour'd to display the means
> Whereby this infant sensibility,
> Great birth-right of our being, was in me
> Augmented and sustain'd.
>
> [*1799*, ii, 314-17]

He goes on to describe both "Nature's finer influxes," to which his mind "lay open," and

> Society made sweet as solitude
> By silent inobtrusive sympathies
> And gentle agitations of the mind
> From manifold distinctions, difference
> Perceived in things where to the common eye
> No difference is ....
>
> [*1799*, ii, 345-50]

This, we may assume, is the true way in which the analyzing powers of the mind should be awakened: opening out in such a context, there is less danger that they will take over to dominate the mind. These gentle processes were, however, complemented for him by a "sublimer joy," created by walks at night in storm or under starlight when he would stand

> Beneath some rock listening to sounds that are
> The ghostly language of the ancient earth
> Or make their dim abode in distant winds.
>
> [*1799*, ii, 357-59]

These worked still more effectively (if more obliquely), setting up in a mind that can remember *how* it felt, even if it does not remember *what* it felt, "an obscure sense / Of possible sublimity."

After further examples of this working, Wordsworth again emphasizes his main point:

> But let this at least
> Be not forgotten, that I still retain'd
> My first creative sensibility
> That by the regular action of the world
> My soul was unsubdued.
>
> [*1799*, ii, 407-11]

He then goes on to describe the development of this sensibility in terms of "a plastic power" ("at times / Rebellious ... but for the most / Subservient strictly to the external things / With which it communed") and of an "auxiliar light,"

> which on the setting sun
> Bestowed new splendour, the melodious birds
> The gentle breezes, fountains that ran on,
> Murmuring so sweetly in themselves, obey'd
> A like dominion, and the midnight storm
> Grew darker in the presence of my eye.
>
> [*1799*, ii, 418-23]

In such passages the magic power of the organic is projecting itself into the "auxiliar light" while the vital spirits respond to, and in their turn express, the "plastic power": the theme of the sensibility being strengthened and quickened into new forms of life by contact with the energies of nature is at its most dramatic. That which Coleridge conceived as a process by which to interpret the working of nature and the human mind is being reported by Wordsworth as fact of his own boyhood experience. The discussion reaches its climax as he describes how—whether through operation of this habit, now deeply "rooted", or through excess of the "great social principle of life," helping him to transfer his own enjoyments to "unorganic natures,"[30] or whether it really was a revelation of truth—he felt the "senti-

[30] *1799*, ii, 435-43.

ment of being" spread over all existence, including all that displays energy:

> O'er all that leaps, and runs, and shouts and sings
> Or beats the gladsome air, o'er all that glides
> Beneath the wave, yea, in the wave itself
> And mighty depth of waters....
>
> [*1799*, ii, 455-58]

So he reaches the crucial statement of his youthful beliefs:

> ... wonder not
> If such my transports were, for in all things
> I saw one life and felt that it was joy.
>
> [*1799*, ii, 458-60]

This ability to project his whole sense of being into nature, so that its whole diversity was brought into one by its subordination to his single, central sense of joy brings the ecstatic note of the 1799 *Prelude* to a climax. In such a moment of unified experience the young man is realizing to its full extent what was implied by the simpler union with nature which he had enjoyed when, even as a child, he

> held unconscious intercourse
> With the eternal Beauty drinking in
> A pure organic pleasure from the lines
> Of curling mist or from the level plain
> Of waters coloured by the steady clouds.
>
> [*1799*, i, 394-98]

As he talks here about the "first-born affinities" which in childhood constitute "the bond of union betwixt life and joy," the highly idiosyncratic use of the word "organic" suggests that he is drawing once again on the idea of an organic center in each human being which is capable of responding in certain situations directly and immediately to the beauties of nature. The word

[180]

"drink," equally, suggests the unmediated quality of the activity. (We recall the central importance of drinking in Coleridge's "Ancient Mariner.") The idea recurs in a still more unusual form later, when, after his description of standing under a rock and listening to sounds that were "the ghostly language of the ancient earth," he continues,

> Thence did I drink the visionary power.
>
> [*1799*, ii, 360]

Sound is, as it were, transmuted effortlessly into "light" by this act of absorption into the central being.

It should by now be clear that the kind of analysis that is being brought to bear on some of Wordsworth's poetry in these years is not intended to reduce it to some kind of abstract formula. What is being suggested rather is that reflection on Coleridge's ideas gave new substance to Wordsworth's memories of his early physical nature and its development. As he continued to work at *The Prelude,* this particular source of excitement ceased to be so directly active; yet it is also fair to point out how many of the most strikingly evocative passages in the final poem are already there in this first version. Coleridge's distinction between the organic and the vital seems, in fact, to have induced in all three friends—himself, Dorothy, and William—a new way of looking at nature herself, encouraging constant distinctions between the effects of her still forms and those of her active energies. A reading of Coleridge's notebooks, Dorothy's journals, and Wordsworth's *Prelude* offers many examples of the kind:[31] I will here consider only one, an unused draft for *The Prelude* in which Wordsworth recalls an experience near Coniston when through the operations of nature's energies the whole scene became totally disordered to his vision:

---

[31]The question is touched upon briefly in *CPI,* pp. 272-73.

> The wind blew through the hills of Coniston
> Compress'd as in a tunnel, from the lake
> Bodies of foam took flight, and the whole vale
> Was wrought into commotion high and low—
> Mist flying up and down, bewilder'd showers,
> Ten thousand thousand waves, mountains and crags,
> And darkness, and the sun's tumultuous light.

Yet, in the middle of the chaos,

> A large unmutilated rainbow stood
> Immoveable in heav'n, kept standing there
> With a colossal stride bridging the vale,
> The substance thin as dreams, lovelier than day,—
> Amid the deafening uproar stood unmov'd,
> Sustain'd itself through many minutes space;
> As if it were pinn'd down by adamant.
>
> [*Prelude*, notes to xiii, 95]

It was with "pins of adamant" that Satan and his fellow-daemons constructed their causeway through Chaos in *Paradise Lost*;[32] in the case of the rainbow's bridge, however, effortlessly imposing its prismatic colours (a notable, if precarious, grace of the New-tonian universe) across a scene of total disorder, any such daemonic element is to be seen as a link with the original unfall-en divine creativity, a triumph of nature's ultimate organic power to produce forms which can supervene upon all the pos-sible disordered operations of energy. The same assertion may be seen in one of the best-known passages in his works, that which describes how, when walking through the Simplon pass, he was oppressed by the contradictory workings of nature's powers there, only to be struck later by the fact that Imagination is after all able to hold all those contradictions in its grasp and, by the working of its own alchemy, to see them as being

---

[32] *Paradise Lost*, x, 318.

> like workings of one mind, the features
> Of the same face, blossoms upon one tree,
> Characters of the great Apocalypse,
> The types and symbols of Eternity,
> Of first and last, and midst, and without end.
>
> [*Prelude* (1805), vi, 568-72]

Many readers must have been disturbed to find an organic image placed in such close proximity to that of the Apocalypse; in terms of the theories we have been discussing, on the other hand, it may be argued that any occasion when the organic assumes its precedence over the warring energies of time must always be of apocalyptic import.

It has to be acknowledged, of course, that the attempt to develop a comprehensive theory of the organic which would apply metaphysically as well as physically, which would bind together the life of nature with that of the human mind, was a difficult and even perilous venture. In particular, Coleridge's attempt to wed the organic to the primary imagination and to see it as a source of light as well as growth (the secondary imagination being, in his own words, "essentially vital" and so active, whereas the primary was passive and transmissive) was at once brilliant yet in certain respects clearly unsatisfactory. In his efforts during these years to bring all phenomena within the purview of this one great idea and energy, Coleridge may sometimes remind one of Blake, endeavoring during the same years to find a total mythology which could be applied universally to human experience and history. With so many brilliant insights and illuminations, the system must often have seemed to be on the point of quivering into total coherence—yet it could never fall into a finally satisfying interpretative pattern.

Coleridge's attempts to relate the ideas to his own experience had something to do with the darkening of his vision during the subsequent years. His personal unhappiness reduced his own sense of vitality. More tragically still, it seems likely that his growing opium addiction was accompanied by a palliative belief that under the influence of drugs the mind became open to its own organic nature: years later he suggested that

> the dire poison for a delusive time has made the body, ⟨i.e. the *organization,* not the articulation (or instruments of motion)⟩ the unknown somewhat, a fitter Instrument for the all-powerful Soul. [*N,* III, 3320]

(Here the "organization" seems to be related to the organic, the "articulation" to the vital.) Awakening to a sense of the deleterious effects of opium upon his system, he came to feel (with a dark modulation of his organic imagery) that he had been "intoxicated with the vernal fragrance and effluvia from the flowers and first-fruits of Pantheism, unaware of its bitter root."[33] In the same way he had explored the darker aspects of the Aeolian harp image in his use of it in "Dejection."[34]

During the earlier years, nevertheless, the form of his theory had continued to exercise its hold on his mind. In one letter of 1804, particularly, we may see it at work in his discussion of three successive topics. Writing to Richard Sharp he first described his state of mind during his illness:[35]

> . . . not that my inner Being was disturbed—on the contrary, it seemed more than usually serene and self-sufficing—but the exceeding Pain, of which I suffered every now and then, and the

[33]Marginal note by Coleridge to *The Works of Jacob Behmen,* ed. G. Ward and T. Langcake, 4 vols. (London, 1764–81), I, 127. This copy is now in the British Library.

[34]See Letter to Sara Hutchinson, 4 April 1802, lines 6–8, 186–215 (*CL,* II, 790, 795); "Dejection: An Ode," lines 6–8, 96–125 (*CPW,* I, 363, 367–78).

[35]Letter to Richard Sharp, 15 Jan. 1804, *CL,* II, 1031–35. In the first passage quoted, the nature of the final parallels is not altogether clear, since one would expect the "Part of us by which we know ourselves to be" to be the same as the "organic." When he comes to "the Vital and the Organic" Coleridge may simply be reversing his terms, but the question needs close examination in relation to his other discussions of the matter.

fearful Distresses of my sleep, had taken away from me the con-
necting Link of voluntary power, which continually combines that
Part of us by which we know ourselves to be, with that outward
Picture or Hieroglyphic, by which we hold communion with our
Like—between the Vital and the Organic—or what Berkley, I sup-
pose would call—Mind and it's sensuous Language.

A few lines later he wrote of Thomas Wedgwood that he made it

a sort of crime even to think of his Faults by so many Virtues
retained, cultivated and preserved in growth & blossom, in a
climate—where now the Gusts so rise and eddy, that deeply-rooted
must *that* be which is not snatched up & made a play thing of by
them . . . .

Wedgwood, then, is a man of organic virtues under attack from
the powers of nature. In the same letter Wordsworth is his great
exemplar of a human being who has kept alive the connections
which he himself is finding it hard to retain:

the only man who has effected a compleat and constant synthesis
of Thought & Feeling and combined them with Poetic Forms, with
the music of pleasurable passion and with Imagination or the
modifying Power in that highest sense of the word in which I have
ventured to oppose it to Fancy, or the *aggregating* power—in that
sense in which it is a dim Analogue of Creation, not all that we can
believe but all that we can *conceive* of creation. [*CL,* II, 1032-34]

Wordsworth, who can produce poetic forms and combine them
both with the music of pleasurable passion (corresponding to the
"symphony and song" of vital power in "Kubla Khan") and with
the modifying power of imagination (the creative and organic
center) is exhibiting the ideal of human creativity as Coleridge
conceives it.

This faith of his in his friend's powers helps to explain the
note of reverence which he often adopted in speaking of him—a
note which caused Lamb to refer semihumorously to

Wordsworth on one occasion as Coleridge's "God."[36] If he was so in Coleridge's eyes it was in the sense that every "son of genius" was seen by him to be a shadowy "son of god."[37] We may turn to that version of "Dejection" which was addressed to Wordsworth himself to see the conception of creative genius embodied in images of a light and love which Coleridge would ascribe also to the deity:

> Calm stedfast Spirit, guided from above,
> O Wordsworth! friend of my devoutest choice,
> Great Son of Genius! full of Light & Love!
> 　　Thus, thus dost thou rejoice.
> To thee do all things live from pole to pole,
> Their Life the Eddying of thy living Soul!
> 　　　　　　　　　　　　[CL, II, 817–18]

This conception of genius as radiant had its immediate counterpart in the organic, however. Thinking of the future happiness of Wordsworth's household he writes (in the original version addressed to Sara Hutchinson):

> Wherefore, O wherefore! should I wish to be
> A wither'd branch upon a blossoming Tree?
> 　　　　　　　　　　　　[CL, II, 794]

Surveying Wordsworth's future, similarly, he writes:

> . . . Mortal Life seems destined for no continuous Happiness save that which results from the exact performance of Duty—and blessed are you, dear William! whose Path of Duty lies thro' vine-trellised Elm-groves, thro' Love and Joy & Grandeur—. [CL, II, 1060]

---

[36] "Coleridge has left us, to go into the North, on a visit to his God, Wordsworth." Letter to Manning, 5 April 1800 (*Letters of Charles and Mary Lamb*, ed. Edwin W. Marrs, Jr., Ithaca: Cornell University Press, 1975, I, 191).

[37] Cf. my *Coleridge the Visionary* (London: Chatto and Windus, 1959), pp. 82–83.

In the Dejection Ode, mourning his own plight, he remembered the former time "When Hope grew round me, like the climbing Vine"; a year later he wrote to Southey concerning his own matrimonial troubles:

O dear Southey! I am no Elm!—I am a crumbling wall, undermined at the foundation! Why should the Vine with all it's clusters be buried in my rubbish? [*CL*, II, 929]

By the summer he had elaborated a new image for his own condition:

—a haunting sense, that I was an herbaceous Plant, as large as a large Tree, with a Trunk of the same Girth, & Branches as Large & shadowing—but with *pith within* the Trunk, not heart of Wood—that I had *power* not *strength* .... [*CL*, II, 959]

He repeated it to Davy:

I have read somewhere that in the tropical climates there are Annuals [as lofty] and of as ample girth as forest trees. So by a very dim likeness, I seem to myself to distinguish power from strength & to have only the power. [*CL*, II, 1102]

This imagery is to be compared with that which he applied to Wordsworth—both his reaction to the early poetry ("an harshness and acerbity connected and combined with words and images all a-glow, which might recall those products of the vegetable world, where gorgeous blossoms rise out of the hard and thorny rind and shell, within which the rich fruit was elaborating"[38]), and the passage from Bartram's *Travels* which he had transcribed in 1801 as a description of his friend's intellect and genius:

The soil is a deep, rich, dark Mould on a deep Stratum of tenacious Clay, and that on a foundation of Rocks, which often break

[38]*BL*, I, 56. The image is being applied to Wordsworth's *Descriptive Sketches*.

through both Strata, lifting their back above the Surface. The Trees, which chiefly grow here, are the gigantic Black Oak, Magnolia, Fraxinus excelsior, Platane, & a few stately Tulip Trees. [*N*, I, 926; *BL*, II, 128–29]

Coleridge continued to project his picture of Wordsworth as a poetic giant, a figure of absolute genius combining the godlike and the organic. Speaking to Hazlitt in 1798, he had, after a few criticisms, declared that Wordsworth's genius "was not a spirit that descended to him through the air; it sprung out of the ground like a flower, or unfolded itself from a green spray, on which the goldfinch sang." He also declared, however, that "his philosophic poetry had a grand and comprehensive spirit in it, so that his soul seemed to inhabit the universe like a palace, and to discover truth by intuition, rather than by deduction."[39]

It is not clear how far Wordsworth would have accepted this picture of himself. By the time that Coleridge returned from Malta in 1806, certainly, he had renounced any role as visionary that he might ever have assumed. In the famous lines of his "Elegiac Stanzas," he bade farewell to the young poet in himself who might once have wished to celebrate

> The light that never was, on sea or land,
> The consecration, and the Poet's dream

and turned to the more stoic virtues of "fortitude, and patient cheer, / And frequent sights of what is to be borne!"[40]

Coleridge presumably registered the change in his friend, but still assimilated what he heard to his former picture of him. So when the completed *Prelude* was read to him early in 1807, Coleridge wrote of its account of Wordsworth's youth as an attempt to convey

[39]Hazlitt, "My First Acquaintance with Poets," paragraph 10, *Complete Works*, Centenary Edition, 21 vols., ed. P. P. Howe (London: J. M. Dent, 1930–34), XVII, 117.

[40]"Elegiac Stanzas . . . , " *WP*, IV, 258–60.

> what within the mind
> By vital breathings secret as the soul
> Of vernal growth, oft quickens in the heart
> Thoughts all too deep for words!

and as expressing the feelings of a time

> When power streamed from thee, and thy soul received
> The light reflected, as a light bestowed . . . .

If Wordsworth had lost his more spontaneous powers, he was still to be seen as a fortified visionary, moreover:

> thenceforth calm and sure
> From the dread watch-tower of man's absolute self,
> With light unwaning on her eyes, to look
> Far on—herself a glory to behold,
> The Angel of the vision![41]

As a result of the painful quarrel which ensued a few years later, Coleridge became somewhat disillusioned with his friend, but he never lost the sense of an overwhelming strength in Wordsworth, which he celebrates again in *Biographia Literaria,* declaring that when at his best he always evinces "the Vision and the Faculty Divine."[42]

And this surviving faith of Coleridge's points us to a final facet of the affair. Although Wordsworth could hardly sustain the stance of godlike and vitally organic man in which Coleridge tried to place him, and although, as we have said, Coleridge's theory could hardly be moulded into the comprehensive interpretative tool that he would like to have made of it, there is a sense in which that theory was strangely self-validating in the careers of both men. In their time the forms of eighteenth-century language had been steadily hardening into objects, so

---

[41]"To William Wordsworth," *CPW,* I, 403–08, lines 8–11, 18–19, 39–43.
[42]*BL,* II, 45, quoting *The Excursion,* i, 79.

that it seemed to the rising poets of the time as if they could hardly be treated as more than counters to play with. By insisting that language, like all natural process, consisted of an interplay between forms and energies, Coleridge gave himself and his friend a way of looking at experience which in turn liberated their own poetry-making powers. Wordsworth's poetry is not contained by the theory, nor is his own achievement fully to be measured in its terms; yet one may reasonably doubt whether the extraordinary efflorescence which gave it birth could have taken place had it not been for the stimulation given by contact with it—particularly as it revealed itself in the workings of Coleridge's own intelligence. In that sense, the title-page inscription which *The Prelude* bore throughout Wordsworth's lifetime— "Poem / Title not yet fixed upon / by / William Wordsworth / Addressed to / S. T. Coleridge"[43]—may strike one as peculiarly apt, and even poignant.

[43]Reproduced, *Prelude*, p. lxxvi.

]5[

What Did Coleridge Say?
John Payne Collier and the
Reports of the 1811–12 Lectures

R. A. FOAKES

When John Payne Collier published his edition of the notes he took at seven of the lectures Coleridge gave in his 1811–12 series, there can have been few people still alive who might remember them. Collier claimed to have mislaid his notes, and his *Seven Lectures on Shakespeare and Milton, By the Late S. T. Coleridge,* appeared in 1856 after an interval of more than forty years. Although by this time Collier had earned a reputation as a man of letters, he also was beginning to be exposed as a literary forger, none of whose work could be trusted too readily. There was no general reason for distrusting his records of Coleridge's lectures, for he certainly attended them, and took shorthand notes, and his accounts seemed to be confirmed by the rediscovery of newspaper reports in the *Morning Chronicle* of Lectures 3, 4, 7, and 8, and by the publication of extracts from Crabb Robinson's Diary and correspondence in 1869; the accounts of and comments on Coleridge's lectures in these bore enough similarity to Collier's notes to support his claim to be presenting an authentic text.[1] The accusations of "literary fraud" and "fabrica-

---

[1]See *Coleridge on Shakespeare: The Text of the Lectures of 1811–12,* ed. R. A. Foakes (London: Routledge & Kegan Paul, 1971), pp. 7–9—hereafter cited as Foakes.

tion" made by Andrew Brae in *Literary Cookery* (1855) and in
Collier, Coleridge and Shakespeare: A Review (1860)[2] were forgotten; Collier's 1856 text was accepted into the canon of Coleridge's works, and it appears in the present standard edition of
his Shakespearean lectures, edited by Thomas Middleton
Raysor.[3]

Raysor saw no need to comment much on the text of the
lectures other than to assert their authenticity and qualify the
assertion with the caveat, "No one will believe that they are accurate in detail; nor does Collier claim that they are so" (II, 22). In
fact, Collier claimed at one point in his 1856 preface that, although he might have missed or omitted or mistaken some
points in Coleridge's lectures, he had "added no word or syllable" of his own; later he confessed to relying on his memory to
"fill up chasms" in his notes, but the impression he sought to
convey was that of presenting a text as close as possible to what
Coleridge actually said.[4] He did not admit to inaccuracy, and
Raysor gives no hint as to what details he thought might be
inaccurate. The result was for long a general assumption that
Collier's notes were accurate. Yet Andrew Brae had demonstrated that Collier must have altered the original words of Coleridge, if only in recording him as referring in Lecture 6 to "Sir
Humphry Davy," since the knighthood was not conferred on
Davy until some months after Coleridge delivered this lecture
(Foakes, pp. 11–12; Brae, p. 41); and Collier had himself stated
that he took his notes down in the third person but translated
them into the first person for the 1856 edition (p. xiii). This
evidence could be construed merely as indicating a certain casu-

[2]The accusatory terms are quoted from the latter work (London: Longman,
1860), p. 43.
[3]*Shakespearean Criticism,* ed. Thomas Middleton Raysor, rev. ed., 2 vols. (London: Dent; New York: Dutton, 1960)—hereafter cited as Raysor.
[4]*Seven Lectures on Shakespeare and Milton,* By the Late S. T. Coleridge, ed. J.
Payne Collier (London: Chapman & Hall, 1856), pp. vii, xiii—hereafter cited as
Collier.

alness in Collier's treatment of his notes, and it only became clear that Collier had in fact revised his notes very thoroughly for his edition when his own longhand transcripts came to light and were printed in 1971.[5] These showed that in 1856 he changed almost every sentence, expanding phrases and making substitutions; he also both added material not in his longhand notes and omitted some passages recorded in them.[6]

In editing these transcripts, I found it possible to demonstrate that the received text, derived from Collier's 1856 edition, represents Collier's rewriting of his own longhand notes and must be a less accurate record of what Coleridge said. The longhand notes, transcribed from shorthand records made in the lecture room and written out perhaps soon after the delivery of the lecture, evidently provide a better text than that of 1856. (Collier's diary entries in November 1811 show that he transcribed his notes of Lectures 1 and 2 on the days when these lectures were delivered, but it is not possible to determine exactly when he wrote out the transcripts of other lectures). So much was clear when I edited these notes in 1971, for it proved easy to show how Collier had imposed his own style on the 1856 text and how he had omitted topical allusions or weakened characteristic words or phrases of Coleridge, so that, for example, "concentring" became "concentrating,"[7] justifying Andrew Brae's charge that the "vivid and peculiar phraseology" of Coleridge was not to be found there (p. 19). However, there remained the matter of

---

[5]In Foakes. The text presented in that volume was based largely on photostats, and I was unable to make a thorough check against the original. John F. Andrews has recorded a number of errors and omissions in his review-article "The *Ipsissima Verba* in My Diary?" in *Shakespeare Studies,* 8 (1975), 333–67. I have since found more, and something more nearly approaching a definitive text will be included in the appropriate volume in the *Collected Coleridge.* The quotations from the book in this essay have been corrected against Collier's manuscript.

[6]See Foakes, pp. 14–16; and also R. A. Foakes, "The Text of Coleridge's 1811-12 Shakespeare Lectures," *Shakespeare Survey,* 23 (1970), 101–111—hereafter cited as Foakes (1970).

[7]In Lecture 8; Foakes, p. 96; Raysor, II, 119.

Collier's shorthand notes; facsimiles of the original shorthand notes for Lectures 9 and 12 were available, and a first shot at decoding these showed, as expected, that they coincided more closely with the longhand transcripts than with the 1856 text, and on the evidence I then had I concluded that the longhand notes provided

> a relatively polished text, worked up, probably with the help of memory, from the framework of notes Collier took at the lectures, but so soon afterwards as to guarantee a good degree of accuracy. That is to say, a full new transcription of the shorthand notes, if this could be made, would represent in a more or less curtailed and mangled form what survives in the manuscript brochures. [Foakes, p. 22]

Since I wrote this, I have deciphered nearly all of Collier's shorthand notes of Lectures 9 and 12 and am forced to come to somewhat different conclusions. A study of these notes also raises questions about the accuracy of these and other records of Coleridge's lectures and leads to some general conclusions of a disconcerting kind.

The analysis that follows will focus on points of difference between the shorthand notes and Collier's longhand transcripts. It should therefore be established first that the transcripts are evidently based on the shorthand notes, and that, for all the differences they show, it is not unreasonable still to refer to them as transcripts. However, in spite of his stated anxiety to present "the very words Coleridge had employed" (p. xiii), Collier did not treat them as an accurate record to be preserved conscientiously so much as notes he could freely vary or expand. The changes are of various kinds. Perhaps the simplest are the substitutions of one word for another. Many of the twenty or more examples that occur in each lecture are more or less neutral equivalents, such as "days" (longhand) for "times" (shorthand), "acquired" for "secured," "stray" for "depart," or "discovers" for "finds."[8] Such substitutions can be explained as natural to many writers in copying their own work, as E. A. J. Honigmann has shown in relation to manuscripts by Keats, Thomas Middleton, and others;[9] certainly, it seems to have been Collier's habit to "improve" what he copied in this way, for the text he printed in 1856 includes a great many more replacements for words in his longhand transcripts. There is no obvious reason, in other words, for many such substitutions. In some cases a change is made to avoid a repetition, as at the end of Lecture 9 "greatest Poet" is substituted for "exquisite poet" (Foakes, p. 115), because the word "exquisite" occurs again in the same sentence. In other instances the change flattens out an unusual or individual phrase of Coleridge's, in a seemingly arbitrary and pointless way. So, in Lecture 9 the phrase "like a lively cadenza in music" (shorthand) becomes "like a lively piece of music" (it was altered again in the 1856 text to become "like a finished piece of music").[10] Such alterations perhaps show no more than the natural tendency in a copyist to replace the unusual by the more common expression; so, again, Collier varied "transplaces himself into the very being of each character" by changing the first word to "transports."[11] This subtly weakens the sense, and alters a Coleridgean expression. Some other substitutions remain unexplained, like that of "Milton" for "Pindar" in a reference to the "picturesque power" of "Pindar and Dante";[12] here Collier could not have misinterpreted his shorthand, as he did on occasion—for example, in rendering "pointing them out" (shorthand) as

---

[8]For the longhand transcripts, see Foakes, pp. 104, 112, 118, and 127.

[9]See *The Stability of Shakespeare's Text* (1965), especially pp. 47-77.

[10]Foakes, p. 113; see also Collier, p. 122 (Raysor, II, 138).

[11]Foakes, p. 107; "transplace" is a word used elsewhere by Coleridge, as in a marginal note on Jeremy Taylor in *The Literary Remains*, ed. Henry Nelson Coleridge, 4 vols. (London: Pickering, 1836-39), III (1838), 205 (cited in *O.E.D.*)

[12]Foakes, p. 110; "Milton" appears also in the text in Collier, p. 115 (Raysor, II, 134).

"painting them" (Foakes, p. 126)—for he wrote out the word "Pindar" in longhand in his shorthand notes.

In view of his readiness to substitute words and "improve" phrases, it is perhaps not surprising that he also expanded the shorthand notes with numerous additional phrases and sentences. Many of these additions can be explained as expansions of the shorthand notes necessary to clarify and provide continuity, for the shorthand notes often contain only the bare bones of a sentence. Perhaps one example (from Lecture 9) will suffice to illustrate a common feature of the relation between the two sets of notes (the shorthand version is given first):

> i. Shakespeare's characters from Macbeth down to Dogberry are ideal they are not the things but abstracts of the things which great mind may take into itself and naturalize to its own happiness. The Dogberry strikes at some folly reigning at the day and which must forever reign.
>
> ii. Shakespeare's characters from Othello or Macbeth down to Dogberry are ideal: they are not the things, but the abstracts of the things which a great mind may take into itself and naturalize to its own heaven. In the character of Dogberry itself some important truths are conveyed, or some admirable allusion is made to some folly reigning at the time, and which the Poet saw must forever reign. [Foakes, p. 101]

Here Collier expanded considerably the sentence about Dogberry, without changing its drift, and perhaps transformed it into something more like what Coleridge said. At the same time the vigor of "strikes at" is gone; something of Coleridge is lost. The addition of "Othello" at the beginning seems pointless, and could be Collier's. The replacement of "happiness" by "heaven" probably is to be explained as a misreading by Collier of his own shorthand; more will be said about this sort of thing later. It is noteworthy that Collier was not satisfied with "heaven" and changed this word to "conception" in 1856 (p. 100; Raysor, II, 125). The kind of expansion shown in this passage, where the additions on the whole swell what is set down in an abbreviated form in shorthand, seems merely a reasonable attempt on the part of Collier to flesh out his notes and make them more readable.

The longhand notes also contain some more substantial additions, which either develop what is briefly indicated in the shorthand, or, in some instances, introduce something completely new. The most striking example of the first of these kinds of expansion occurs at the end of Lecture 12, where Collier seems to have been unable to cope with Coleridge's peroration, and his shorthand record ends flatly:

> Shakespeare has shown in this the fulness of his powers all that is amiable in nature is combined in Hamlet but in one article: The man living in meditation does no action independent of all meditation.

This is expanded in the longhand version into a much more resonant and powerful close, which it would be pleasant to think is closer to what Coleridge said in the lecture room:

> Shakespeare has shown the fulness and force of his powers; all that is amiable and excellent in nature is combined in Hamlet, with the exception of this one quality: he is a man living in meditation, called upon to act by every motive, human and divine, but the great purpose of life [is] defeated by continually resolving to do, yet doing nothing but resolve. [Foakes, p. 128]

The second kind of addition, of material not even hinted at in the shorthand version, is rarer, but there are several examples, such as this sentence in Lecture 9:

> The reader often feels that some ideal trait of our own is caught, or some nerve has been touched of which we were not before aware, and it is proved that it has been touched by the vibration that we feel, a sort of thrilling, which tells us, that we know ourselves the better for it. [Foakes, p. 102]

[197]

Coleridge had been distinguishing classes of readers, picking up a theme of Lecture 2 in the 1811–12 series.[13] This added sentence is not necessary to the sequence of thought, but Coleridge could have said something like it. There is no way of knowing whether Collier recalled it or invented it.

The various changes and additions so far considered could all be regarded as "improvements," filling out Collier's shorthand notes. It is understandable that Collier should have treated his shorthand in this way, for the notes contain plenty of indications that his shorthand was not good enough to enable him to take down all that Coleridge said. This should not be surprising, since Henry Nelson Coleridge recorded the inability of the famous William Gurney to make sense in shorthand of Coleridge's lectures:

> A very experienced short-hand writer was employed to take down Mr. Coleridge's lectures on Shakespeare, but the manuscript was almost entirely unintelligible. Yet the lecturer was, as he always is, slow and measured. The writer—we have some notion it was no worse an artist than Mr. Gurney himself—gave this account of the difficulty: that with regard to every other speaker whom he had ever heard, however rapid or involved, he could almost always, by long experience in his art, guess the form of the latter part, or apodosis, of the sentence by the form of the beginning; but that the conclusion of every one of Coleridge's sentences was a *surprise* upon him. He was obliged to listen to the last word.[14]

Gurney was eminent enough as a legal and parliamentary shorthand writer to earn a mention in Byron's *Don Juan*, and if such a professional expert could not cope with Coleridge's lectures, Collier must have found them very difficult to record. His difficulties are revealed in various ways. One is his rendering of

---

[13]Collier, p. 13 (Raysor, II, 39; see also I, 220–21).

[14]*Coleridge the Talker: A Series of Contemporary Descriptions and Comments*, ed. Richard W. Armour and Raymond F. Howes (Ithaca: Cornell University Press; London: Oxford University Press, 1940), p. 145.

unfamiliar quotations. With Shakespeare's plays he had no problem, for he could simply jot down a few phrases from the beginning and end of a speech quoted by Coleridge, and copy out the full text into his transcript, a procedure he adopted notably in recording Lecture 12. However, in Lecture 9 Coleridge quoted a poem on Shakespeare first printed in the Second Folio of 1632, and Collier tried to take this down verbatim. Collier did pretty well to start with, after a puzzling error in the first line ("full and clear" for "clear / And equal," wrecking the lineation, as it happens), but it seems that he could not keep up with the speaker. After taking down 14 lines with only minor inaccuracies, he gave up in the middle of line 15, omitting the next 3½ lines altogether. He then took down a further 10 lines, with a much larger number of errors in them, again giving up in the middle of a line, and omitting a further 10 lines before resuming. The omission of the first passage makes no sense, but it is just possible that Coleridge might have left out the second; however, in his transcript Collier copied out both the omitted passages, which suggests that the whole poem was cited in the lecture (Foakes, pp. 104–105). Earlier, in Lecture 8, Coleridge quoted two passages from Hooker's *Laws of Ecclesiastical Polity,* which Collier transcribed into longhand without checking, and his rendering of both is confused and very inaccurate (Foakes, p. 91; these passages were omitted from the 1856 text). Perhaps it was easier to take down verse, where the rhymes must have helped; both instances show that Collier could take down much of what Coleridge said, but had neither the speed nor the competence to record his words accurately and in full.

Another way in which the limitations of Collier's shorthand are shown is in a number of passages which make no sense, and which he either omitted or reconstructed in his longhand transcripts. In Lecture 9 there are three notable examples of shorthand passages Collier did not attempt to transcribe into longhand:[15]

---

[15]See contexts in Foakes, pp. 99, 112, and 115 respectively.

a. He wholly felt it that exquisite feeling in imperfect being might preface of his future existence being wholly [holy?] is often that object presented to him.

b. (the aversion of the sylph) to be tied down to any definite doing who seems to require a mortal to compel him to do anything but when compelled he loves [lives?] *surprise* into it.

c. Effects of which one of the greatest excellencies of Sh and yet more than all in other *nature* of his works and yet with all *splendours* has character of great saints who felt himself to have facts and appearance of life only as means of realising and giving thus replica feelings of *human* creatures that of individual which could not but be found without them.

Since Collier registered consonants, but rarely vowels, in his shorthand, it is not possible to determine whether he meant "wholly" or "holy," "loves" or "lives," and the third passage required a great deal of teasing out—the words italicized remain uncertain. The first passage Collier simply omitted. The second, though obscure, suggests a very interesting observation about Ariel in *The Tempest,* if Coleridge said that Ariel requires a mortal to compel him to act, but when compelled, he loves his service, but Collier seems to have decided it was impenetrable, and in his longhand wrote, "This aversion of the Sylph is kept up throughout the whole." The third passage is hard to decipher, and Collier simply gave up, and wrote, "Coleridge concluded by a panegyric upon Shakespeare," so indicating in his transcript that he was omitting what the lecturer actually said at this point (Foakes, p. 115; Collier, p. 125; Raysor, II, 140; it is worth noting that Collier cut this phrase out of his 1856 text, so concealing the omission of this passage).

In each of these cases Collier's difficulty is apparent; his shorthand does not make sense as it stands, and he decided simply to omit these passages. It may be that his awareness of the inadequacy of his shorthand to record Coleridge's lectures fully left him feeling free to expand and revise his notes; but if so, it might seem the more puzzling that he did not wrest some meaning from passages such as these, rather than omit them.[16] In fact, when he did choose to rework a passage in his shorthand he found difficult to decipher, or obscure in sense, it could be in such a way as to change the original radically and to omit interesting ideas. Perhaps the most notable examples of this occur in the account of *Hamlet* in Lecture 12. In the longhand transcript Collier wrote:

> The first question was, what did Shakespeare mean when he drew the character of Hamlet? Coleridge's belief was that the poet regarded his story before he began to write much in the same light that a painter looked at his canvas before he began to paint. What was the point to which Shakespeare directed himself? He meant to pourtray a person in whose view the external world, and all its incidents and objects, were comparatively dim and of no interest in themselves, and which began to interest only when they were reflected in the mirror of his mind. Hamlet beheld external objects in the same way that a man of vivid imagination, who shuts his eyes, sees what has previously made an impression upon his organs. [Foakes, p. 124]

This flows nicely and makes good sense, but what Collier did was to tidy the beginning and then omit a sentence that loops away from the straight line of argument, reminding us of Gurney's remark that he could not guess the conclusions of Coleridge's sentences from their beginnings. In shorthand the passage runs as follows:

> The first question is what meant Sh by the character of Hamlet. I believe he regarded his stories little more than a painter does his

---

[16]The most striking omission in Lecture 12 is a comparison between Bolingbroke and Macbeth. The reference to Macbeth was omitted from the transcript; see Foakes, p. 123. The shorthand is not easy to make out, but runs thus: "then checked by the eye of York proceeds 'my stooping duty tenderly will show' another example   in Macbeth where Sh gives him the most natural rhodomontade   ." The blank spaces indicate indecipherable signs, partly due to a long smudged inkblot. Perhaps Coleridge referred to Macbeth's sudden changes in III.iv, when he encounters the Ghost of Banquo.

canvas as the circumstance on which he was to write his plays
What is the point to which Sh directed himself? In H he meant to
show us a being whose dizzying intellectual circumstances a man in
whom all we have when we shut our eyes was more strong more
vivid than is consistent with that perfect balance of our being in
which the outward impressions we throughout day force to be
corrected by our uneven circumstances. But in Hamlet he meant
to describe a character in whom the play's external world and all its
incidents are comparatively dim of no interest in themselves but
commencing to interest as soon as they are recollected in causes as
soon as they have formed a part of that other world in which a man
of vivid imagination exists.

In reconstructing this passage for his longhand transcript, Collier carried the image of shutting one's eyes over into the final
sentence, but he sacrificed a great deal else, apparently for the
sake of tidiness of argument and clarity of expression.

It would be misleading to give the impression that Collier took
such license with his shorthand notes frequently; he much more
often expanded than abbreviated them, but even in expanding
he might change or omit what seem characteristic usages of Coleridge. Some excuse may be found in the fact that from time to
time the shorthand notes evidently garble or telescope what Coleridge said, and, in making sense of them, Collier perhaps got
into the habit of rewording as he saw fit. An example of confusion in the shorthand notes is the following from Lecture 9:

The passing in 6 or 12 hours though this depicted 24 hours though
in fact we might have supposed that as easily 20 months as 20
hours because it has become an object of imagination.

Here Collier seems to have lost track of Coleridge's argument in
the lecture room, where, perhaps following Schlegel, he seems
to have begun from the classical principle of confining the action
of a tragedy to a day, and to have gone on to claim that a day is so
much longer than the playing time of a drama that any license
beyond this is permissible, echoing Dr. Johnson's "I know not

where the limits of imagination can be fixed."[17] In this case Collier might have done better to expand, but he contented himself with transcribing it thus:

> The limit allowed by the Greeks was 24 hours, but we might as well take 24 months, because it has already become an object of imagination.[18]

As against such instances of revision that are at least understandable, and arguably necessary to make sense of the shorthand notes, there are many more where Collier's revisions in the transcript translate what Coleridge said into a different idiom, and change the meaning, if only in small ways. So in Lecture 9 Coleridge referred to the phenomenon of the spectre of the Brocken in this way according to the shorthand notes:

> Or as travellers in the north of Germ when the sun rises at the immense tops askance the mountain they see figure gigantic of dimensions so distant and mighty so great in size that they scarce think it credible but which corresponds with their own simulacrum . . . .

In the longhand transcript this is changed, and made more readily intelligible, but the effect is quite different:

> or as a man traversing the Brocken in the north of Germany at sunrise, when the glorious beams are shot ascance the mountain; he sees before him a figure of gigantic proportions and of such elevated dignity, that he only knows it to be himself by the similarity of action . . . . [Foakes, p. 102]

The first recorded use of "simulacrum" in this sense listed in the *O.E.D.* is dated 1805, and perhaps Collier could not make out his

---

[17]This is from the essay on the rules of writing in *The Rambler*, No. 156 (15 Sept. 1751).

[18]Foakes, p. 101. Collier was understandably dissatisfied with this, and revised it thoroughly in 1856; see Collier, p. 99 (Raysor, II, 124).

shorthand, and rendered it as "similarity." There is nothing in the shorthand notes to suggest the phrase "of such elevated dignity," while the longhand leaves out the comment "so great in size that they scarce think it credible."

Another interesting example occurs in Lecture 12, where Coleridge referred to Dr. Johnson's comments on Richard II (Foakes, p. 119). Here Collier added an indecipherable word or two in shorthand in the margin, prefacing the word "adversity," the signs for which he interlined, also as part of the addition; the sentence reads: "he is insolent and presumptious Quotes D^r. J^n. [   ] adversity wise Roman and passive fortitude." Collier rendered this in his longhand as "In his prosperity he is insolent and presumptuous, but in adversity Dr. Johnson says that he was humane and pious," but went on to add a sentence not in the shorthand notes at all: "Dr. Johnson gave him the virtue of a Confessor rather than of a King." What Dr. Johnson actually wrote was that Shakespeare "gave him only passive fortitude, the virtue of a confessor rather than of a King. In his prosperity we saw him imperious and oppressive, but in his distress he is wise, patient, and pious."[19] Coleridge seems to have misquoted Dr. Johnson, but Collier probably took down only part of what he said. It is curious that the shorthand includes two of Dr. Johnson's adjectives, "wise" and "passive," which are both omitted from the longhand version, but this in turn has "pious," which is not in the shorthand. If Collier had consulted Dr. Johnson's commentary when writing out his longhand notes, he presumably would have corrected the quotation. It seems, then, that Collier recalled Coleridge as citing the phrase "the virtue of a confessor rather than of a King," and added this in the longhand, but, in tidying up his shorthand, characteristically muddied what Coleridge said, replacing an interesting misquotation of Coleridge's by a dull one of his own. I suspect that he misread

---

[19] *Johnson on Shakespeare*, the Yale edition of the *Works of Samuel Johnson* (New Haven: Yale University Press, 1968), VII, 440.

his own shorthand, interpreting "Roman" ('rmn' in shorthand) as "humane" ('hmn' in shorthand), and that this misreading added to the confusion.

There is other evidence that Collier could not always decipher his shorthand, or did not take the trouble to do so. Toward the end of Lecture 9 he left a blank where he failed to read his own signs, which are not too difficult to interpret as signifying the word "individual," in the comment on Ariel in *The Tempest:* "all that belongs to Ariel is all that belongs to the delight the mind can receive from external appearances abstracted from any inborn or individual purpose."[20] Here the longhand provides an exact transcript, except for the omission of the word "individual." At other places, Collier seems to have misinterpreted his shorthand, by reading it casually, perhaps, and transcribing what was immediately suggested by the shorthand notation and made sense; so, a little further on in Lecture 9, he transcribed a phrase as "all the strength of contrast is thus acquired" (Foakes, p. 112), where the shorthand has "all the strength in which the contrast is thus secured." "Secured" is much the more appropriate word, besides being the correct reading, but in shorthand symbols the only difference is the addition of the sign for "s" to those for the consonants "c(=q)rd." Then again, in the poem quoted in Lecture 9, Collier, as elsewhere in his shorthand, wrote out some names or difficult terms in longhand, or in longhand abbreviations; there, for instance, boggling at the word "physiognomy," he wrote "phi," and left a blank in the longhand transcript.

Enough evidence has been adduced to illustrate a number of significant aspects of Collier's reporting of Coleridge's lectures. To begin with, his shorthand was not good enough to enable

[20]Foakes, pp. 111-12. In 1856, Collier simply omitted the phrase "abstracted from any inborn or individual purpose" (p. 119; Raysor, II 136), which suggests he either did not collate his longhand notes with the shorthand, or else could not decode his shorthand here.

him to take down all Coleridge's words; the proportion of each lecture that he took down probably varied. The shorthand notes for Lecture 9 are considerably longer than those for Lecture 12—about 4,800 as against 2,500 words—suggesting that Collier made some notation of a large part of the first, but perhaps not much more than half of the second, even allowing for the expansion by quotations from Shakespeare. Both shorthand reports contain a few garbled or incomprehensible passages, where Collier seems to have lost the thread of the argument, and both show that Collier frequently resorted to registering the main words, but not the whole, of sentences. His expectation, as a newspaper reporter, was presumably that he could rely on his memory to fill out his notes when transcribing them as soon as possible afterward. However, it is not certain what interval elapsed between his attendance at Lectures 9 and 12 and the longhand transcripts he made of his notes taken at them.

Collier's habit of expanding his notes, partly from memory, to fill in gaps or make sense of abbreviated phrases or sentences, passes into and overlaps with his inclination to revise and clarify as he transcribed his shorthand. He seems to have wanted above all to present a smooth-flowing, lucid, and coherent text; his concern was to remove roughness, and to make all tidy, rather than to present as accurately as he could what Coleridge said. So he sometimes substituted his own words for those of Coleridge, at the risk of effacing characteristic usages (as "transplaces" is changed to "transports"), or rewrote sentences or paragraphs more in his own than in Coleridge's idiom. Moreover, in a number of instances he found his shorthand notes did not fit into the flow of the transcript, or were confused and obscure, or indecipherable, and simply omitted phrases or passages from his longhand version. In the preface to his edition of *Seven Lectures* in 1856, Collier acknowledged that his text was "full of omissions, owing in some degree to want of facility" on his part, or imperfect because he was "not unfrequently so engrossed, and absorbed by the almost inspired look and manner of the speaker," that he was rendered incapable of taking notes. At the same time, he insisted that he was presenting his notes "merely as they are" (p. xiii), and that he "did not knowingly register a sentence, that did not come from Coleridge's lips" (p. vi). The first statements appear to be true; the last are certainly false. The 1856 text is a much revised, and to some extent Victorianized, reworking of the longhand transcripts, as I have shown elsewhere.[21] It is now clear that the longhand transcripts, in turn, are modified, expanded, and from time to time rewritten versions of what Collier took down in shorthand, at least as far as Lectures 9 and 12 are concerned. Even if many of the added phrases and sentences can be attributed to Collier's memory of what Coleridge said, a great deal of his reworking seems to have been done merely in the interests of providing a tidy and readable version, with little serious concern for the sentences that came from Coleridge's lips.

Having regard to the inadequacies of Collier's shorthand, and the gaps and obscurities in these notes, as well as the uncertainties of transcribing them, it is reasonable to argue that the longhand versions of Lectures 9 and 12 remain the best texts available for these lectures. No shorthand notes survive for Lectures 1, 2, 6, 7, and 8, and for these the longhand notes must be the best text, since the only other version, that of 1856, reprinted in Raysor's standard edition, was much revised and generally made more diffuse by Collier. However, it is important to keep in mind just how uncertain the relation is between the shorthand notes and the full text of the lectures as Coleridge gave them. The longhand notes are at yet a further remove, and neither these, nor by analogy any other contemporary reports of his lectures, can be regarded as providing reliable evidence of his style and vocabulary, quotations and allusions, sources, or possible plagiarisms. Coleridge's lectures on Shakespeare, especially those of 1811–12, have become accepted as a familiar part of his

[21]Foakes (1970), pp. 106-11.

writings, and it is easy to take them for granted as having the same textual authority as works he saw through the press himself. The features of Collier's notes discussed in this essay provide a salutary reminder that Coleridge published none of his lectures on literary subjects, and that for many of them what survives is a more or less inadequate record, dependent not only on a reporter's competence as a shorthand writer, but also on his ability to understand and transmit the essentials of Coleridge's argument.

One detailed difference between the shorthand record and the transcript shows how easily distortions can occur: this relates to the famous allusion to Schlegel in Lecture 9. The various versions of this passage are as follows:

a. Shorthand notes,

> Yesterday friend had left for him a work by German writer and of course had only time to read small part of the vols

b. Longhand transcript

> Yesterday afternoon a friend had left for him a Work by a German Writer, of which Coleridge had had time only to read a small part [Foakes, p. 103]

c. 1856 text

> Yesterday afternoon a friend left a book for me by a German critic, of which I have only had time to read a small part. [Collier, p. 103; Raysor, II, 126]

The received text alters "work" to "book," which could mean the whole of Schlegel's *Vorlesungen Ueber dramatische Kunst und Litteratur*, which were published in Heidelberg in three volumes, two in 1809, the third late in 1810, with the date "1811" on the title page; or "book" could mean merely the last volume, the one containing the lecture on Shakespeare. "Work," in the longhand transcript, seems less ambiguous, and might be taken as referring to the whole set. If my interpretation of Collier's signs is correct, the shorthand notes refer to "the vols," which must mean the whole set. This bears upon the vexing question of Coleridge's reading of Schlegel and borrowing from him. If Coleridge saw the set of Schlegel's volumes for the first time in December 1811, then it would appear to leave unexplained the entry in Crabb Robinson's Diary on 29 January of that year in which he wrote, "Coleridge seemed willing to censure Schiller's and Schlegel's ideas concerning the German idea of the Greek chorus, but he did not fix any reproach upon them that I could comprehend."[22] This comment is itself scarcely comprehensible, and might well be an echo of a conversation in which neither party had more than a vague idea of what was being discussed. What can be said is that Crabb Robinson was reading A. W. Schlegel's lectures, apparently for the first time, in February 1812 (I, 63), but had earlier looked at "Schlegel's fragments," which he read aloud to Charles Lamb in August 1811 (I, 44). Coleridge had read widely in Schiller, and owned a set of the *Athenaeum,* the periodical edited and largely written by Friedrich and A. W. Schlegel between 1798 and 1800, which included about three hundred "fragments," aphorisms, and brief essays written by the two brothers.[23] The "German idea of the Greek chorus" was probably that proposed by Lessing in his *Hamburg Dramaturgy* (1767–69), which Coleridge also knew. Schiller introduced a Chorus into his play *The Bride of Messina* (1803), defending in a preface his use of this device; but it is impossible to guess what either Crabb Robinson or Coleridge thought "Schiller's and Schlegel's ideas" were, and neither Schiller nor

[22]*Henry Crabb Robinson on Books and Their Writers,* ed. Edith J. Morley, 3 vols. (London: Dent, 1938), I, 21.

[23]See George Whalley, "England: Romantic—Romanticism," in *"Romantic" and Its Cognates: The European History of a Word,* ed. Hans Eichner (Toronto: University of Toronto Press, 1972), p. 203.

]6[

Sara *fille:* Fairy Child

CARL WOODRING

On the eve of Christmas Eve, 1802, was born a child of nature and of faerie destined paradoxically to be a scholar and an editor. Her conception might be considered post-romantic, coming about the time of her father's "Letter to [Asra]." Although complaining in that verse letter that his two "Angel Children" bound and plucked out "the Wing-feathers" of his mind, he was procreating a third—who would, by a further turn of irony, fall in love with that mind and devote herself to it. Her myriad-minded and several-souled father was tormented in almost equal degrees by love for Sara Hutchinson (Asra) and an inability to live with the mother of his children. The child Sara's beauty was one of her gifts from another land: at least it could have come from neither of the two women whose name she bore. Sara lived for the next twenty-seven years in Greta Hall, so situated above Keswick and Derwentwater as to teach a child the beautiful, the sublime, and the mundane without book. At two, she was baptized into the dynamic rigors of nature by an accidental fall into the Greta River, an enclosing episode to match her father's night in the damp after taking up a kitchen knife in pursuit of his brother Frank (*CL,* I, 353). Her father, seeking a home near Wordsworth, had found the picturesque kingdom of Greta, had collected post-Pantisocratic in-laws, and had left in a cloud. Her uncle Southey, an efficient paterfamilias, who

[211]

thought her father financially and morally irresponsible to the edge of insanity or beyond it, collected at Greta Hall some 14,000 volumes in eight or nine languages in order to write for a living in the first of several he helped to teach to Sara. In 1813 he became Poet Laureate, an office not included in the *British Imperial Calendar* among such lists as the "Artists of His Majesty's Household," but notable enough to a niece of eleven under his intellectual care. Nearby was the giant Wordsworth who spoke of what her father *could* be, while the female dependents around Uncle Southey spoke reprehendingly of what he had become.

With her mother, Sara had twenty-seven years of a cramped room in a rambling house, self-conscious dependency, and social condescension, but she did not have enough of Catherine Morland in her to discover any wicked wizards or witches in the cupboards. Southey, from his private remarks about Coleridge and his obtuse public combats with Byron, has come down to us as one of the most self-righteous figures in English literature, but Sara knew him as a thoughtful, irreplaceable foster parent. To D. H. Lawrence's rocking-horse boy the walls spoke endlessly of money; to Sara the walls spoke, often in verse, of endless learning. For symmetry opening beyond her pedantic enclosure, she was one of three: there was neat and precise Edith Southey; Dora Wordsworth, nut brown as her aunt Dorothy; and studious, wistful, agile, beautiful Sara. Everything points to Sara as Cinderella, with her maligned absent father as the fairy godmother. Loving her mother, uncle, and cousins, Sara did not see her situation in that way until it became clear that all the elders offered her languages, skills, and stories to prepare her as a governess or—if the star above Greta brought luck to all—a wife.

Properly to show her love for her father she had to go in 1808 to sleep in his bed at Allan Bank, where he lived with the Wordsworths and had an amanuensis for the *Friend* in Sara Hutchinson. There her father told her fairy tales at midnight. The visiting child drew a firm line when asked to call her father's dear friends Dorothy and Sara beautiful. She remembered long enough to tell her own daughter how she had drawn that line.

From day to day and year to year, she was pliancy itself. She accepted intellectual chores too tedious even for Southey, such as translating in three volumes *An Account of the Abipones* from the gnarled Latin of Martin Dobrizhoffer (1822). In translating the *Memoirs of the Chevalier Bayard,* by the Loyal Servant (1825), she recalled the battles of Amadis de Gaul, who had hurled at her in childhood challenges of language and imagination. The intense effort of translation strained her eyes and something hurt her back. There were better writers to translate, Cervantes for example, but a damsel could avoid public distress only by declining to follow literature down the unmaidenly roads of Cervantes—not to speak, as her father did, of Rabelais. Considering the general public voice, including her father's, on such subjects, it is noteworthy that she referred seldom, and never coyly, even in evaluating Jacobean drama, to sexual aspects of literature that propriety asked her to notice only with shock.

Far to the south of England she had a cousin Henry who had even more perplexing trouble with his eyes and severe rheumatic difficulties in his spine. With periods off for recuperation, he had won honors at Cambridge and had become a Chancery barrister at Lincoln's Inn. When the several Coleridges came together in London in December 1822 it can be said that Henry was instantly enamored of his uncle Samuel, so long as a much stronger term is reserved for the rapidly formed, secretly plighted love of Henry and Sara. At first he feared that Sara would accept a proposal from his friend John May; next, and for several years, he feared that she would succumb to pressures from the family. His father, Colonel James Coleridge, no Comberbache, had married into wealth and dignity, and the sickly and impecunious Henry was regarded as proposing marriage to a charming but penniless princess of no earthly abode.

John Moultrie, a friend of Henry's at Eton and of Henry's and her brother Derwent's at Cambridge, tried to describe her in several poems, and perhaps succeeded in "The Poet's Daughter":

A vision crossed my path in youth,—
A brighter none have seen . . . .
The glory of that angel face
Too fair for words to paint:
An emanation she might seem
Of some intense, seraphic dream
By bard or prophet saint
Conceived: and such an one I ween
The author of her birth had been.[1]

As the Southeys were later on to prove fanged combatants of each other, it is no wonder that envy seeped through their references to S.T.C.'s beautiful and accomplished daughter. At the time of the journey southward in 1822, the Southey relatives hoped that she was not to be shown off too much above her station by Lady Beaumont. Wordsworth, with no envy aroused, looked fondly on what she had been and what she had become, "one of the loveliest and best of creatures."[2] William Collins, when Sara was a fairy lass, and George Richmond, when Sara was a widow, portrayed her with an impatient absence around the eyes but with hands crossed in resignation on her lap.

The nervous tears commenced in subserviency continued through her long engagement. One of her attempts to reach her fiancé and her father, in 1826, was stopped, if we adopt the perspective of Sara Hutchinson, because "unluckily her mother accompanied her to Kendal & there persuaded her she was not fit for the journey, dosed her with Laudanum to make her sleep at a time when she could not have been expected to sleep if she

---

[1]John Moultrie, *Poems,* with a Memoir by Derwent Coleridge, rev. ed., 2 vols. (London, 1876), II, 392–93.
[2]*The Correspondence of Henry Crabb Robinson with the Wordsworth Circle,* ed. Edith J. Morley, 2 vols. (Oxford: Clarendon Press, 1927), I, 207.

had had the feeling of a stone . . . and brought her back."[3] Henry's dominant brother John Taylor Coleridge explained some of the reasons why the engagement should be annulled. Sara answered that she was affianced for life, whether for marriage, spinsterhood, or whatever. When they married, after nine years of frustration, her fierce clear-sightedness about his personal traits seems to have reduced in no way, for the next twenty-three years, her devotion. They moved to Hampstead, in walking distance of her father at Highgate.

It would be comforting to accept Earl Griggs's assurance that Sara and her father "were constantly to visit one another" from 1829 until his death in 1834.[4] Records that I have seen disclose few opportunities for such visits. Sara's husband went regularly from Hampstead to Highgate, or from Lincoln's Inn to Highgate on the way to Hampstead, sometimes on foot all the way. Though not strong, he was relatively free in these years of the debilitating pains that more often than not racked Sara and S.T.C. Often ill during pregnancies, Sara had periods of mental anguish from causes that included puerperal fever and "over-nursing." Whether well or unwell, she was annually in Devonshire or at the seaside for a month or six weeks, and in London for similar periods. Her times away were different from S.T.C.'s periods at Ramsgate. Mrs. Coleridge's astonishment at S.T.C.'s "continuous talking" on the day Sara's daughter Edith was christened, in August 1832, can be counted as a further bit of evidence that he had visited Hampstead seldom before that date.[5] Illnesses were afterward more frequent and more prolonged. Sara had not followed Henry's advice of 1827 to write down her

---

[3] *The Letters of Sara Hutchinson from 1800 to 1835,* ed. Kathleen Coburn (Toronto: University of Toronto Press, 1954), p. 322.

[4] Earl Leslie Griggs, *Coleridge Fille: A Biography of Sara Coleridge* (London: Oxford University Press, 1940), p. 67. See also pp. 88, 90.

[5] *Minnow among Tritons: Mrs. S. T. Coleridge's Letters to Thomas Poole 1799–1834,* ed. Stephen Potter (London: Nonesuch Press, 1934), pp. 169, 165.

father's conversation; one reason may have been infrequency of opportunity. Increasingly, a bedridden father and daughter prayed for each other across the heath that separated them. Sara was ill before and after her twins, Berkeley and Florence, were born and died in January 1834. She kept in close touch through Henry until S.T.C.'s death on July 25th. The funeral was attended only by men.

Surviving evidences of Sara's strength are as abundant as evidences of her beauty. She kept a remarkable journal, maternal but searingly honest, of the birth and infancy of Herbert, born at 11:00 A.M. on 7 October 1830.[6] In 1850, fatally afflicted with cancer of the breast, she resisted the pleas of friends like Chauncey Hare Townshend to consult the famous John Elliotson for mesmeric treatment. Contemplating her father's agnosticism with regard to explanations of animal magnetism, she gave in to the extent of accepting treatment, on Elliotson's advice, from Morgan Peter Kavanagh and her own cook, Hannah; but then abandoned the aberrancies in self-respect, explaining that Elliotson was "a good creature" but self-deceived.[7]

When the fairy child, once regaled with midnight fairy tales, grew into the author of *Phantasmion: A Fairy Tale* (1837), what sort of work appeared? The answer, briefly, is a Victorian *Amadis de Gaul,* a *Thalaba* in prose, a *Don Quixote* without Sancho Panza; or, to find later comparisons, a *Lord of the Rings* with less of Disney's Seven Dwarfs, and a Christian, this-world relation of Ursula Le Guin's *Earthsea.* Battle and single combat are subordinated, as in the nearest Oriental analogues, to illusion, spells,

[6]Humanities Research Center, The University of Texas at Austin (hereafter cited as Texas), Sara Coleridge papers, X.B 1.8. Most of Sara's surviving letters are among the Coleridge family papers at the University of Texas, with important exceptions at Dove Cottage and the Victoria University Library, Toronto, and a scattering among major libraries holding the papers of intellectual leaders and prominent figures with whom she corresponded.

[7]Texas, Grantz 360. On the mesmeric treatments, see also Grantz 410–21, 541, 857, 1133, 1141–42, 1212, 1322. There is a useful account of Elliotson in Fred Kaplan's *Dickens and Mesmerism* (Princeton: Princeton University Press, 1975).

unnatural sleep, and dreams. Of the thirty-five or so inset lyrics, mostly fine, some are Southeyan, some notably Shelleyan. There are touches from *The White Doe of Rylstone*.

The inspiring forces were not all literary. Painting and other arts have their place, most pervasively in the descriptions of landscape, more surprisingly as in the iconographic allusion in Chapter 36 to some version of Henry Fuseli's then most notorious work: "Ulander beheld his own Leucoia lying bound at the feet of Malderyl, and the hideous dwarf crouching like a nightmare on her breast."

Next after literature, however, the book draws on Sara's childhood in the Lake country. There are three slender damsels, often together—the heroine Iarine and the sisters Leucoia and Zelneth. The action is overseen and sometimes redirected by fairies recognized in the vicinity of Greta Woods: the dangerous, fishy, slippery water-spirit, Seshelma; the kindly but usually ineffective Spirit of Flowers, Feydeleen; the spirit of the Blast and of clouds, Oloola; the unattractive Valhorga, male Spirit of the Earth, especially of caverns; the Spirit of the Woods; and Phantasmion's guardian, Potentilla, the fairy artisan of insects. The most memorably exciting passages are not those of combat between Phantasmion and his enemy Glandreth or his rival Karadan, but those descriptive of Potentilla's intervention. Thrust into a dungeon by Glandreth's forces (Ch. 22), "Phantasmion beheld a multitude of saw-flies with yellow bodies and black heads, flitting toward the light of the lamp; along with them came numbers of wasps, and the youth shrank as he beheld the mingled swarm approaching himself." The flies and wasps, alighting on the cords that bound his arms and wings, weakened the threads until he could snap them. Next a swarm of bees deposited above his head "the honey which they had just collected in the gardens of the island." The spirit of insects is exactly the right fairy guardian for any boy who wishes without evil intent for wings.

The story and its topography return us to the legends of a

faith exercised and recorded indoors. In antecendent events, narrated in the course of present action, Penselimer of Almaterra dropped the Silver Pitcher awarded by the Spirit of Flowers, whereupon his betrothed, Anthemmina, gave the Pitcher to Dorimant of Palmland, who in turn gave it to Albinian of Rockland, soon coaxed unhappily to marry Anthemmina, who then disappeared. By this first misadventure and a second unfortunate marriage to Maudra of Tigridia, Albinian is reduced to a withered uselessness not greatly different from the moonless insanity (*not* lunacy) of Penselimer. In the older generation, the good want strength. To marry Iarine, Phantasmion must surpass her cousin Karadan (son of Magnart of Polyanthida, and brother of Zelneth and Leucoia) for possession of the Silver Pitcher. The name Polyanthida suggests a land of many flowers, but not entirely floral. Magnart belongs to the literary line of Merlin. His son Karadan morally vacillates. Clearly, then, without expecting help from Polyanthida, Phantasmion must gather allies to overthrow the usurpers of Rockland (Maudra and Glandreth), to restore Albinian and Penselimer to personal health and kingly power, and to afford thrones and brides to worthy claimants. Much of this is what it sounds like, a vastly more sober version of such botanical tales by E. T. A. Hoffmann as "Datura Fastuosa" and his nearer analogue, "The King's Bride," in which the daughter of Herr Dapsul von Zabeltau marries the King of Carrots.

Signs of Zelneth's interest in Phantasmion are accompanied by a lyric concerning the dangers of loving the heights when a "blossomed vale" beckons (Ch. 11), but all three slender maidens are presumed to be appropriately rewarded when Penselimer marries Zelneth, and Ulander, made king of Tigridia, takes Leucoia as Queen. Though unacceptable to later feminists, this pecking order seems in the tale as faithful to the trials of existence as the pointed descriptions of perplexity, anxious dreams, and illness. "Hence," said Mona Wilson of Sara's accounts in *Phantasmion* of death and insanity, "the imaginative child will find this book a better preparation for life than a simpler story with a direct moral purpose."[8] Whatever the justice to the damsels, for the male rivals the law later to be expounded by Bronson Howard, that three good hearts cannot beat as one, is put into force. Karadan, not, one supposes, because he woos his cousin, but because his rival is superior in interest to *us*, must and does die. The important law for Sara is one reiterated by her father, by Wordsworth, and by Lamb. She declares it in "L'Envoy of *Phantasmion*": imagination, not moral precept, brings growth. Worldlings can escape the "mickle harm" of worldly toil by avoiding cautionary moral tales and performing the sacred duty of escape into airy dreams. A second stanza goes further: even to the tender spirit who aspires to "blessed works and noblest love," an imaginative flight (of beautiful insects) can do no harm.

In more obvious ways than are shown in *Phantasmion*, Sara *fille* had a sympathetic understanding of her father's mind, and of his chief subjects, superior to that of her brothers and seldom matched by later scholars. By 1823 she had already become one of the most thoughtfully appreciative readers her father's prose has ever had. In letters to her brothers Hartley and Derwent after S.T.C.'s death, she will begin with references to "our father" but then later in each letter refer to him as "my father." The transition, conscious or not, is justified by her performance as interpreter. Of her public references to "my Father" also, in the dedication of the *Biographia Literaria* of 1847 to Wordsworth, as in the Advertisement, Introduction, and notes to those two volumes, one soon feels the appropriateness, if not in the clarity of her style then in the reasoned discriminations. One sees the kinship with S.T.C., for example, in her distinction between a suitable analogy for infant baptism and an unsuitable analogy: "If we throw a stone into the still unmoving pool, the waters leap

---

[8]Mona Wilson, "Sara Coleridge," *Those Were Muses* (London: Sidgwick & Jackson, 1924), pp. 222–23.

up: the pool has not stirred itself, but it co-operates in the pro-
duction of motion." So the corresponsive act of the baptized child.
Not so in the usual erroneous analogy: ". . . *as* a seed is set in the
ground and remains inert and latent for a time, then germi-
nates, shoots up and bears fruit, *so* grace may be poured into the
soul of a child incapable of moral acts, may remain latent for a
time, then, when reason and the moral sense have come into
play, may produce good thoughts and good works, the fruit of
the Spirit."[9] Whoever could accept the latter analogy might
make the double error of believing S.T.C. a pantheist and of
seeing no wrong in the passive view of mind and soul thereby
attributed to him.

The narrowest of her arguments with Derwent is of keen importance for the text of Coleridge's poems. In 1851, when she
and Derwent were preparing a new edition of the poetry, she
was determined to omit juvenile trivia and "certain sportive effusions of Mr. C.'s later years" on the plea that it was her husband who had added them to the edition of 1834. And in fact
Henry had written on 20 March 1834, to his brother John
Taylor Coleridge: "I have endeavored to collect every thing, &
the arrangement & corrections give me much trouble."[10] Sara
wrote on 23 January 1852, to Derwent, with regard to "The
Nose," "Inside the Coach," "Devonshire Roads," "Happiness,"
and other pieces:

> My dear Henry found these poems in old MS. books & in all the
> ardour of first love, would insert them in the new edition. He had in
> him the strangest mixture of high taste and low taste, passion &
> unselectness, delicacy (or *particularity*) and exceeding freeness—
> dignity and familiarity. I think by this time he would have been
> ready to discard these *puerilia*. But the truth is, *it is our judgment*

---

[9]*Biographia Literaria or Biographical Sketches of My Literary Life and Opinions,*
Second Edition Prepared for Publication in Part by the Late Henry Nelson
Coleridge, Completed and Published by His Widow, 2 vols. (London: Pickering,
1847), I, lxxxi n.
[10]British Museum Add. MS. 47,557, f. 103^v.

versus H.N.C. not our judgment against STC, either unbiassed, or swayed by friends, which constitutes our great exertion of editorial boldness. The fact must have been that my Father never troubled his head about the edition of 1834—left it entirely to Henry— Had he given the matter a thought, he never COULD have sanctioned the publication of poems he scorned in 1796.[11]

An editor today, once he has excluded the poems and fragments by others copied from the notebooks and published as Coleridge's by E. H. Coleridge, would not be inclined to banish altogether any effusions or trivia identifiable as Coleridge's. But Sara's *caveat* is important, particularly as it bears on the question of text.

E. H. Coleridge concluded that Coleridge himself was responsible for the text of his *Poetical Works* of 1834 (*CPW*, I, iii–iv), but Sara's testimony, along with Henry's description of his procedure, gives such assurance a shake. As early as 1830, when Henry was readying the prefatory matter to the second edition of *Aids to Reflection* (and also the second edition of *On the Constitution of the Church and State*), Coleridge wrote: "I assure you, that I have quite confidence enough in your taste & judgement to give you a Chart Blanch for any amendments in the style"— including the style of expressing the relation of the work to its origins in Leighton (*CL*, VI, 849). It is unlikely that Henry would deliberately have made changes in the texts of Coleridge's poems, but he felt free to adjust titles, notes, the "arrangement & corrections," and concerning the text he was fallible. No change between the editions of 1829 and 1834 should be admitted into a modern edition without evidence other than the edition of 1834 for Coleridge's authority to introduce the change.[12] Sara's prin-

---

[11]Texas, Grantz 96. See also Grantz 133, 134, 136.
[12]I have pointed on an earlier occasion to "Ode on the Departing Year," published under that title in all appearances until 1834, when the preposition *on* became *to*. On the change from "A Trifle" to "A Character" see Griggs, *Coleridge Fille*, p. 89.

ciple with regard to the edition of 1834 shares her customary soundness.

After Henry's death in 1843—in editions of *Biographia Literaria* (1847), *Aids to Reflection* (1848), and *Essays on His Own Times* (1850), and elsewhere—Sara was not only to deal subtly with Coleridge's opponents and misinterpreters in politics and religion, but also to deal subtly with both his relation to his sources and the general Victorian significance of his sources, from St. Paul and Luther to Fichte and Schelling, while establishing her own positions next to his on such subjects as baptism, atonement, the Eucharist, catholicity, and Stuart dramatists. She retained her loyalty to Southey as well as to her mother, both important to her personally, but her father was a mind important to English-speaking and English-reading societies, everywhere and for the prophesiable future. As thinker, he was not from faerie.

]7[

James Marsh as
Editor of Coleridge

ANTHONY JOHN HARDING

Roswell Marsh, writing to his brother James on 17 July 1824, expressed satisfaction at seeing James at last settled in a reasonably secure employment:

> You do not mention the particular department in which you are likely to be permanently engaged at Hamden Sidney College, but I presume it is somehow connected with the theological Seminary founding there. If so, I rejoice that you have fallen in a situation where you can gratify what appears to be your taste for general Science in unison with the duties of an useful & lucrative employment.[1]

[1]James Marsh Collection, Guy W. Bailey Memorial Library, University of Vermont, Folder 2.2 (hereafter cited as JMC plus folder number). I am grateful to Mr. T. D. Seymour Bassett and Mr. John Buechler for their permission to use the xerox facsimiles of papers in the Marsh Collection, and for their help and advice, and to Dr. Walter Knowlton Hall for granting permission to quote from the Marsh Papers. I should also like to thank Professor Claud Thompson, of the University of Saskatchewan, for valuable bibliographical assistance; Dr. Norman Pittenger, King's College, Cambridge, for reading the MS and making many helpful comments; Professor David Hiatt, University of Saskatchewan, for his useful suggestions; Professor David Waite, of Butler University, Indiana, for (in a manner) introducing me to Marsh; the staff of the Reference Department, University of Saskatchewan Library, for coping so well with my exorbitant de-

Marsh's new post, as Professor of Languages, was in fact his second at Hampden-Sydney College, Prince Edward County, Virginia (he has been Tutor there in 1823), but the "taste for general Science" which so puzzled his brother would within little more than two years win Marsh a position of even more usefulness, and not a little fame: the Presidency of the University of Vermont.

The story of James Marsh's rescue of the University of Vermont from near-bankruptcy, his curricular innovations, and the prodigious reputation he gained as a teacher, does not need retelling here.[2] This essay is concerned rather with the connection between Marsh's "taste for general Science" and one other venture of his, the publication of Coleridge's *Aids to Reflection* (Burlington, 1829), the first American edition of that work.

Like Coleridge himself, Marsh possessed a mind which was not capable of remaining content with half-knowledge. Coleridge's frequent expressions of dissatisfaction with Locke and his school, his feeling that to reduce the human mind to a repository for accumulated, classified sense data was a "wilful res-

---

mands upon their services; and my wife, for her immense patience and encouragement.

After this essay had been prepared for publication, my attention was drawn by a 1977 bibliography to Peter C. Carafiol's article "James Marsh's American *Aids to Reflection*," in *New England Quarterly*, 49 (1976), 27–45. Carafiol examines more fully than I have been able to the response of Emerson, Alcott, and other transcendentalists to Marsh's edition of *Aids*, but he does not pay as much attention to Marsh's motives and interests in publishing the work.

[2]The standard source is Joseph Torrey's "Memoir" in his edition of *The Remains of the Rev. James Marsh, D.D.,* 2d ed. (New York: Mark H. Newman, 1845). Useful accounts of Marsh's intellectual development may be found in John Wright Buckham, "James Marsh and Coleridge," *Bibliotheca Sacra*, 61 (1904), 305–17; John Dewey, "James Marsh and American Philosophy," *Journal of the History of Ideas*, 2 (1941), 131–50; Marjorie H. Nicolson, "James Marsh and the Vermont Transcendentalists," *Philosophical Review*, 34 (1925), 28–50; and Ruth Helen Williams White, "James Marsh—Educator," Diss., University of Southern Mississippi, 1963. Lewis S. Feuer, in "James Marsh and the Conservative Transcendentalist Philosophy: A Political Interpretation," *New England Quarterly*, 31 (1958), 3–31, evaluates Marsh's career from the standpoint of dialectical materialism.

ignation of intellect" against which human nature itself must rebel (*BL*, I, 93), had spoken home to Marsh as he commenced his theological studies. Joseph Torrey's "Memoir" describes in some detail the religious experience Marsh underwent in 1815: first the conviction of his unworthiness and hardness of heart, the troubling doubts of his own existence which came upon him when reading Euclid, the overwhelming sense of the glory of God and the certitude of His reality which dispelled these horrors, and the public declaration of faith he made on 7 August 1815 (pp. 17–21). Frequently overlooked in accounts of Marsh's intellectual development is Torrey's statement that, as a result of this conversion, Marsh rededicated himself still more devoutly to the pursuit of knowledge. For Marsh, as for Coleridge, there could be no undefined terms in the language of the intellect; no tacit agreement to consign God, or Being, to the inaccessible outer ranges of the mental landscape. Coleridge's conviction that "Truth is the correlative of Being," and that "intelligence and being are reciprocally each other's substrate" (*BL*, I, 94), is echoed in Torrey's summary of Marsh's lifelong aim: to find and express "that which imparts to truth its living reality; which connects knowing with being" (p. 114). No philosophy that solved its problems by severing this vital link between what exists and what is "known" could henceforth satisfy Marsh.

In one respect, however, the intellectual journey Marsh undertook—from conventional outward piety to a revelatory experience of God, a public profession of faith, and a lifelong quest for a truly Christian philosophy—differed markedly from Coleridge's. Marsh had become a convinced theist and Christian without ever embracing Spinozism, and so could not follow Coleridge in suffering the creative tension between the rival systems of "it is" and "I Am," the splendors of *Naturphilosophie* and the moral certainties of revealed religion.[3] Paradoxically, perhaps, Marsh's entire innocence of pantheism was to be his most serious

[3]See Thomas McFarland, *Coleridge and the Pantheist Tradition* (Oxford: Clarendon Press, 1969), Ch. 3.

weakness as a commentator on Coleridge; but when Torrey says of him that, while at the Andover Theological Seminary, he "felt himself bound to know the grounds of every thing he professed to understand and believe" (p. 29), we can see at once why Marsh would have been attracted to Coleridge, and also why he would have been lacking in *rapport* with Coleridge in this one important respect.

Andover Seminary was in any case an exception to the general rule of New England theological colleges, where Calvinism was so often taught alongside the Lockean philosophy that the two sets of doctrines seemed to have become a single belief, a new unchallenged orthodoxy. Though Calvinist in affiliation, having been founded in 1805 in a reaction against the Unitarian leanings of Harvard under Henry Ware, Andover had in its Professor of Sacred Literature, Moses Stuart, perhaps the most distinguished of the early importers of German philosophy and biblical scholarship into America.[4] Marsh's search for the principles by which the various departments of knowledge might be unified into a living whole thus began under the aegis of a teacher well qualified to point the way. From Coleridge's *Biographia Literaria* and Madame de Staël's *De l'Allemagne* Marsh graduated, in the winter of 1820–1821, to Kant's *Critique of Pure Reason* (Torrey, p. 43), which (like Emerson after him) he found to be at once a liberating experience and—when too strictly interpreted—an unsatisfying alternative to traditional faith. Kant's distinction between the Pure and the Practical Reason later became, in Marsh's hands, a means of clearing the ground for the unrestricted operation of the Practical Reason, the reconstruction of metaphysics upon a firmly theological basis. In a manuscript dated March 1834 and headed "Memoranda," Marsh wrote:

[4]Harold Clarke Goddard, *Studies in New England Transcendentalism* (New York: Columbia University Press, 1908; rpt. New York: Hillary House, 1960), p. 88; Nicolson, pp. 38–39. On Stuart, see Nicolson, p. 32.

Metaphysics is therefore also in strict propriety one with theology
& metaphysics without theology is an absurdity. But on the other
hand too theology is essentially only metaphysics & a knowledge of
it can proceed only out of the reason as its source. —Reason is
therefore not indeed the fountain but the corresponding sense &
the proper test of all revelation ... [;] faith, to which revelation
originally directs itself is nothing else than the yet undeveloped
reason as reason again is nothing more nor less than faith distinctly
manifested to our consciousness. [JMC 3.5]

Religious *experience,* therefore, not theoretical assent to a
half-comprehended dogma, was Marsh's point of departure,
and his teaching was in turn intended to equip his students for
their active service as ministers of the Gospel. A philosophy of
mind which treated religious experience as lying outside the
realm of legitimate inquiry would be of no use to the young
ordinands Marsh taught. Even when the subject under discussion was not a specifically theological one, Marsh upheld the
validity of religious experience; for example, a lecture on
"Mind" quotes (*variatim*) Coleridge's "Credidi, ideóque intellexi,
appears to me the dictate equally of Philosophy and Religion"
(*BL,* II, 216) and proceeds: "Why should we cling to abstract
principles and lifeless dogmas while the sentiments the feelings
of which the dogmas are nothing more than the *expositors* are
treated as if without the bounds of all philosophy? Let the dead
bury their dead. Moral and religious feelings are after all the
living ground of all moral and religious knowledge" (JMC 3.3).
This is close in spirit, if not in phraseology, to Coleridge's assertion that the sense of the "exceeding *desireableness*" of Christianity is "the true FOUNDATION of the spiritual Edifice," and the
"actual *Trial* of the Faith in Christ" is its roof and keystone. What
Coleridge's original metaphor of the Temple of Faith is meant to
demonstrate is that no one can "know" truth without conform-
ing to that truth—that is, becoming a Christian and experiencing
Christianity's conformity with Reason: "Credidi, ideóque intellexi." The doubter who objects that this argument is circular

[227]

will be told that by the lesser light of the Understanding it indeed appears circular, but Reason will be found to be its own sufficient evidence. The division between "knowing" and "being" that troubles the empirical philosopher is thus seen to be a false division, created by the exclusion of intelligence itself—or rather the knowledge that the world is intelligently ordered, and is therefore congruent with the mind of man—from the philosopher's realm of inquiry (*BL,* II, 215–16).

But for Marsh the existence of a harmony, congruence, or compatibility between the human mind and the universe did not mean that matter and mind, the natural world and the spiritual, were ultimately one and the same. As has been noted, Marsh's desire for unity of knowledge never led him toward pantheism (nor indeed toward Panentheism, Karl Christian Friedrich Krause's more orthodox doctrine, published in 1828, that everything finite is *in* God, but essentially different from God).[5] As much as the crassest materialism, pantheism seemed to Marsh to run counter to the truth of individual religious experience, including his own: we do not find him comparing Spinoza with St. Paul, as Coleridge does in Chapter XXIV of *Biographia* (II, 217). The strength of the Puritan tradition in America, for Marsh, was that it recognized the eternal antipathy between the natural and the spiritual, on which any understanding of "regeneration" according to the Gospel must be based. Reading *Aids to Reflection* in 1826 (Torrey, p. 91), Marsh came across such statements as "the most general and negative definition of nature is, whatever is not spirit; and *vice versa* of spirit, that which is not comprehended in nature; or in the language of our elder divines,

---

[5]Krause's "orthodoxy" is questioned by Thomas McFarland, *Coleridge and the Pantheist Tradition* (New York: Oxford University Press, 1968; Oxford: Clarendon Press, 1969), pp. 269–70: but theologians such as W. R. Inge and von Hügel approved Panentheism, and some affirmations of St. Thomas Aquinas and St. Augustine will bear a "Panentheistic" interpretation. (I am indebted for this observation to Dr. Norman Pittenger.)

that which transcends nature."[6] Such language must have struck Marsh as the authentic language of "Spiritual Religion," a sufficient corrective not only to the "shallow empiricism" of the materialists but also to the specious splendors of pantheism: "He saw, or thought he saw, in the current systems of explanation, a strong and necessary tendency to materialism on the one hand. He knew also, that the rejection of these theories might easily lead to their corresponding opposite, a seductive and pernicious pantheism. Both theories agreeing in the denial of the true spiritual character of man."[7] Marsh's use of Coleridgean phraseology in his sermons, which the Rev. Noah Porter criticized as "subservient" in his otherwise predominantly favorable assessment of Marsh,[8] is explained if not excused by the fact that Coleridge alone seemed to speak a language that recognized the validity of religious experience without abandoning the attempt at a consistent theory of mind, the kind of theory Marsh needed in order to achieve the long-sought-after principles of unity in knowledge.

Coleridge's contradistinction between the spiritual and the natural thus enabled Marsh to describe the transcendental philosophy (in a letter to George Wilson, a minister who had evidently asked for some elucidation) as simply a philosophical statement of the evangelist's claim, "I live, yet not I, but Christ liveth in me." Through the spiritual part it was possible to know Christ "inwardly & spiritually" as well as "after the flesh as we know our fellow men i.e. historically & from outward experience" (JMC 3.9). Marsh could not have been expected to foresee the parting of the ways between Christianity and tran-

---

[6]"Aphorisms on That Which Is Indeed Spiritual Religion": "Reflections Introductory to Aphorism X."

[7]John Wheeler, *A Discourse, Delivered July 6, 1842, at the Funeral of James Marsh, D.D.* (Burlington, Vt.: Chauncey Goodrich, 1842), p. 13.

[8]Noah Porter, "Coleridge and His American Disciples," *Bibliotheca Sacra,* 4 (1847), 163.

scendentalism, when later transcendentalists, as O. B. Frothingham points out, applied the Christological language of St. Paul
and St. John to the human soul itself, destroying the concept of
regeneration and treating Christianity as nothing more than "an
illustrious form of natural religion."[9] It is thus a distortion to
ascribe to Calvinism merely a negative influence on the beginnings of the transcendental movement (as in Goddard, p. 42).
Marsh inherited from Andover, not the hatred of moribund
dogma that is sometimes supposed to be one of the roots of
transcendentalism, but a sense of the inwardness that was—for
him—an essential part of religious faith, allied with a respect for
the intellect that (as Porter observed, p. 138) was in the 1820s all
too rare among New England theologians.

Before Marsh read *Aids to Reflection* in 1826, Torrey asserts (p.
91), he had already conceived the idea of bringing the profound-
er theology of Baxter's era to the notice of a public rapidly
becoming dead to the things of the spirit. However, the very
"pseudo-rationalism" which was the most obvious symptom of
the disease would be likely to impede the patient's recovery by
making the cure seem inaccessible and remote, perhaps even
undesirable. An undiluted dose of seventeenth-century theology
would do no good to a public who venerated the empirical philosophy of Locke, Reid, and Stewart. So closely had their "system" become linked with Christian orthodoxy that a rejection of
Locke seemed a rejection of Christianity itself.[10] Yet an alternative philosophy of mind must be provided before Leighton, Baxter, Burnet, and Jeremy Taylor could speak home to the New
England reading public. That philosophy of mind lay ready to

[9] O. B. Frothingham, *Transcendentalism in New England* (New York: Harper,
1959), p. 204.
[10] Marsh, "Preliminary Essay," in *Aids to Reflection, in the Formation of a Manly
Character* ... ; First American, from the first London Edition; with an Appendix ... together with a Preliminary Essay, and Additional Notes, By James
Marsh, President of the University of Vermont (Burlington, Vt.: Chauncey
Goodrich, 1829), pp. xliv–xlv.

hand in Coleridge's latest work—an unexpected source, it seems, as most American readers, even those who had read the *Lay Sermons,* thought of Coleridge's prose as addressing itself more to general philosophical and political problems than to metaphysical and theological ones. Marsh found in *Aids to Reflection,* as Buckham expressed it, "the enflowered and perfect statements of truths which had been struggling for expression in his own mind" (p. 308). Buckham's suggestion of the organic metaphor in the word "enflowered" expresses well the sense of completion and fulfilment with which Marsh—already familiar with the Kantian basis of Coleridge's arguments—must have read *Aids.* Out of the nettle of danger (for metaphysical speculation was indeed considered dangerous) must the flower of safety be plucked.

Aids to Reflection was not to be presented as a strictly philosophical work, however. James Murdock observed in 1842 that young theologians in the 1820s and 1830s used Coleridge's writings, especially Marsh's edition of *Aids,* as a more palatable version of Kant, even though Murdock himself described the book as "not so much a treatise on philosophy, as a treatise on practical or experimental religion."[11] While it does use some Kantian tools to achieve its main purpose, the reassertion of the essentials of Christian faith, that the book should at the same time be a prolegomenon to Kant was no part of Marsh's intention. But those for whom Coleridge and Kant were equally untrustworthy authorities (for example, the reviewer for the conservative *Quarterly Christian Spectator*) did not scruple to lump Kant together with Coleridge as a cloudy and heterodox reasoner. Thus not only the "transcendentalists" themselves, but also those hostile to transcendentalism, were guilty of blurring or ignoring the real differences between Kant and Coleridge (most significantly, Coleridge's belief, which permeates *Aids to*

---

[11] James Murdock, *Sketches of Modern Philosophy* (Hartford, Conn.: J. C. Wells, 1842), p. 158—hereafter cited as *Sketches.*

Reflection, that the ideas of Reason—Conscience, Free Will, Immortality—are constitutive, not merely regulative, as Kant had argued).

This taint of "German metaphysics" was not the only feature of *Aids to Reflection* which might render it unpalatable to New England readers educated in the tradition of Locke and eighteenth-century neoclassicism. Its very form—a series of "aphorisms" from old authors, collected under various heads, and interspersed with reflective passages of wildly varying length—would make it appear to the classically educated reader an extravagant piece of Gothic mystification. Where could be found the unifying principle of such a work? Should not Marsh have feared the accusation that he was foisting on the public what was really little more than an elaborate kind of commonplace-book?

Marsh had already confronted the issue of classical "unity" versus modern conceptions of "organic unity" in his important essay "Ancient and Modern Poetry" (1822).[12] Although the essay is not primarily concerned with prose forms, it shows how well Marsh would have been prepared to defend the "irregularity" of a work such as *Aids,* in that it places him firmly with Madame de Staël, Schlegel, and Coleridge, and against Boileau, Addison, and Johnson. He praises di Breme for having adopted "German" notions of creative genius, and for having respected the "forms and objects" of modern literature, in his defense of Madame de Staël against the attacks of the Italian neoclassicists. It was an excellent thing for the pre-Christian poets to represent noble and heroic outward actions, and to exhibit in their works the corresponding kind of unity, that is, unity in the grouping of external objects and events. Modern, which is to say Christian, literature must of necessity place a lower value on merely "ex-

---

[12]Unsigned review by Marsh hereafter cited as "Ancient and Modern Poetry": "*Intorno all'ingiustizia di alcuni guidizii letterarii Italiania. Discorso di Lodovico Arborio Gattinara di Breme, figlio . . .* 1816" (running titles: "Present Literature of Italy," "Ancient and Modern Poetry"), *North American Review,* 15 (1822), 94–131.

ternal" objects. Invoking *Biographia Literaria,* and Coleridge's discussion of the subjective-objective distinction in *Blackwood's* (1821), Marsh argues that whereas the classical poets rightly applied their efforts to the depiction of "objective" events, the moderns have turned inward, finding in the subjective sphere "higher interests" and "sublimer conceptions" than all the objects of the external world can supply (pp. 106–07). This is not to say that those laws which the Greek writers established can comfortably be forgotten; as F. W. Schlegel has shown, true genius will always conform to such laws, without any sense of having to strive after them, for these laws originate within the human mind itself. Both the ancients and the moderns, therefore, recognize laws of unity; but modern literature substitutes a unity of emotional and spiritual development for that unity of outward events which the ancient writers cultivated. "Mind and its attributes, the spiritual and 'the things that are not seen,' are more the direct and immediate objects of our thoughts" (p. 108).

Insofar, then, as *Aids to Reflection* was organized around a single spiritual purpose, it could be seen by Marsh as a "unified" work. Marsh evidently anticipated such criticisms as those made by Murdock—that Coleridge, in relying on aphorisms instead of "logical definitions and fully developed arguments," was asking too much of his readers and assuming that they would be able to understand him from mere hints and brilliant fragments of thought (*Sketches,* p. 159). The opening paragraphs of Marsh's "Preliminary Essay" therefore stress that *Aids* offered not a "speculative system of doctrines built upon established premises," but a means of turning the mind "back upon the premises themselves" (p. viii). It is possible for someone else to aid us in the work of "reflection," turning the mind back upon its own laws, for these laws are the same for everyone; but the work of such an explorer must be tested and verified in each individual's consciousness. In this sense, Coleridge could claim to have made a contribution to the "science of words" (pp. ix, viii). With this argument, Marsh establishes a new distinction to be set alongside

Coleridge's own: a distinction between "speculation," which works outward from established premises, and "reflection," which attempts to uncover in the mind itself the basis for such premises.

> [T]he primary tendency and design of the work is, not to establish this or that system, but to cultivate in every mind the power and the will to seek earnestly and steadfastly for the truth in the only direction, in which it can ever be found . . . . If the work become the occasion of controversy at all, I should expect it from those, who, instead of *reflecting* deeply upon the first principles of truth in their own reason and conscience and in the word of God, are more accustomed to *speculate*—that is, from premises given or assumed, but considered unquestionable, as the constituted point of observation, to look abroad upon the whole field of their intellectual vision, and *thence* to decide upon the true form and dimensions of all which meets their view. [pp. x, xi–xii]

Marsh's reiteration of his belief that the truth will by this method be discovered to be in accord with the Word of God— "the first principles of truth in . . . reason and conscience and in the word of God"—suggests that another enemy to true faith, besides deism and ultra-Calvinism, is present to his mind: that more insidious European import, German biblical criticism. Marsh's attitude toward the higher criticism, like Coleridge's, was ambivalent; while wishing to see American scholarship set free from the shackles of dogmatism and a narrow literalist reading of Scripture, he spoke of the "extravagances of German criticism or of Andover exegesis" (JMC 3.3), and his essay "Ancient and Modern Poetry" (1822) ends with a warning against "turning all our religion to poetry." Whereas the ancients, and Christians in the Middle Ages, experienced no conflict between the ventures of the imagination and their usual criteria of objective truth, poetry and history being to them one and the same, the modern believer has to know where well-founded belief ends and fantasy begins; and even if doubt is conquered, the prior battle between doubt and faith must inevitably change the nature of faith. "In regard to the objects of faith, the very habit of examining them philosophically destroys one half their power over us, because, though we may be rationally convinced, we still admit them with a salvo on the side of reason, and our faith is at last but an imperfect one . . . " (pp. 131, 123).

The essential character of Christianity could be preserved, it seemed, only by placing the groundwork of belief where Coleridge had placed it, in the mind's knowledge of its own laws. In the correspondence between the mind's knowledge of itself and the Pauline affirmations concerning the "mind of Christ," the Christian would find the only remaining solid confirmation of his faith, beyond all danger of erosion from historical criticism.

And yet, Marsh faced another danger in directing his readers to "reflect" in transcendental fashion rather than merely to "speculate": namely, that he would be accused of reducing Christianity to a particular set of philosophical doctrines, that despite his protestations to the contrary many readers would take his careful explications of theory to be an attempt to substitute Coleridgean metaphysics for the Gospels themselves. (This accusation was in fact made by Noah Porter.)[13] But without Coleridgean metaphysics, that which made Christianity unique among religions, the antithesis of "natural" and "spiritual," would inevitably be lost—either to a degrading materialism or to an ostensibly noble but essentially pernicious pantheism. Materialism, or rather the materialistic tendencies of Lockean empiricism, was Marsh's chief object of attack in the "Preliminary Essay," however, being closer at hand—and, perhaps, easier to prove ungodly—than pantheism.

According to Marsh, the chief difficulty experienced by those of his contemporaries who were called to propagate the Gospel message was that, though the New Testament distinctly spoke of "spiritual" and "natural" as opposite terms, it was received and taught in conjunction with a philosophy that tended to deny the

[13]Porter, p. 141. See also Dewey, p. 136.

meaning of that distinction. According to the system of Locke, Reid, and Stewart, wrote Marsh in the "Preliminary Essay," "the same *law of cause and effect* is the *law of the universe*. It extends to the *moral* and *spiritual* ... no less than to the properly *natural* powers and agencies of our being. The acts of the *free-will* are pre-determined by a cause *out of the will*, according to the same law of cause and effect, which controls the changes in the physical world" (p. xxx). But however many susceptibilities and capacities are added to the nature of X, a hypothetical creature, as long as X is bound by the laws of cause and effect which control the material universe it cannot be considered "human." Does not the human race exhibit observable traits and faculties which cannot be accounted for by any conceivable "natural law"? Marsh asked. "Would any supposable addition to the *degree* merely of those powers which we ascribe to brutes render them *rational* beings, and remove the sacred distinction, which law and reason have sanctioned, between things and persons? Will any such addition account for our having—what the brute is supposed not to have—the pure *ideas* of the geometrician, the power of ideal construction, the intuition of geometrical or other necessary and universal truths?" (p. xlii).

This may appear familiar ground to the reader of *The Friend* and *Lay Sermons*. There is, however, an important difference between Coleridge arguing for the existence of a rational faculty in the human race and Marsh addressing himself to the same problem: in the phrase "the *degree* merely of those powers which we ascribe to brutes" Marsh implies that we can be sure of our absolute superiority over the animal kingdom because our powers are self-evidently different in kind from theirs. (He will then argue that these uniquely human powers of Reason, as distinct from the powers of Understanding which are in some sense shared with the animal kingdom, constitute the sphere in which spiritual realities are apprehended.) As Owen Barfield has lucidly shown, Coleridge was aware that the terms "degree" and "kind" did not have the universal applicability often attributed to them: that an apparent difference in "kind" might if correctly understood be found to be no more than a difference in "degree":[14] and (more importantly) that the term "Reason" could not, in the long run, be restricted to the meaning Marsh evidently attaches to it here. Reason for Coleridge was ultimately not a "faculty" or a "power," human or otherwise, but a presence in all nature, including humanity, the presence which "impels the chrysalis of the horned fly to leave room in its involucrum for antennae yet to come" (*BL*, I, 167). Instinct, in other words, is potential understanding, just as sensation is potential instinct, and there is no discontinuity in nature between the lowest and the highest (*natura non facit saltus*). But only when Reason is revealed to the Understanding, as it is in the fully awakened human being, the philosopher, does it become aware of itself as Reason.[15]

Marsh's aims in the "Preliminary Essay" were admittedly limited to preparing the way for "reflection"; moreover, it is not difficult to imagine what would have been the reaction of his New England readers, had Marsh offered and defended this totally unfamiliar redefinition of the term Reason. However, the difference between Marsh and Coleridge on this point is real enough, and can be supported by other evidence. Marsh was the more conservative theologian: and it was the "conservative" reading of Coleridge's thinking as regards Reason that prevented Marsh from conquering the problem so troublesome to later Transcendentalists, Emerson in particular, the apparently unbridgeable gap between matter and mind. Coleridge, though at the end of his life certainly no pantheist, had learned from Schelling that the Cartesian mind/matter dualism would pose

[14]Coleridge's example is the chemistry student learning that there is heat in ice.

[15]Owen Barfield, *What Coleridge Thought* (Middletown, Conn.: Wesleyan University Press, 1971; London: Oxford University Press, 1972), pp. 81–83, 94–96. Of Barfield's sources in these two chapters, it should be noted, Marsh had access only to *Biographia, Lay Sermons, The Friend,* and *Aids.*

insoluble problems for the theologian. Marsh, however, saw the dangers of pantheism too clearly to accept any reasoning that appeared to compromise the basis of Christian theology, as he saw it, the division between nature and spirit. A note on "Distinctions of physical & final cause" gives this warning: "Must be careful of applying our notions to God. Science of nature to be kept distinct from Theology. Experience & observation of nature cannot of itself carry us beyond nature. Teleology of nature is a principle adopted as a ground of judgment in order to understand nature but we cannot pass [from] nature to the author of nature as from the watch to the watchmaker" (JMC 3.2). This is not to argue that Marsh did not understand the hints thrown out by Coleridge in *The Friend*, *Biographia Literaria* and *Aids* to the effect that a progressive development of powers (sensation, instinct, understanding) could be observed in all gradations of the natural order: he did understand them, and profited from them in his teaching.[16] But when Marsh speaks of an "ascent from the lower to the higher in the developement of living powers," it is the division between the natural and the spiritual that is emphasized, not the Coleridgean rejection of such a division:

> In the progressive ascent from the lower to the higher in the developement of living powers the lower is always taken up into the higher & made a partaker of its dignity & glory. Thus while we distinguish in the animal organism a vegetable sphere or the sphere of productivity & growth it is obvious that it is no longer on a level with the same power in the vegetable world. The whole has become more instinct with life or rather is entirely interpenetrated by a higher life. Irritability & sensibility are not confined to their peculiar organs the muscular & nervous fibres but pervade the whole.
>
> So when in man the spiritual is superadded to the natural it does not leave the natural in its own lower sphere & preclude it from that which pertains to the spiritual but interpenetrates, exalts,

[16]See the note entitled "Moral Philosophy & Evidences of Religion," JMC 3.2, and the MSS on Religion, *passim*.

spiritualizes nature itself   The natural is transformed into the spiritual & partakes of its power & worth. [JMC 3.2]

My diagnosis of Marsh's intention in stressing the uniqueness of humanity's spiritual faculty—that he wished to uphold it as the only possible basis for the peculiar doctrines of Christianity—can also be applied to his treatment of the Kantian distinctions between the Pure and the Practical Reason, and between Reason and Understanding. The case against Marsh as expositor of Kant is well argued by Henry A. Pochmann. Marsh underestimated Coleridge's reliance on Kant, being predisposed by his admiration for the seventeenth century to take at face value Coleridge's purported proof that the Reason/ Understanding distinction originated with Bacon and Leighton, not with Kant. Moreover, Marsh ignored Kant's warning about mistaking *regulative* principles of Reason for *constitutive* principles of transcendent knowledge, a deficiency for which Coleridge is partly responsible, since Coleridge, as has been noted, gives Reason a quite different role from that which Kant allows it in the *Critiques*. Worst of all, Marsh accepted uncritically Coleridge's unKantian definition of Understanding as "the faculty judging according to sense."[17] These charges receive additional support from Marsh's admission (in a letter of 23 March 1829 to Coleridge, never answered): "though I have read a part of the works of Kant it was under many disadvantages, so that I am indebted to your own writings for the ability to understand what I have read of his works—& am waiting with some impatience for that part of your works which will aid more directly in the study of those subjects of which he treats."[18] What must, therefore, be seen as Marsh's failure to provide in his "Preliminary

[17]Henry A. Pochmann, *German Culture in America* (Madison: University of Wisconsin Press, 1957), pp. 134–38.
[18]JMC 3.8; printed in *Coleridge's American Disciples: The Selected Correspondence of James Marsh*, ed. John J. Duffy (Amherst: University of Massachusetts Press, 1973), pp. 79–82 (hereafter cited as Duffy). See also the comments on this letter in Nicolson, p. 32.

Essay" an independent and accurate delineation of the Critical Philosophy did, undoubtedly, have serious consequences for the Transcendental movement, for many beginners in philosophy—Emerson among them—were led by Marsh's "Essay" to expect entirely the wrong thing of Kantism. Marsh does indeed assert that "spiritual religion" inheres in the *Practical Reason* (p. xxiii), but this remark merely serves to introduce the observation that a man may be, in practice, religious, even though he is philosophically bewildered. No warning about the distinction between the Pure and the Practical Reason follows (although a note on p. 279 speaks of the "distinct offices" of Reason as "*speculative,* and as *practical* reason"), and it would be a very astute reader who could construct that distinction for himself from the materials Marsh provides, since the tendency of the discussion throughout is to assume that the inward discipline which the reader is invited to undertake will furnish a true *knowledge* of the mind's laws—of constitutive principles, that is to say, not of regulative principles only. "I maintain, that instead of pretending to exclude philosophy from our religious enquiries, it is vastly important, that we philosophize in earnest—that we endeavor by profound reflection to learn the *real* requirements of reason, and attain a true knowledge of ourselves" (p. xxi). (Kant had written, in the second edition of the *Critique,* "I have no *knowledge* of myself as I am but merely as I appear to myself. The consciousness of self is thus very far from being a knowledge of the self.")[19]

As is clear from the letter quoted above, Marsh expected Coleridge to provide in due course a major work on the philosophy of mind which would complement or supersede the two great *Critiques* of Kant. The point that has been overlooked, I think, is that Marsh seems to have believed that Kant's work already had been superseded, at least insofar as it dealt with articles of reli-

[19]*Immanuel Kant's Critique of Pure Reason,* trans. Norman Kemp Smith (London: Macmillan, 1929), p. 169 (B 158).

gious faith: that Kant had merely cleared the ground by limiting Pure Reason to its rightful sphere, the deduction of the Categories, and that Coleridge—on the basis of his own as yet unpublished but still philosophically sound system—had "completed" the work begun by Kant, demonstrating the philosophical grounds for the possibility of a spiritual religion. Marsh knew, that is, that his "Preliminary Essay" went beyond the limits of the Critical Philosophy (even when the latter was read in Coleridgean fashion), but he believed there was firm ground under his feet, namely, Coleridge's promised *Logosophia*. This seems to be the sense of the following passage from the manuscript of a lecture on "Mind":

> The critical philosophy draws the limits between pure reason and sensuousness and by thus setting limits to the latter contributes to the progress of Metaphysics. Though it may seem at first to do nothing but what is merely negative. But again pure reason is restrained by it to the narrow bounds of experience. True in its proper office but it leaves the way open for practical reason to extend its empire & removes the necessity of setting reason in opposition to itself as would otherwise be the case in regard to all that is beyond the limits of experience. [JMC 3.5]

The supposition that Marsh took for granted the philosophical soundness of Coleridge's "system" may account for the rather cavalier way in which Marsh here speaks of Pure Reason as "restrained ... to the narrow bounds of experience," and of a potential conflict between two functions of Reason thus being averted. It also goes some way to account for the confident tone in which Marsh refers to Coleridge's whole system as underpinning his "precise, exclusive, and steadfast" usage of the terms Reason, Understanding, Free Will, and Conscience (note 23, pp. 261–62).

Whatever the truth of Marsh's understanding of Kant, however, it is evident that the refutation of Locke was to Marsh, as to Coleridge, merely a preliminary clearing of the ground in order to arrive at a more vital, less "Arminian" faith. In human nature as represented by Lockean empiricism, "there is, and can be ... no true will; even as there can be in nature nothing that is above or over against nature."[20] To Coleridge, humanity was set "over against" Nature by its possession of Free Will; the spiritual in humanity was, indeed, the Will. Those passages in *Aids to Reflection* which concern the Will have none of the caution proper to a disciple of Kant who knows he is speaking of a merely regulative idea: they betray the fervor which is born of successive personal encounters with a spiritual fact. It was through his proclamation of Free Will, however, that Coleridge (and Marsh insofar as he defended Coleridge) attracted the most virulent denunciations of his heterodoxy.

Noah Porter noted that Coleridge's intention in writing *Aids to Reflection* was to release Christian belief from two different kinds of "dead weight" that had been hung upon it, the "low Arminian" being responsible for one of them, the "ultra Calvinist" for the other. The "formal" and "meaningless" Christianity of the low Arminian was sufficiently answered by the assertion of humanity's truly spiritual nature: against the "iron fatalism" of the ultra-Calvinist, said Porter, Coleridge argued "that man in his deepest guilt was still himself the offender and the guilty; that this was possible because his nature was spiritual and therefore *free;* and that the interposition of God for man was in the line of that high nature and in consistency with all its faculties" (pp. 143–44). Commentators like Porter accepted without demur the argument that a Christian must believe that the Will may be influenced by "the spiritual force of the higher universe" (Porter's phrase); where they found Coleridge to err, and err gravely, was in making this the one essential doctrine of Christianity, the sole object of the Incarnation, Crucifixion, and Resurrection. No passage in Scripture, Porter continued, will bear

[20]Torrey, p. 381; see also *Aids* (1829), pp. 273–75.

this interpretation; and indeed St. Paul's doctrine of the Atonement—the "forensic justification"—is perfectly contrary to it (p. 163). Marsh, inasmuch as he defended Coleridge's view, was also criticized.

Marsh and Coleridge were not the only Christian believers of their time who felt that the ultra-Calvinist doctrine of the utter sinfulness of humanity, and their need to be redeemed by an acceptable sacrifice, the death of God's only Son, was shocking to the reason of humankind, and inimical, therefore, to an active, positive faith. William Ellery Channing, a Calvinist until 1815, had in 1826 compared Calvinist theology to choosing a gallows as Christianity's central symbol, the symbol of the execution of God's own Son. The sermon in which he made this charge, "Unitarian Christianity most Favorable to Piety," marked the dedication of New York City's second Unitarian church, and was thus an important milestone in the advance of "Unitarian Christianity."[21]

It would surely have been impossible for Marsh—and others for whom Unitarianism was not an acceptable alternative to Calvinist orthodoxy—to ignore this evidence that the older creed was being made to seem not only antirational but also inimical to piety and positive faith. Yet Marsh knew—had himself discovered under the ministry of Roswell Shurtleff—that the older creed was not at all incompatible with immediate religious experience, but did indeed promise "regeneration" to those who were able to offer themselves to it. Coleridge's affirmations in *Aids to Reflection* seemed to promise a continuation of a genuine spiritual life within the older church. Moreover, as Marsh had cautiously attempted to show in his review of Moses Stuart's *Commentary on the Epistle to the Hebrews*, the doctrine of the forensic justification itself depended mainly on certain disputed in-

[21]Vernon Louis Parrington, *Main Currents in American Thought*, 2 vols. (New York: Harcourt, Brace, n.d. but 1954), II, 322–23.

terpretations of St. Paul's language concerning Redemption. (The review was attacked by the Calvinists for its heterodoxy on just this point.)[22]

It cannot be doubted that Marsh fully accepted Coleridge's definition of the "peculiar" doctrines of Christianity in Aphorism VII of the "Aphorisms on That Which Is Indeed Spiritual Religion." The "Preliminary Essay" refers the reader to this passage, and advises "those who are anxious to examine further into" its orthodoxy to look ahead to Aphorism X, "On Original Sin," and Aphorism XIX, which contains a "Synopsis of the constituent points in the doctrine of Redemption." The *effect* of Redemption, in the latter passage, is defined as "the being born anew." As Marsh points out, this coincides with what would be called, in New England, Evangelical doctrine, but it challenges Calvinist orthodoxy on the very issue that had provoked William Ellery Channing to argue that the Unitarian position was more "favorable to piety": its interpretation of the Crucifixion in terms of the blood sacrifice for sins prescribed to the Israelites in Leviticus 16:16–19. Moreover, Marsh is careful to explain that Coleridge indeed understands "the being born again" as a rebirth under a higher law than that of Nature:

> If the reader clearly apprehends the *law of life*, as a living power or agency, antecedent to and independent of the visible and tangible forms, which it constructs, he will have little difficulty in understanding what is said of the transfusion of a higher gift and specially inbreathed, of a soul, having its life in itself, and independent for its subsistence of the inferior powers, with which it co-exists. He will be prepared to apprehend at least the meaning of the doctrine, that distinct specific forms or laws of being are superadded to that life, which is common to all. [p. 253 n3]

Or, as it is phrased in a manuscript note by Marsh, "What the senses are to the instinct of the brute that the understanding is to

[22]Marsh, "Review of Stuart on the Epistle to the Hebrews," *Quarterly Christian Spectator*, 1 (March 1829), 134–35. See Nicolson, p. 37.

the ⟨natural⟩ will of man & faith to the regenerate will" (JMC 3.2).

No aspect of *Aids to Reflection* provoked as much religious controversy as this one: to some, Coleridge's views on the Atonement seemed "admirable & unanswerable" (JMC 2.7; Duffy, p. 123); to others they were an attack on the very meaning of the Gospels, a substitution at the very core of Christian belief of a subjective and "Unitarian" concept—the change to be wrought in the sinner's own heart—for the traditional view of Christ's death as a satisfaction of Divine justice, the sacrifice being itself the ground of the sinner's acceptance by his Creator. But consequences unforeseen by either Marsh or his critics were to follow from the reorientation effected by Coleridge's subjective interpretation of the Atonement: when Richard Henry Dana wrote to Marsh in 1838 about a young lecturer, Ralph Waldo Emerson, and complained, "I cannot find that he is bottomed on any thing" (JMC 3.9; Duffy, p. 214), it would have surprised him to learn that Emerson might reasonably have claimed to be "bottomed" on *Aids to Reflection*.

On 23 October 1829, Marsh wrote to his brother Leonard of his fears that *Aids to Reflection* might not be well received. "I have various reasons to feel some solicitude about it & among others the prejudice which you know has existed against me at Andover & the fact that the work will do some violence to certain prejudices of the religious public" (JMC 2.6; Duffy, p. 96). Marsh knew his public well. Many were bewildered by *Aids,* some outraged, but (as Torrey later observed) "few could deny the great moral and intellectual power which it every where exhibited."[23] The young, in particular, gave to *Aids* the moral authority that more traditional theological writers (Paley, Brown) seemed to lack. The orthodox were shocked: but the shock waves traveled

---

[23]Torrey, pp. 99-100. Chauncey Goodrich, Marsh's publisher, sent twenty-four copies of *Aids* (1829) to Coleridge's publisher in London, and Marsh sent one to Coleridge with "a long letter" (see JMC 2.6).

beyond their immediate target, as shock waves will, and eventually rebounded to hit the larger target of institutional Christianity itself—a consequence that Marsh certainly did not intend. It was with Marsh, rather than with Coleridge, that the responsibility for the devastation lay; when Rufus Griswold wrote his *Prose Writers of America* in 1847, he credited Marsh's "Preliminary Essay," not *Aids* itself, with administering the first serious shock to the orthodox of New England.[24] Coleridge's *Lay Sermons* and *Biographia Literaria* were already available to New England readers: had *Aids* itself been published in the same way as the earlier prose works, it would conceivably have made much less of a stir. "Coleridge's metaphysics" were already a byword for unintelligibility, and German idealism still indisputably a foreign product. Marsh, however, held a position of considerable authority in one of the older States of the Union: he commanded great respect both as scholar and as teacher, and his credentials were impeccable. The orthodox were taken aback, not by what Coleridge had dared to think in the name of religion, but by the fact that a respected New Englander could give his sanction to Coleridge's speculations, and indeed publish them with the professed aim of helping to advance the cause of Christianity.

Published reactions to *Aids* were few, but Alcott, Emerson, and Hawthorne were among those who read it, and (at least in the first two cases) were profoundly influenced by it.[25] Emerson's letter of 31 May 1834 to Edward Emerson, in which he attempts to expound "the distinction of Milton Coleridge & the Germans between Reason & Understanding," is well known, as also is the description by Frederic Henry Hedge of the first

[24]Rufus Griswold, *Prose Writers of America* (Philadelphia: Carey & Hart; London: R. Bentley, 1847; often reprinted), p. 400.

[25]Pochmann, pp. 163, 179; Frank T. Thompson, "Emerson's Indebtedness to Coleridge," *Studies in Philology*, 23 (1926), 56; *The Journals of Bronson Alcott*, ed. Odell Shepard (Boston: Little, Brown, 1938), pp. 29–30, 67; F. O. Matthiessen, *American Renaissance* (London: Oxford University Press, 1941), p. 231.

meeting of the so-called "Transcendentalists" on 19 September 1836, partly as a result of Marsh's editions of *Aids to Reflection* and *The Friend*.[26]

Marsh evidently asked his friend Ebenezer C. Tracy—sometime editor of the *Vermont Chronicle,* the organ of the Congregationalist church in Vermont—if he would review *Aids* for the *Quarterly Christian Spectator,* a theological journal published at New Haven, but Tracy doubted whether the kind of review he would write would be accepted by such a conservative journal. "Our theological journals," he wrote to Marsh, "are all party publication [sic], and tacitly or avowedly pledged, each to its own public for the support of particular doctrines" (JMC 3.8; Duffy, p. 98). The *Quarterly Christian Spectator* could not ignore Coleridge altogether, however, and published an attack on his doctrines and, more surprisingly, those of Kant, in 1835.[27] The *New Jerusalem Magazine* of Boston, a Swedenborgian publication, found "some valuable thoughts" in Marsh's "Preliminary Essay," but could not "join the editor in his unqualified admiration" of Coleridge.[28] The *North American Review* mentioned *Aids,* among other prose works by Coleridge, in a temperate but generally favorable review of his *Poetical Works* (Philadelphia, 1831).[29] For the student of New England transcendentalism, however, perhaps the most interesting review is the article "Coleridge's Literary Character," by Frederic Henry Hedge, in the Unitarian

[26]*The Letters of Ralph Waldo Emerson,* ed. Ralph L. Rusk, 6 vols. (New York: Columbia University Press, 1939), I, 412; James Elliot Cabot, *A Memoir of Ralph Waldo Emerson,* 2 vols. (Boston: Houghton Mifflin, 1887), I, 245.

[27]Anon., "Present State of Metaphysics," *Quarterly Christian Spectator,* 6 (1835), 609–31.

[28]Anon., "American Edition of *Aids to Reflection,*" *New Jerusalem Magazine,* 3 (1830), 189–91.

[29][Robert Cassie Waterston], "Coleridge's Poems. The Poetical Works of S. T. Coleridge. Complete in one Volume. Philadelphia. 1831," *North American Review,* 39 (1834), 437–58.

Christian Examiner for March 1833.[30] Hedge thanks Marsh for introducing *Aids* to America, and hopes that Marsh's philosophical talents "will some day be employed in more extensive undertakings." In the same essay, however, he challenges Coleridge's claim to have reconciled "head" and "heart," philosophy and religion, and warns that Coleridge's supposed Trinitarianism is a gross misinterpretation of the doctrines of the Church of England, and his views on the Atonement far from orthodox.

> The strong expressions used by St. Paul in reference to this subject, he tells us are not intended to designate the *act* of redemption, but are only figurative expressions descriptive of its effects. The *act* of redemption he calls a "mystery," which term, as it may mean any thing, means, in reality, nothing. The other doctrines fare in the same way. Every thing is first mystified into a sort of imposing indistinctness, and then pronounced to be genuine Orthodoxy. The truth is, Mr. Coleridge, though a great scholar, was not qualified in point of biblical learning for an undertaking like this. [pp. 127-28]

With these rather considerable reservations, however, Hedge praised *Aids to Reflection* as "a very valuable work," especially insofar as it correctly distinguished between morality and mere prudence, and between natural and spiritual religion. Writing to Caroline Healey Dall in 1877, Hedge modestly disclaimed personal responsibility for the overthrowing of orthodox prejudice against German metaphysics by his article, but added that the printing of such a relatively favorable review of Coleridge's works in a respected Unitarian journal lent an authority to his

---

[30]Frederic Henry Hedge, "Coleridge's Literary Character: 1. *Biographia Literaria* ... New York. 1817. 2. *The Poetical Works of S. T. Coleridge* ... 3 vols. ... London. 1829. 3. *Aids to Reflection* ... Burlington. 1829. 4. *The Friend* ... Burlington ... 1831," *Christian Examiner*, 14 (1833), 108-29.

(Hedge's) views which must have contributed to the defeat of the old "sensualistic" philosophy.[31]

The interest aroused by Marsh's edition of *Aids to Reflection* led in 1831 to the publication in Burlington of *The Friend,* a work which had been "but little known in this country" (according to Marsh's note 1, p. 251, in *Aids*). In his "Preface to the American Edition" of *The Friend,* however, Marsh took the success of *Aids* as an indication that *The Friend* was also assured of a wide sale:

> When nearly two years ago the "Aids to Reflection," another work of the same author, came before the public, there were many occasions of doubt with regard to its probable reception. Those doubts are now removed. The result has justified the most flattering anticipations, and furnishes abundant proof, that the "fit audience" to be found among us for works of this kind is not so small as had been apprehended.[32]

Not until 1840, though, was there a second American edition of *Aids* itself, partly because Marsh had wished to wait until Coleridge's "last additions and corrections" were received, and these were not available until Henry Nelson Coleridge published the fourth London edition (1839), which was the basis for Marsh's Burlington edition of 1840.[33] (Marsh's "Preliminary Essay" was retained, but the Notes and Appendix, consisting chiefly of extracts from Coleridge's other prose works, Marsh judged it wiser to leave out.)

In a sense, however, Marsh had been preempted. One sign of the unexpected and unauthorized uses to which Coleridge's

[31]George Willis Cooke, *An Historical and Biographical Introduction to Accompany the Dial as Reprinted in Numbers for the Rowfant Club,* 2 vols. (Cleveland: Rowfant Club, 1902; rpt. New York: Russell & Russell, 1961), I, 72–73.

[31]*The Friend: A Series of Essays* .... First American, from the Second London Edition (Burlington: Chauncey Goodrich, 1831), p. [v].

[33]"Advertisement" (signed "J.M.") to *Aids to Reflection ... with a Preliminary Essay, by James Marsh, D.D.* From the fourth London edition (Burlington: Chauncey Goodrich, 1840), p. 5.

thought was now being put was the appearance in 1839 of a reprint of *Aids* with a new "Preliminary Essay" by one John M'Vickar, Professor of Moral Philosophy at Columbia College, New York. Bolder than Marsh, M'Vickar claimed that Marsh's Calvinist leanings, so far from being a recommendation, disqualified him from giving a true interpretation of Coleridge's ideas. M'Vickar's usurpation of Marsh's role as interpreter of Coleridge to the American public, and particularly his insinuation that he, M'Vickar, had Henry Nelson Coleridge's approval for this reprint, were denounced by an anonymous writer in the *Vermont Chronicle:*

> The purchaser, not looking beyond the title-page, would of course suppose this to be the work as edited in accordance with the author's Will, with no other change than the addition of a Preliminary Essay. But it is not so. An important part of the volume has been omitted.

> *Query.* Had the question of the *copy-right* of Dr. Marsh's Essay, any influence with the publishers of Professor M'Vickar's Edition? Will the public countenance an edition, by which a genuine SCHOLAR is thus to be wronged of that pecuniary reward for his labor which belongs to him even by the rules and courtesies of business,—not to mention higher considerations?[34]

But the question whether a Calvinist could properly interpret Coleridge, or whether Coleridge's doctrines were consonant with Evangelicalism, mattered little to most of the "radicals" and "new lights" who launched *The Dial* in the summer of 1840. When George Ripley in October of that year sent the first two

---

[34]Anon., "Singular Management," *Vermont Chronicle,* 1 Jan. 1840, p. 2. A letter from Benjamin Ball Newton to James Marsh, 20 Jan. 1840 (JMC 2.10), reads in part: "I presume that Mr. Tracy has written you before this—and that you have recieved [sic] a copy of the paper containing a notice of 'Coleridge & his Editors'—G. N. Adams." If this is the article referred to, as seems certain, the letter would appear good ground for attributing it to Adams, but I have not been able to trace this name.

issues of *The Dial* to Marsh, and invited him to contribute, his tone was apologetic, and his expectation not high that Marsh would sympathize with the contents of the new magazine (Duffy, pp. 239-40). If transcendentalism had at first been Marsh's foster-child, it was already evident that the child had deserted the parent.

]8[

Coleridge and the
Idea of the Clerisy

STEPHEN PRICKETT

Few Victorians thought of Coleridge primarily as a poet. John Stuart Mill had set the tone a decade after Coleridge's death with his essays contrasting Bentham and Coleridge as the two seminal thinkers of the age. His portrait of Coleridge as one of the great conservative theoreticians of the century sounds slightly odd to the ears of a modern reader who is unaware that he is reading a review of the second edition of *Church and State.* For many years after Coleridge's death it was his best-selling work. To a minority, including such people as Julius Hare, F. D. Maurice, and F. J. A. Hort, it was Coleridge the theologian and philosopher who was important, but for the majority of those prepared to take the trouble to read him, he was above all a prophet of social and educational ideas. This is how Mill saw him:

> The influence of Coleridge, like that of Bentham, extends far beyond those who share in the peculiarities of his religious or philosophical creed. He has been the great awakener in this country of the spirit of philosophy, within the bounds of traditional opinions. He has been, almost as truly as Bentham, "the great questioner of things established;" for a questioner needs not necessarily be an enemy. By Bentham, beyond all others, men have been led to ask themselves, in regard to any ancient or received opinion, Is it true? and by Coleridge, What is the meaning of it? The one

took his stand *outside* the received opinion, and surveyed it as an entire stranger to it; the other looked at it from within, and endeavoured to see it with the eyes of a believer in it; to discover by what apparent facts it was at first suggested, and by what appearances it has ever since been rendered continually credible—has seemed, to a succession of persons, to be a faithful interpretation of their experience.[1]

A similar, though perhaps less enthusiastic verdict could have been drawn from Matthew Arnold. Newman's admission that Coleridge had "instilled a higher philosophy into inquiring minds, than they had hitherto been accustomed to accept" and that he had "in this way made trial of his age"[2] suggests that he had seen the unity of Coleridge's thinking more clearly than many of his contemporaries, and it is hard not to see the shade of Coleridge behind his vision of the dialectical relationship between theology and the other disciplines in an idealized Oxford at least as clearly as in his more specifically theological studies.[3]

Similarly, Mark Pattison, who had been first attracted to Coleridge by his religious philosophy during the 1830s,[4] was by the 1850s more interested in his ideas about the clerisy. Pattison's interest, moreover, was a firmly practical one. Like his mentors, Mill, Arnold, and Newman, he was concerned with what Coleridge had called, picturesquely, "the plebification of knowledge," and he was struggling with the problem of how to create

[1]John Stuart Mill, "Coleridge," *London and Westminster Review*, 33 (1840), 257; rpt. in *John Stuart Mill on Bentham and Coleridge,* Introduction by F. R. Leavis (London: Chatto & Windus, 1950), pp. 99–100. It is the worst feature of Leavis's interesting introduction that he nowhere mentions that Mill's essay is a review-article.

[2]John Henry Newman, *Apologia Pro Vita Sua, Being a History of His Religious Opinions,* ed. Martin J. Svaglic (London: Oxford University Press, 1967), p. 94. First published 1864.

[3]Newman, *On the Scope and Nature of University Education* (London: Dent; New York: Dutton, 1915), first published 1852, especially Discourses I–III.

[4]Mark Pattison, *Memoirs,* ed. Mrs. Pattison (London: Macmillan, 1885), pp. 164–65.

and defend an academic elite free from the immediate pressures of middle-class commercial philistinism to engage in the disinterested pursuit of knowledge for its own sake. His terms betray the source of his ideas. Writing of a mass technical education he comments: "I have no wish to depreciate this species of education, which I would willingly see much more widely diffused in this country, but in its proper sphere—for the classes, that is, whose callings in life will not admit of the more protracted process which a solid education requires.... Each system has its own place; they should not be rivals; the one for the mass of the people, the other for a cultivated clerisy."[5] In his evidence to the Commission of Inquiry on Oxford in 1852 he argued the ideal of a liberal education in terms of his conception of the "clerisy":

> It is one which, as it originated in a profound study of the nature of the mind, can only be appreciated by the maintenance of that study and knowledge. It needs protection therefore. There is no natural demand for it. The pressure and competition of actual life not only do not call for such an education, but have a continual tendency to substitute for it the more immediately available education of professional skill and accomplishment. To secure this popular education the state has only to remove intellectual obstacles, and leave it to the operation of the law of supply and demand. Remove restrictions on the Universities, and they will contribute their share towards popular education. But this is not their proper business, and never has been regarded so among us. The higher education is that which the Universities seek at once to give, and to give the means of appreciating, and in this function they need protecting....[6]

Behind this spirited defense of "pure" academic learning and cultivation of the mind is Mill's model of the teachers in the universities and other intellectual leaders forming potentially a

[5]Pattison, quoted in John Sparrow, *Mark Pattison and the Idea of a University* (Cambridge: Cambridge University Press, 1967), p. 93.

[6]Pattison, quoted in "Report of H. M. Commissioners Appointed to Inquire into the State, Discipline, Studies, and Revenues of the University and Colleges of Oxford," *Parliamentary Papers*, 22 (1852), Evidence, p. 45.

separate class or "estate" of the realm—who could be endowed to act as a kind of secular clergy. For both, the acknowledged original was Coleridge's "National Church," "the third remaining estate of the realm, [which] was to secure and improve civilization, without which the nation could be neither permanent nor progressive." For Coleridge, this "third estate" or National Clerisy "comprehended the learned of all denominations" but had three main constituents: the parish clergy and the teachers in the parish schools and in the universities. Between them these provided a custodianship of the national values in centers of learning and piety, and representatives of this culture in every parish in the land (*CS,* pp. 34, 36). The details of this conception are left vague: it is not clear, for instance, whether Coleridge is being prescriptive or descriptive in his account, or how far such a body should serve as an instrument of change, or as a defender of the existing establishment.

For Pattison, however, with less idealism and perhaps a stronger sense of the actual state of the parish teachers and clergy, there is no question that the clerisy is primarily to be identified with the university teachers—and in particular with those of Oxford and Cambridge. "We are beginning to see," he wrote in 1876, "that science and letters are a vocation, and that they have a value in themselves, and are not merely useful as teachable material. . . . That universities have other functions than that of educating youth. That liberal and scientific culture, intelligence, and the whole domain of mind, is a national interest, as much as agriculture, commerce, banking, or water supply."[7] By general agreement the reforms of 1854, essential as they were, constituted only a breathing-space in the hard-fought battle for renovating Oxford, and by 1868 Pattison, now Rector of Lincoln College, returned to the subject with his much more detailed *Suggestions on Academical Organization.* By now the terms of the debate had resolved themselves for him into a much more

[7]Pattison, "Review of the Situation," in *Essays on the Endowment of Research,* By Various Writers (London: H. S. King, 1876).

narrow and clear-cut question: that of professionalism. He urged the creation of a qualified and specialist profession of university teachers, lecturers and professors, engaged in research and teaching—as one found, say, in German models, like Humboldt's University of Berlin—yet the ways of thinking about education remain unmistakably "clerisical." A concurrent debate in Cambridge, for instance, was severely censured for assuming that students "must be taught in that on which they can be examined, so as to be pitted against each other." The result is that "competition, instead of being regarded as a necessary evil, has ousted education from the system, of which it has become the end and purpose."[8] Since the preservation of liberal and scientific culture is a paramount value, scholars must be insulated from the pressures of the marketplace in terms of both finance and competition—and it is in the best interests of the entire community that they be so.

> If it be objected that you cannot override economical laws with impunity, without originating mischief, the answer is, that such endowment of learning is not an exception to the law of supply and demand. It is only an indirect application of the law. It is only because, in a civilized community, there arises a demand for theoretical science, that the community becomes willing to pay for, and creates the conditions of its supply—viz. independence and leisure. [p. 198]

That last clause provides the key to the new mood. The fulfillment of Coleridge's ideal, secularized and professionalized, is to be achieved by the creation of a new privileged class—a new meritocracy[9]—whose sine qua non is to be independence and leisure.

[8]Pattison, *Suggestions on Academical Organization, with Especial Reference to Oxford* (Edinburgh: Edmonton & Douglas, 1868), p. 348.
[9]For the origins of this term see Michael D. Young, *The Rise of the Meritocracy, 1870-2033; An Essay on Education and Equality* (1958; rpt. Harmondsworth: Penguin Books, 1961).

Pattison's proposals are historically very important in the history of English universities. Contained within them are the seeds of the modern British university system—and, indeed, only within the last twenty years have we begun to catch up with some of his proposals to broaden the curriculum. They help to explain also why higher education in the United Kingdom has evolved in a particular way that makes it distinctively different from its counterparts in either the United States or continental Europe. Oxford and Cambridge, in particular, have come, partly as a result of this line of argument, to be associated with a group of academic qualities as delightful to their admirers as they are infuriating to their critics. At their center is the notion of the scholar and gentlemen: the tutor who carefully nurtures his pupils not merely into learning, but also into a quality of civilization, at once aesthetic and moral. It was, perhaps, epitomized in the popular myth of the Oxford Greats man, rowing for his college and gaining his double first before entering Parliament, the civil service, or the literary seclusion of a country rectory. Pattison's ideal, popularized and sentimentalized, was taken over as the dream of a class and of an age—in many ways a great class, and a great age, admittedly, which produced distinguished exempla of that ideal—but its attractions should not blind us to its faults. It was unashamedly an elitist ideal, implying inevitably a hierarchical view of society, at the very time when this static and hierarchical model was beginning to be questioned. Not merely were the ancient universities for a tiny minority even of the wealthy upper and upper middle classes, but, as Pattison and Arnold both freely admitted, those who subscribed to their ideals were only a minority even of those within the universities. Their golden age was, in effect, a mythical period whose image is shattered afresh every time one reads a new set of reminiscences. Was it the Oxford of Evelyn Waugh? Or the Cambridge of Russell, or of Leavis? In fact, it must have come as near to fulfillment as it ever did in Pattison's own youth, when, in particular, the Rugby men, who had been educated under Thomas another form of this same prejudice.[11] If the critical canons were already laid down, founded on the great literature of the past, new kinds of art could only threaten the status quo—and, by implication, the whole civilization which favored and protected the clerisy.

Certainly "civilization" in these terms proved to be a hot-house flower of remarkable frailty, hardly expected to flourish outside the confines of a particular social class—or even, for the purists, much outside of the city limits of Cambridge. The Apostles, that most exclusive debating society of Cambridge Coleridgeans who had from the beginning explicitly taken on themselves the mantle of the clerisy, exemplifed all these attitudes in abundance. They were as horrified as Coleridge himself by the aims of the 1832 Reform Bill and the political agitation that led up to it. Some even joined the Cambridge militia in expectation of imminent revolution. Their tendency to think of "reform" primarily in intellectual and educational terms is illustrated by a letter of the same period from Kemble (son of the famous Shakespearean actor) to another apostle: "All reform is misplaced which does not begin by reforming our system of *education,* from the lowest to the highest & from the dame school to the University."[12] Yet apostolic enthusiasm for educational reform at any but the "highest" level was rapidly blunted by experience. In 1836, W. H. Thompson, finding himself teaching in a Leicester school, wrote to a fellow apostle in disgust:

> I doubt very much whether it be possible for boys to be taught by one much less stupid than themselves—unless indeed he make up for possessing an ordinary share of understanding by a most extraordinary one of benevolence; that is, of love of his species *as*

[11]Ben Knights, *Mind and Society* (Cambridge: Cambridge University Press, 1977). I am in general indebted to this lively and stimulating account of the clerisy, even though, as may be seen, I do not support many of its conclusions.

[12]Kemble to Donne, 25 Oct. 1836, in Peter Allen, *The Cambridge Apostles* (Cambridge: Cambridge University Press, 1978), Ch. X.

such. For any amiable quality beyond this,—it were as easy to love Plato's plucked chicken as an average Leicester boy—The only motive one has for giving oneself trouble with them is the fear lest they should grow up like their parents.[13]

On leaving Leicester he concluded thankfully to the same correspondent: "They are an evil and filthy generation: and who knows whether I might not have been made like unto them by a longer sojourn. Perhaps, some fine day, one might have caught oneself intermarrying with the daughters of the people of the land, & so defiling the purity of apostolic descent."[14] Nor do the rural areas, the world of the dame school and the country parson, fare much better when we descend from theory to practice. The apostolic and Arnoldian ideal of the clerisy at work in leavening the lump of parish life could be devastatingly challenged simply by reference to the facts. I quote Edward Miall, M.P. for Bradford and a prominent Nonconformist:

> I wish to say something of the rural parishes of the kingdom. In each of these, we are told, the clergyman, maintained by national endowment, is a living link between the highest and the lowliest of the parishioners—is a cultivated gentleman, located just where there is, if not the greatest need, at any rate the best opportunity, for diffusing both "sweetness and light"—is the fixed centre in the parish of civilization, of education, of charity, of piety—and I am told that I propose to abolish him and leave the people to fall back again into ignorance and Paganism. . . . These rural parishes have been in the undisturbed spiritual occupation of the clergy of the Church of England for generations past. . . . Well, what, on a large scale, has been the result? What are the most conspicuous characteristics of our labouring agricultural population? Do they include "sweetness and light"? Do they include fairly-developed intelligence? Do they include a high state of morality? Do they include affectionate veneration for religion? Are these the most prominent features by which the character of our agricultural population is distinguished, and in respect of which they bear away the palm

[13]Thompson to Blakesley, 5 Nov. 1836, in ibid.
[14]27 April 1837, in ibid.

from the inmates of towns? And the discouraging and painful answers to these queries—are they not to be found in blue-books, verified as they may be by minute personal observation?[15]

The painful contrast between ideal and practice can be focused in a single incident, horrific in itself, which produced one of the most curious and revealing confrontations of the nineteenth century. In 1865 there was a Negro revolt in Jamaica which was put down by the governor, John Eyre, with great brutality. In all, some 22 whites had been killed in the uprising, but in reprisals over 450 blacks were executed, many without even a pretense of a trial, and some under conditions of peculiar savagery—such as being flogged to death. When news of these incidents reached Britain early the following year there was an immediate outcry, and a committee was formed to press for the impeachment and trial of Governor Eyre. Its members and supporters included Mill, Darwin, Huxley, Spencer, Lyell, Leslie Stephen, J. M. Ludlow, and Thomas Hughes—a group with a predominantly scientific and agnostic bias. The main exceptions to this were Ludlow, a lawyer, who is now generally considered to be the founder of the Christian Socialists, and Hughes, author of *Tom Brown's Schooldays,* a prominent Evangelical and also a Christian Socialist. Eyre, however, was not just any colonial governor; he had in his youth been a famous explorer—one of the first to cross the interior of Australia (part of which is now named after him). His *Expedition into Central Australia and Overland from Adelaide to King George's Sound* had been published in 1845, and in the eyes of many he was a hero. Another committee was rapidly formed for his defense, and it included Carlyle, Ruskin, Tennyson, Dickens, Froude, and Kingsley. Though some, like Carlyle and Kingsley, were evidently predisposed to hero-worship, what divides the two groups is something much

[15]Quoted in Donald Davie, *A Gathered Church: The Literature of the English Dissenting Interest, 1700-1930* (London: Routledge & Kegan Paul, 1978), pp. 78-79.

more profound than an attitude toward great men, or even the conventional political alignments that such an attitude might imply. There were, for instance, others besides Hughes who could recognize Flashman, and there were noted radicals in both groups. But by and large it is the men of letters, those who have undergone the nearest existing equivalent of the humane and liberal education advocated by Newman and Pattison, who see the security of society in terms of *authority;* the scientists and utilitarians, narrower and less "cultured" in outlook, who see society in terms of *morality.*

It is instructive in this regard to compare Darwin's attitude towards slavery, and the blacks in general, with that of Kingsley. In the *Voyage of the Beagle* Darwin describes how horrified he was by the look in the eyes of a slave in Brazil who imagined he was about to strike him. "I shall never forget," he writes, "my feelings of surprise, disgust, and shame, at seeing a great powerful man afraid to ward off a blow, directed, as he thought, at his face. The man had been trained to a degradation lower than the slavery of the most helpless animal." On an estate on the Rio Macae he describes how he was nearly "an eye-witness to one of those atrocious acts which can only take place in a slave country":

> Owing to a quarrel and a law-suit, the owner was on the point of taking all the women and children from the male slaves, and selling them separately at the public auction in Rio. Interest, and not any feeling of compassion, prevented this act. Indeed, I do not believe the inhumanity of separating thirty families, who had lived together for many years, even occurred to the owner. Yet I will pledge myself, that in humanity and good feeling he was superior to the common run of men. It may be said there exists no limit to the blindness of interest and selfish habit.[16]

Kingsley's view of the West Indians was certainly not free of "interest"—at least by association. His grandfather had been a

---

[16]Charles Darwin, *Journal of Researches into the Geology & Natural History of the Various Countries Visited during the Voyage of H.M.S. Beagle round the World,* Everyman's Library, 104 (London: Dent; New York: Dutton, 1906), p. 23. First published 1839.

slaveowner in Barbados, where his mother was born. When he visited the West Indies in 1869, only three years after the rising, he, like Darwin in Brazil, was enchanted by the vegetation and fauna, but unlike Darwin, found in the Negroes signs not of oppression but innate inferiority. At St. Thomas in the Virgin Islands the sight of the black laborers in coal barges alongside his boat dancing to the strains of a waltz from the band on the deck revolted him. He observed "the negro shoveller dancing in the black water at the barge bottom, shovel in hand," and "the pleasant white folks dancing under the awning,"

> till the contrast between the refinement within and the brutality without became very painful. For brutality it was, not merely in the eyes of the sentimentalist, but in those of the moralist; still more in the eyes of those who try to believe that all God's humans may be somewhen, somewhere, somehow, reformed into his likeness.[17]

It must be added that Kingsley also had a low opinion of the Irish.

Eyre's case is an interesting one in a number of ways (he was suspended but not prosecuted, and he retired on a full governor's pension), but it illustrates dramatically the dangers of an "establishment," even as loose and notional as that of Victorian England (for the group above would certainly not have thought of themselves as "privileged" or "established" in any sense), as a guardian of moral or spiritual values. It was a danger that was implicit, but not adequately spelled out, in Coleridge's own thinking. As a modern critic of *Church and State* has acutely pointed out, Coleridge comes dangerously near to asserting that the duties of the clerisy are to inculcate habits of obedience toward the state.[18] As a no less acute modern novelist has reminded us, "All through history the elect have made their cases

---

[17]Susan Chitty, *The Beast and the Monk: A Life of Charles Kingsley* (London: Hodder and Stoughton, 1974), p. 260.

[18]John Colmer, *Coleridge: Critic of Society* (Oxford: Clarendon Press, 1959), p. 157.

for election. But time allows only one plea . . . . It is this. That the elect, whatever the particular grounds they advance for their cause, have introduced a finer and fairer morality into this dark world. If they fail this test, then they become no more than despots, sultans, mere seekers after their own pleasure and power"[19]

In short, the charges against Coleridge's idea of the clerisy and its functions are serious ones. Not merely does his exposition contain some special pleading, and even doubtful logic (Colmer, p. 155), but it could be, and was, used as the basis of an argument for a narrowly professionalized secular establishment, privileged and conservative in outlook. So far from refreshing the moral and spiritual standards of the nation, its constituents were as liable to find themselves in dubious moral company as any other section of society on social and political issues—and possibly more so. We recall that Coleridge himself wrote *Church and State* in opposition to Catholic Emancipation—which to most observers, then and now, seemed only simple natural justice.[20] For many of his readers the real message of his work seemed clear: the Church of England, properly endowed, and with its privileged status in the universities unchallenged, was the best bulwark there was against social change and reform. Abuses and hardships in this world could be amply redressed by the rewards for patience and obedience in the next. Intellectually, the clerisy provided a defense of academic standards against the threatened "plebification" of knowledge, and its dilution into "useful" arts and other "practical" studies for the philistines or the swinish multitude.

Clearly, this is a crude parody of the ideas of an Arnold or a Pattison. The idea of the clerisy in Victorian times is not so much a single thread as a whole bundle of interrelated strands, often

---

[19]John Fowles, *The French Lieutenant's Woman* (1969; rpt. New York: Panther Books, 1971), p. 342.
[20]See Prickett, p. 251.

differing widely in detail, that are part of a central cultural debate throughout the second half of the century. Yet it is the crude popularized versions of ideas that often have the greatest effect on what emerges. Donald Davie has rightly described Miall's attack on the ideal of the rural clerisy as "effective parliamentary knockabout," but the stress must be on the word "effective." Ultimately a social idea *has* to be put crudely if it is to be influential. It is not the intricacies of Arnold's argument that remain with us after we have read *Culture and Anarchy,* but his main terms: "Hebraism versus Hellenism," the desirability of "Sweetness and Light," and "Philistine" as an epithet for his opponents—a coinage which has passed into the language.

Yet the case against Coleridge is not an open-and-shut one. It is not unknown for an idea to become influential in a way quite unintended by its progenitor. We notice, for instance, that as the idea is propounded by Mill, Arnold, and Pattison, it is an entirely secular conception. All three were ardent secularizers of what they held to be of permanent social value in religious belief or structures. Even Carlyle, though he seems to have retained a sense of some cloudy theocentric Mystery brooding at the heart of the universe, follows in practice a similar tendency. As early as 1834 we find the outspoken Kemble proclaiming on behalf of the Apostles that "the *Clerisy* of the land must no longer be the parsonry of the land" (Allen, Ch. X). In contrast, the Coleridgeans who remained Christians in a more orthodox sense—Hare and Maurice, and their followers such as Kingsley, Ludlow, and Hughes—were involved with a quite different educational ideal: the Working Men's Colleges. The real counterpart to Pattison's *Suggestions on Academical Organization* is not Newman's *Idea of a University* but Maurice's lectures *On Learning and Working,* delivered at the inauguration of the London Working Men's College. The answer of the Christian Socialists to the problem of preserving the values of disinterested learning from the philistines was to go over the heads of the middle class and appeal to the great thirst for learning that existed in the more articulate working the parish schools, and those in the "great schools" and universities. Numerically, and in terms of influence on the whole population, the most important of these was probably the parish clergy—and this was precisely the group omitted by the secularists. It was this body, or, to be more exact, the Church of England as a whole, that Maurice makes central to his vision in *The Kingdom of Christ* (1838, rev. 1842). At the heart of his thinking is the Coleridgean dialectic. The Church must be a universal spiritual society if it is to stand for anything: but it cannot be universal, and appeal to all men, unless it be also truly spiritual; it cannot be spiritual unless it be also truly universal. To be the National Church is essential, but it is only a first stage toward the organic Universal Church, and the Nation only finds its real significance as a distinctive part of the wider whole. Maurice's book was perhaps the most important single work of Anglican theology to appear in the nineteenth century, at once challenging and confirming the role of the Church of England in a manner that it has never quite been able to come to terms with since.[23] It was this tensional or dialectical way of thinking that Maurice had, above all, learned from *Church and State*. Just as it had never been clear from Coleridge whether his account of the clerisy had been descriptive or prescriptive, so Maurice's description of the universal spiritual society which is for all is similarly deliberately ambiguous. To describe an institution in a new way is to change it. Maurice had seen, in a way that most of his contemporaries had not, that the whole strategy of *Church and State* depended upon a series of such tensional models, and that the idea of the clerisy cannot be properly understood apart from this inherent and essential tension.[24] The word "idea" as Coleridge had attempted to define it was a living semantic embodiment of this principle. It differs from a "conception," he tells us, in that while the latter is conscious, and therefore fully realized,

[23]See Prickett, ch. 5, for a detailed discussion of Maurice.
[24]See Prickett, ch. 1.

[267]

the "idea" of a thing can be neither generalized nor abstracted from particular concrete examples, but can only be grasped if we have a knowledge of its ultimate aim (*CS*, p. 12). The "idea" of a "state," for instance, is not necessarily to be discovered by looking at every example of a state there is. For God, indeed, it may exist as a Platonic absolute, but for us, it comes more often as a perpetual series of revelations or discoveries as new aspects of its meaning come to light. In *Biographia Literaria* he had suggested that "an IDEA, in the *highest* sense of that word, cannot be conveyed but by a *symbol*" (*BL*, I, 100—Ch. IX). Ultimately, we apprehend it not in linear and discursive terms, but as we might a work of art, which speaks afresh with new meaning to every generation, and is not merely intellectual but emotional in its impact.

Thus we find that in Coleridge's scheme of things the Constitution of the Nation is composed of two opposite groups, or "poles" (*CS*, p. 22): they are the "State," the political and secular interest, and the "Church." Like the two poles of a magnet, each is dependent upon the other and cannot exist as itself without its opposite. But each of these interests is composed in turn of a further dialectic of opposites. The "State" is a synthesis of two opposite pressure groups seeking Permanence and Progression respectively (the former representing the interests of the landowners, the latter of the manufacturers). Similarly, the "Church" is a synthesis of two quite different but coexisting entities. One is the National Church, which is, we recall, the repository and custodian of the moral and spiritual values of the Nation. It is "religious" in the broad sense of the word, but not specifically Christian since the nature of a society's particular beliefs depend upon the accidents of geography and history. The other is the Church of Christ. By a "blessed accident" the National Church of England is also Christian, and so just as in its National capacity it is headed by the monarch, in this case still George IV himself, so as a Christian Church it pays homage to Christ alone. Though they exist within a single organization and structure, these two bodies are totally separate and distinct:

> As the olive tree is said in its growth to fertilize the surrounding soil; to invigorate the roots of the vines in its immediate neighbourhood, and to improve the strength and flavour of the wines—such is the relation of the Christian and the National Church. But as the olive is not the same plant with the vine, ... even so is Christianity ... no essential part of the *Being* of the *National* Church, however conducive or even indispensable it may be to its *well* being. And even so a National Church might exist, and has existed, without ... the *Christian* Church.

Nevertheless, under the existing state of affairs, the two principles coexist indivisibly within a single unified entity. As Coleridge explains, "two distinct functions do not necessarily imply or require two different functionaries. Nay, the perfection of each may require the union of both in the same person. And in the instance now in question, great and grievous errors have arisen from confounding the functions; and fearfully great and grievous will be the evils from the success of an attempt to separate them" (*CS*, pp. 44–45). Now the clerisy is a function not of the Christian Church, but of the National Church, but, because it is England of 1830, it is nonetheless a *Christian* clerisy. Thus, from the start, Coleridge's idea of the clerisy exists under tension: each function, the National and the Christian, is both in opposition to, and supported by, the other. In every town and village in the land the Church of Christ bears witness by its teaching and sacraments to those eternal truths against which the State and clerisy alike will one day be judged and found wanting. The clerisy exists not as a privileged caste, but under judgment—endowed with greater responsibility because the possessor of greater knowledge, including greater self-knowledge.

Now, as John Colmer among others has pointed out (p. 157),

the weakest point in this elaborate theoretical structure is Coleridge's failure to distinguish between an "idea" actually existing in people's minds and an "idea" as merely the supposed basic principle behind existing social institutions that have grown out of a specific historical context. The notion that the British Constitution was designed to have such a complex dialectical structure is as absurd as to suppose that the features he purports to discover in the British system have any universal validity whatsoever. The tenuous attempts to find parallels in the Old Testament or among the Druids is simply disingenuous. Coleridge's argument only makes sense if we assume that England, with her peculiar historical development, presents a unique case in almost all respects, and that he is consciously imposing on the existing system a new interpretive structure (complete with suitable tactical definitions) in order to show its potential, and hitherto unrealized, value. And this he is never willing to do, in so many words. It is hardly surprising that, in spite of Mill's general praise for his willingness to look at an ancient or received opinion and ask afresh, "What is the meaning of it?" Coleridge's actual theoretical structure in *Church and State* was almost entirely ignored by those wishing to develop the notion of a clerisy.

Nevertheless, I suspect that this ambiguity between descriptive and prescriptive accounts is deliberate and essential to Coleridge's purpose. He was under no more illusion as to the actual state of the Church of England in 1830 than Edward Miall was in 1871. Though in many places it had been stirred by the Evangelical Revival,[25] a vast number of parishes—probably the majority—were still as lax and corrupt as Grasmere was when Coleridge stayed with the Wordsworths in the early 1800s and found that the curate was commonly drunk in the pulpit on Sundays. Thomas Mozley recalls similar instances of scandal among the clergy as late as the 1830s, and argues that they were

[25]See, for instance, Ian Bradley, *The Call to Seriousness* (London: Jonathan Cape, 1976).

by no means exceptional.[26] Indeed, in many respects Coleridge himself had not lost the early anticlericalism that, even after his return to the Anglican fold, led to his debating the question of his children's baptism in such terms as these: "Shall I suffer the Toad of Priesthood to spurt out his foul juice in this Babe's face? Shall I suffer him to see grave countenances and hear grave accents, while his face is sprinkled, and while the fat paw of a Parson crosses his forehead?" (*CL*, I, 625). Gillman records that he rarely in fact attended Church when living in Highgate, and in the Notebooks for the late 1820s, at the very time when he was at work on *Church and State,* we are liable to find such tart comments as "A very useful article might be written on the History and Progress of the Vice of Lying on the Christian Church" or, even more antiecclesiastical: "Can a man of mind, for whom *the Truth* on *all* subjects, & philosophic Freedom in the pursuit of it, are *good* per se, . . . adopt the Church for a Profession?"[27] Yet the picture was by no means all black. Against the supine clergy of Trollope's Barchester we must set the portraits of men like Mr. Irwine in George Eliot's *Adam Bede.* There *were* thousands of faithful clergymen in both town and country, and the ministries of such adherents to the clerisical ideal as Maurice, Kingsley, and Hare in their own respective parishes in London (St. Peter's, Vere Street), Eversley, and Hurstmonceaux show the kind of powerful moral influence an energetic parson could wield. Nor need we confine ourselves to the Church of England. As Davie points out, "in Miall's time there *was* one body of clergy serving the agricultural labourer in this way. It was not the clergy of the Established Church, but it wasn't (either) the clergy of the middle-class Congregationalism that Miall spoke for. It was the clergy (mostly lay-preachers, in fact) of the Primitive Methodists, who supported Joseph Arch in his struggle to

[26]Thomas Mozley, *Reminiscences: Chiefly of Oriel College and the Oxford Movement,* 2 vols. (London: Longmans, Green, 1882).
[29]Notebook 39, British Museum Add. MS. 47,534, pp. 52, 68.

unionize farmworkers" (p. 79). Moreover, our very notion of clerical abuses is ultimately derived from the teachings of the Church and the life and example of Christ. The paradox of faith and corruption is not peculiar to eighteenth- or nineteenth-century England, but is much older than institutional Christianity, and is the theme of much of the Old Testament as well as the New.

The greatest contribution that Hare and Maurice made to Coleridge's conception of the clerisy is in their sense of this tension in Biblical history, and of its relevance to contemporary affairs. As Maurice brings out in *The Kingdom of Christ,* the prophetic tradition of the Bible is not a process whereby a new set of commandments or ideals comes to supersede the old, but a process of *discovery* by which the meaning of existing forms and institutions is enhanced and transformed. "Prophecy," in this sense, is the discovery of preexisting relationships: the Biblical God has acted toward his people, and is initiating them into an understanding of what they already possess. The quality that Mill discovers in Coleridge's *Church and State* is one that Coleridge has found in the Bible. In many ways, it is true, *Church and State* is a curiously static book, conspicuously lacking that sense of purposeful historical change that Hare and Maurice were able to discern in their own society, but Coleridge had laid the foundations for this insight upon something equally valuable: that sense of potentiality or "entelechy" within existing social institutions, which was to prove no less revolutionary for English and British society in the long run. He was familiar, both through his own Biblical studies and through his reading of the German critics such as Lessing, with the notion that certain basic doctrines, like that of the Trinity, were not explicitly formulated until after the New Testament period—though they could be said to be "latent" in some of the Gospels and Epistles. Referring to 2 Corinthians 11:16–18, Coleridge himself had speculated: "Collated with the Gospel of John, does not this passage confirm the suggestion of my mind, that in the Apostolic *explicit* belief the Spirit in the *personal* sense was not yet distinguished from the

Word—but that as in the Church before Christ the Son was folded up, as it were, in the Spirit, so in the beginning of the Christian Church the Spirit was identified with the Word."[28] Similarly, the "idea" of the clerisy may be said to be "folded up" in the existing social function of the Church of England, but as yet unrecognized for what it already is. Thus Coleridge's account of the clerisy is neither descriptive nor prescriptive in the normal sense of the words; it is rather intended to awaken in the clergy, and in "the learned of all denominations," a consciousness of the role they are already fulfilling in society, and by making it conscious, transform it, and, in the long run, English society as well.

If, for many nineteenth-century intellectuals, this coming to consciousness also implied secularization and the creation of an endowed elite, a minority tradition was to persist in finding a peculiar and indissoluble relationship between the religious and intellectual life of the nation that has found (so far as I know) no parallel in free societies outside the United Kingdom. Yet, significantly, one of the most noted members of that tradition in the twentieth century was an American by birth: T. S. Eliot. His own social writings, such as *The Idea of a Christian Society* and certain essays in *To Criticise the Critic,* suggest that it was the possibility of such a relationship that induced him to make his life in England. His own words in *Little Gidding* mirror Coleridge's theme:

> And the end of all our exploring,
> Will be to arrive where we started
> And know the place for the first time.

When we discover another American scholar as distinguished as Earl Leslie Griggs choosing to enter the Church on his retirement from an academic post, we may have reason to suspect that Coleridge's idea is part of a tradition of which we have still not seen the end.

[28]Notebook 41, British Museum Add. MS. 47536, p. 49.

A Bibliography of
Earl Leslie Griggs

Students of Coleridge will remain forever in the debt of Earl Leslie Griggs. From the time he was invited by the poet's great-grandson, the Rev. Gerard H. B. Coleridge, to work in the vicarage study on the family papers as he prepared his doctoral dissertation, a biography of Hartley Coleridge, his Coleridge studies were always assisted by the wholehearted cooperation of the poet's descendants, who came to think of him as a member of the family. The life of Hartley (1929) was followed by letters (1936) and new poems (1942) of Hartley, and the life of Sara (1940). The capstone of his scholarly career, however, is the magisterial six-volume *Collected Letters* of the poet (1956–71), which superseded his two-volume *Unpublished Letters* (1932). His many journal articles about hitherto unpublished letters supply invaluable background information that could not be included in the notes in the collected edition.

"Five Sources of Edgar Allan Poe's 'Pinakidia.'" *American Literature*, 1 (1929), 196–99.
Hartley Coleridge: His Life and Work. London: University of London Press, 1929. xi, 255 pp.
"Samuel Taylor Coleridge at Malta." *Modern Philology*, 27 (1929), 201–17.
"Coleridge and Byron." *PMLA*, 45 (1930), 1085–97.
"Coleridge and His Son." *Studies in Philology*, 27 (1930), 635–47.
"Coleridge and Mrs. Mary Robinson." *Modern Language Notes*, 45 (1930), 90–95.

[275]

Bibliography

"Coleridge and the Wedgwood Annuity." *Review of English Studies,* 6 (1930), 63–72.

"Notes on a Proposed Edition of the Correspondence of Samuel Taylor Coleridge." *Papers of the Michigan Academy of Sciences, Arts and Letters,* 12 (1929, published 1930), 293–99.

"Coleridge the Dragoon." *Modern Philology,* 28 (1931), 470–75.

"Hartley Coleridge on His Father." *PMLA,* 46 (1931), 1246–52.

"Hartley Coleridge's Unpublished Correspondence." *London Mercury,* 24 (1931), 146–57.

"Coleridge, De Quincey, and Nineteenth-Century Editing." *Modern Language Notes,* 47 (1932), 88–90.

"Robert Southey and the *Edinburgh Review.*" *Modern Philology,* 30 (1932), 100–03.

"Swinburne on Coleridge." *Modern Philology,* 30 (1932), 215–16.

Unpublished Letters of Samuel Taylor Coleridge, Including Certain Letters Republished from Original Sources. 2 vols. London: Constable, 1932; New Haven, Conn.: Yale University Press, 1933.

"Hazlitt's Estrangement from Coleridge and Wordsworth." *Modern Language Notes,* 48 (1933), 173–76.

"James Fenimore Cooper on Coleridge." *American Literature,* 4 (1933), 389–91.

The Best of Coleridge. (Nelson English Series) New York: Nelson, 1934. xxxv, 722 pp.

Coleridge: Studies by Several Hands, on the Hundredth Anniversary of His Death. Ed. Edmund Blunden and Earl Leslie Griggs. London: Constable, 1934. viii, 243 pp.

"The Death of Coleridge, Being an Unpublished Letter from Mrs. Henry Nelson Coleridge (Sara) to Her Brother Hartley." In *Coleridge* (1934), pp. 223–32.

"Wordsworth as the Prototype of the Poet in Shelley's *Alastor.*" By Paul Mueschke and Earl Leslie Griggs. *PMLA,* 49 (1934), 229–45.

"A Scholar Goes Visiting." *Michigan Alumnus Quarterly Review,* 41 (1935), 408–16.

"Benjamin Haydon and Thomas Clarkson." *Michigan Alumnus Quarterly Review,* 43 (1936), 318–23.

"John Greenleaf Whittier and Thomas Clarkson." *American Literature,* 7 (1936), 458–60.

Letters of Hartley Coleridge. Ed. Grace Evelyn Griggs and Earl Leslie Griggs. London: Oxford University Press, 1936. xv, 328 pp.

"The Poet in Shelley's *Alastor:* A Criticism and a Reply." *PMLA,* 51 (1936), reply on pp. 310–12.

[276]

Thomas Clarkson: The Friend of Slaves. London: Allen and Unwin, 1936; Ann Arbor: University of Michigan Press, 1938. 210 pp.

"*Diadestè,* A Fragment of an Unpublished Play by Samuel Taylor Coleridge." *Modern Philology,* 34 (1937), 377–85.

"Christophe, King of Haiti." *Opportunity: Journal of Negro Life,* 16 (April 1938), 103–05, 121.

"*The Friend:* 1809 and 1818 Editions." *Modern Philology,* 35 (1938), 369–73.

"Louis A. Strauss, 1872–1938—An Appreciation." *Michigan Alumnus Quarterly Review,* 45 (Autumn 1938), 38–41.

"An Early Defense of *Christabel.*" In *Wordsworth and Coleridge* (1939), pp. 173–91.

Wordsworth and Coleridge: Studies in Honor of George McLean Harper. Ed. Earl Leslie Griggs. Princeton: Princeton University Press, 1939. viii, 254 pp.

Coleridge Fille: A Biography of Sara Coleridge. London: Oxford University Press, 1940. xiii, 259 pp.

"Unflattering Imitation." *Sewanee Review,* 49 (1941), 285–88. [Review of Arthur H. Nethercot, *The Road to Tryermaine* (1939).]

Hartley Coleridge: New Poems, Including a Selection from His Published Poetry. London: Oxford University Press, 1942. xxii, 135 pp.

"On Reading Poetry Aloud." In *Education in a Nation at War: Twenty-Ninth Annual Schoolmen's Week Proceedings, . . . March 18–21, 1942.* [Ed. F. C. Gruber] Philadelphia: University of Pennsylvania, 1942. Pp. 221–29.

"The Humanities, Scholarship, and the War." *The General Magazine and Historical Chronicle* (University of Pennsylvania), 46 (Autumn 1943), 3–16.

"Knowing How to Live." *School and College Placement,* 4 (May 1944), 5–9.

"Robert Southey's Estimate of Samuel Taylor Coleridge: A Study in Human Relations." *Huntington Library Quarterly,* 9 (1945), 61–94.

"The Willing Suspension of Disbelief." In *Elizabethan Studies and Other Essays in Honor of George F. Reynolds.* (University of Colorado Studies, Series B, Studies in the Humanities, 2, No. 41) Boulder: University of Colorado Press, 1945. Pp. 272–85.

"Four Letters of Hartley Coleridge." *Huntington Library Quarterly,* 9 (1946), 401–09.

"Date Shells and the Eye of the Critic." *Virginia Quarterly Review,* 23 (1947), 297–301.

Articles in *Chambers's Encyclopaedia* (1950): "Hartley Coleridge," V, 720; "Samuel Taylor Coleridge," V, 722; "Sara Coleridge," V, 722.

Bibliography

"Samuel Taylor Coleridge and Thomas Pringle." *Quarterly Bulletin of the South African Library,* 6 (September 1951), 1–6.

"Wordsworth through Coleridge's Eyes." In *Wordsworth Centenary Studies.* Ed. Gilbert T. Dunklin. Princeton: Princeton University Press, 1951. Pp. 45–90.

Henry Christophe and Thomas Clarkson: A Correspondence. Ed. Earl Leslie Griggs and Clifford H. Prator. Berkeley: University of California Press, 1952. 287 pp.

"The Ancient Mariner on the Screen: II. The Film Seen and Heard." *Quarterly of Film, Radio and Television,* 8 (1953), 93–99.

"Coleridge's Army Experiences." *English,* 9 (1953), 171–75.

"A Note on Wordsworth's *A Character.*" *Review of English Studies,* 4 (1953), 57–63.

Articles in *Colliers Encyclopedia* (1954): "Christabel," V, 225; "Samuel Taylor Coleridge," V, 441; "Thomas Holcroft," X, 108; "Kubla Khan," XII, 12.

"Notes concerning Certain Poems by Samuel Taylor Coleridge." *Modern Language Notes,* 69 (1954), 27–31.

"The Romantic Movement." In *English Literature: A Period Anthology.* Ed. Albert C. Baugh and George Wm. McClelland. New York: Appleton-Century-Crofts, 1954. Pp. 775–88.

"Samuel Taylor Coleridge and Opium." *Huntington Library Quarterly,* 17 (1954), 357–78.

"Ludwig Tieck and Samuel Taylor Coleridge." *Journal of English and Germanic Philology,* 54 (1955), 262–68.

"Coleridge and His Friends." *Charles Lamb Society Bulletin,* No. 132 (1956), 119–21.

Collected Letters of Samuel Taylor Coleridge. 6 vols. Oxford: Clarendon Press, I–II 1956 (corrected edition 1966), III–IV 1959, V–VI 1971.

["The Library in the Expanding University."] In *Proceedings of the Third Annual Meeting, Council of Graduate Schools in the United States, ... Washington, D.C., December 12–14, 1963.* [Washington: The Council, 1964.] Pp. 210–15.

Contributors

JOHN BEER, who is Reader in English Literature at Cambridge University and Fellow of Peterhouse, is the author of *Coleridge the Visionary, The Achievement of E. M. Forster, Blake's Humanism, Blake's Visionary Universe, Coleridge's Poetic Intelligence, Wordsworth and the Human Heart,* and *Wordsworth in Time.* He also edited and contributed to the bicentenary volume *Coleridge's Variety* and the Forster centenary studies *E. M. Forster: A Human Exploration* (with C. K. Das); and has produced a new edition of Coleridge's *Poems.* For the *Collected Coleridge* he has edited Coleridge's marginalia to Archbishop Leighton and is editing his *Aids to Reflection.*

WALTER B. CRAWFORD is Professor of English at California State University, Long Beach. Among his Coleridge publications is *A Portfolio of Twenty Drawings Commemorating the Bicentenary of the Birth of Coleridge* (1972), a limited edition of works by ten California artists, with a foreword by him on Coleridge illustration. He is also nearing completion of the first of three projected volumes of *Samuel Taylor Coleridge, 1900–1979,* a computerized, comprehensive, annotated bibliography of scholarship, criticism, and Coleridgeana, with a supplement of material not appearing in *Samuel Taylor Coleridge: An Annotated Bibliography of Criticism and Scholarship,* Vol. I, 1793–1899, by Josephine and Richard Haven and Maurianne S. Adams (1976).

Contributors

R. A. Foakes is Professor of English at the University of Kent in England. Among his publications are *The Romantic Assertion* and *Coleridge on Shakespeare: The Text of the Lectures of 1811-12*. He is also well known for his work on Shakespeare, which includes a study of *Shakespeare, the Dark Comedies to the Last Plays* and editions of *The Comedy of Errors, Much Ado about Nothing, Macbeth* and *Henry VIII*. For the *Collected Coleridge* he is editing the *Literary Lectures,* which will include the major part of Coleridge's Shakespeare criticism.

Anthony John Harding is Associate Professor of English at the University of Saskatchewan. After reading for his Ph.D. at Jesus College, Cambridge, from 1969 to 1972, he worked under John Horden on the revision of Halkett and Laing's *Dictionary of Anonymous and Pseudonymous English Literature* until 1974, when he joined the University of Saskatchewan. His study of human relationship in Coleridge's thought, *Coleridge and the Idea of Love* (Cambridge University Press), appeared in 1975. He has recently published in *The Wordsworth Circle* and *Studies in Romanticism.*

Laurence S. Lockridge is Associate Professor of English at New York University. A graduate of Indiana University and a Woodrow Wilson and Danforth Fellow, he received his M.A. and Ph.D. degrees from Harvard University. He has previously taught at Rutgers University and Northwestern University. Recently awarded a grant from the National Endowment for the Humanities, he is author of *Coleridge the Moralist* (Cornell University Press, 1977), a work he is extending to the larger context of the British Romantic movement in a subsequent volume.

Thomas McFarland was educated at Harvard, Yale, and Tübingen, and he is at present Professor of English Literature at Princeton University. He is currently editing Coleridge's *Opus Maximum* for the *Collected Coleridge.* Among his previous contributions to Coleridge studies are *Coleridge and the Pantheist Tra-*

dition (1969); "The Origin and Significance of Coleridge's Theory of Secondary Imagination," in *New Perspectives on Coleridge and Wordsworth: Selected Papers from the English Institute* (1972); and "Coleridge's Anxiety," in *Coleridge's Variety: Bicentenary Studies* (1974). He has recently completed a general study of Romanticism called *Romanticism and the Forms of Ruin: Wordsworth, Coleridge, and Modalities of Fragmentation*, which will be published by Princeton University Press.

STEPHEN PRICKETT was educated at Trinity Hall, Cambridge, and University College, Oxford, and is now a Reader in English in' the School of English and American Studies, University of Sussex. He has also taught in the United States at Smith College and at the University of Minnesota. Besides a detective story, *Do It Yourself Doom* (1962), he is author of *Coleridge and Wordsworth: The Poetry of Growth* (1970), *Wordsworth and Coleridge: The Lyrical Ballads* (1975), *Romanticism and Religion: The Tradition of Coleridge and Wordsworth in the Victorian Church* (1976), and *Victorian Fantasy* (1979).

MAX F. SCHULZ is Professor of English and Chairman of the English Department at the University of Southern California. He is the author of *The Poetic Voices of Coleridge* (1963) and of the chapter on Coleridge in the revised edition of *The English Romantic Poets* (1972), as well as of numerous articles on Coleridge. He is currently at work on an extensive interdisciplinary study of the changing image of paradise in eighteenth- and nineteenth-century England as it is revealed in landscape gardens, literature, art, architecture, and technology.

CARL WOODRING, George Edward Woodberry Professor of Literature at Columbia University, is the author of *Politics in the Poetry of Coleridge, Politics in English Romantic Poetry, Wordsworth*, and other studies of literature in the cultural contexts of the nineteenth century, with occasional forays into earlier and later periods. In the *Collected Coleridge* he is the editor of *Table Talk*.

Index

This index includes specific citations to the most frequently cited works by Coleridge: the *Collected Letters* (*CL*), *The Friend* (*F*), and the *Notebooks* (*N*). Authors and titles of secondary sources named only in the notes are not indexed.

Index

Index

Index

Library of Congress Cataloging in Publication Data
Main entry under title:

Reading Coleridge.

Bibliography: p.
Includes index.
1. Coleridge, Samuel Taylor, 1772–1834—Criticism and interpretation—Addresses, essays, lectures. 2. Griggs, Earl Leslie. I. Crawford, Walter Byron.
PR4484.R4   821'.7   79-7616
ISBN 0-8014-1219-6